FOR THE PUBLIC GOOD

POLICY T🌐 PRACTICE
Ethnographic Perspectives on Global Health Systems

SERIES EDITORS: Svea Closser, Emily Mendenhall, Judith Justice, & Peter J. Brown

Policy to Practice: Ethnographic Perspectives on Global Health Systems illustrates and provides critical perspectives on how global health policy becomes practice, and how critical scholarship can itself inform global public health policy. Policy to Practice provides a venue for relevant work from a variety of disciplines, including anthropology, sociology, history, political science, and critical public health.

For the Public Good

*Women, Health, and
Equity in Rural India*

PATRICIA ANTONIELLO

VANDERBILT UNIVERSITY PRESS
Nashville, Tennessee

Library of Congress Cataloging-in-Publication Data

Names: Antoniello, Patricia, 1946– author.
Title: For the public good : women, health, and equity in rural India
  / Patricia Antoniello.
Description: Nashville : Vanderbilt University Press, [2020] | Series:
  Policy to practice | Includes bibliographical references and
  index.
Identifiers: LCCN 2020007878 (print) | LCCN 2020007879 (ebook) |
  ISBN 9780826500243 (hardcover) | ISBN 9780826500236 (paperback)
  | ISBN 9780826500250 (epub) | ISBN 9780826500267 (pdf)
Subjects: LCSH: Rural health services—India—Maharashtra. | Com-
  munity health aides—India—Maharashtra. | Women's health
  services—India—Maharashtra.
Classification: LCC RA771.7.I4 A58 2020 (print) | LCC RA771.7.I4
  (ebook) | DDC 362.10954/79—dc23

LC record available at https://lccn.loc.gov/2020007878
LC ebook record available at https://lccn.loc.gov/2020007879

With love (—*Sine te nihil potest*)
Sara, Ben, Alexander, and John

With respect
Dr. Shobha Arole and Ravi Arole
and Mrs. Ratna Kamble

CONTENTS

ACKNOWLEDGMENTS

I am grateful to an incalculable number of people both in India and at home for the support, kindness, and collaboration that made this book possible. As Muktabai said, one lamp lights another, reminding us that we stand in the history of others. My eternal gratitude to Dr. Raj Arole who was a truly dedicated, pious, and heroic physician and educator. He was at the same time dynamic and unassuming in his leadership of CRHP, his commitment to work for the poor, and his concern for a just health system for India, as his work on the National Rural Health Mission showed. Dr. Arole generously gave me his support for my research and spent time talking about India, health, anthropology, and caste. Our chats on winter nights in the garden around a wood fire are most memorable. His life and work have left an indelible mark as he is a true humanitarian.

Dr. Shobha Arole, medical director of CRHP, was a whirlwind of professional energy and commitment. In a typical day she would do rounds at the hospital, go with the mobile health team to do a village clinic visit, teach a class of VHWs, teach a group of students from an American or Australian college, and then, when called at 3:00 a.m., perform an emergency cesarean surgery—all accomplished effortlessly. Shobha became a colleague and friend as I negotiated my own education about India and CRHP. I traveled with Shobha to professional conferences in the US, where she gave insightful research papers on CRHP at the American Public Health Association annual meetings and Global Health conferences, and to the many talks she was invited to give in India. Our trip to foundations in Delhi to search for appropriate funds for continuing projects and programs was memorable. In the process I thoroughly enjoyed our daily meals and the always insightful and instructive conversations at her home, as well as our exploits away from Jamkhed travelling in India and the US.

Ravi Arole, in his own dynamic and inimitable way, has charted an amazing new course for CRHP. As the current director, he has provided a stable direction for the organization. In my early days of research he helped conceptualize parts of the project and found the time to translate some of the most enduring interviews. Ravi has worked with VHWs whom he has known his entire life. What is brilliant about Ravi is his ability to multitask endlessly, keeping everything afloat in his own charismatic way. I thank him for his support of my project and for his kindness and generosity.

Mrs. Ratna Kamble, colleague and friend, contributed countless hours of her precious time to this project as one of the primary translators of interviews and interactions. This book would not have become a reality without her care and generosity in accompanying me to villages, engaging in conversations with villagers, organizing village visits, and answering a prodigious number of questions. I especially enjoyed sharing roasted jowar at sorghum harvest. She has my unending gratitude. I would also like to thank Jayesh Samuel Kamble, a teacher and source of knowledge both academic and local for me and my students; Monica Kamble, who guides the Adolescent Girls Club; Meena Naidu Sansare, an exceptional preschool teacher who is always offering help and personal support; and Chris Vermeniren, who volunteers at the hospital to help those in desperate need. I would also like to thank my Elon University colleagues Amanda Tapler and Martin Kamela.

The entire adventure would not have been possible without Dr. Alex Kaysin, assistant professor of family and community medicine at the University of Maryland. I met Alex at Brooklyn College when he was a first-year student in the newly initiated CUNY Honors College. He became my advisee and conducted a brilliant internship at SUNY Medical Center. As a medical student Alex was instrumental in starting a free clinic in Bedford-Stuyvesant, Brooklyn. Alex decided to take a gap year between college and medical school was accepted to the Mabelle Arole Fellowship program in Jamkhed, India. It was because of Alex that I was first invited to CRHP and able to begin what became a ten-year ethnographic project. We have visited Jamkhed together many times and worked on various projects together. It has been my great pleasure to have had an amicable and enduring relationship with him. Through Alex I met vivacious Smisha Agarwal, a brilliant researcher and now an assistant professor at Johns Hopkins Bloomberg School of Public Health, who also conducted a project at CRHP. I thank them both for their kindness and friendship.

I am grateful for the women of CRHP for generously giving their time to me over the years of my research: Lalanbai Kadam, Yamunabai Kashinath

Kulkarni, Babaibai Rambhau Dalvi, Halima Ratan Shaikh, Surekha Sadaphule, Rambhabai Sanap, Muktabai Pol, Rekha Bajirao Paudmal, Sakhubai Babasaheb Gite, Kantibai Devrao Shirsath, Sharada Thackrey, Baby Khandu Moholkar, Dwarkabai Nana Sawant, Kalpana Ashok Gaikwad, Disha Karvande, Sangeeta, Gite, Sarubai Sahebrao Salve, Sophia Abbas Pathan, Nanda Shankar Jadhav, Mangal Kishan Khawle, Saraswati Rama Dhawale, Pushpa Popat Sutar, Mumtaj Badshah Shaikh, Shalan Tukaram Lashkar, Padmini Sadashiv Lad, Parubai Maruti Chande, Babai Hari Sathe, Leelabai Rama Amte, Salubai Sadaphule, Sujata Balasaheb Khedkar, Bhamabai Kale, Mukta R. Gunjal, and Jijabai Dashrath Bangar.

I would also like to thank the educators and staff of CRHP: Surekha Sonawane (social worker and MHT); Shaila Deshpade; and of course Connie Gates, whose dedication to CRHP has been a life's work; the Ajay Jadhave library staff who accompanied students to various World Heritage sites throughout India; office staff: Abel Desai, Abhay Jadhav, Amul Khetre, Atul Khetre, Atul Khetre, Daniel Bhanushali; hospital staff: Dr. Prashant Gaikwad, Dr. Elia Ghorpade, and Moses Gurram (jack of all trades); kitchen staff: Janabai Karle, Asha Garadkar, Kashibai, Kavita; and of course two women who are central to the everyday functioning of CRHP, Sultana Shaikh and Shhabai Kapse. Special thanks to Dr. Ramaswamy Premkumar permission and help with statistical analysis. And of course, Kaat Landuyt and Sister Sylvia who have given so much.

For their continuing good wishes and support I thank the anthropology department at Brooklyn College, all of whom I consider both colleagues and friends—a rarity in most academic departments—Arthur Bankoff, Kelly Britt, Shahrina Chowdhury, Stephen Chester, Meghan Ference, Katie Hejtmanek, Rhea Rhaman, and especially Naomi Schiller and Jillian Cavanaugh for running the show; our efficient department administrative assistant Leticia Medina, for making every aspect of our academic day genial; Christa Paterline, for unending and fun-filled political discussions and for an unforgettable writing weekend in Williamstown with Meghan; special thanks to Shahrina for last minute help with graphic design. My research was supported by Brooklyn College sabbatical year, and Tow Travel Grants and PSC-CUNY research grants helped finance the multiyear project. I would also like to thank the students of Brooklyn College and other CUNYs who enrolled in the India Global Health Study Abroad course and independent studies at CRHP, especially the first two, Punam Thakkar and Preyasi Kothari, and the participants of the last summer research trip, Tasnia Mahmud, Peter

Lee, and Neelima Dosakayala—particularly Neeli, whose help collating the bibliography for this book was incredibly efficient and greatly appreciated.

I thank Alisse Waterson for all her amazing support for anthropology and creating the AAA salon, for beginning this process with her recommendation, and especially for her effervescent goodness. I am grateful to the members of the advisory board of the New York Academy of Sciences Anthropology and the members of the Columbia Seminar—Culture, Power, Boundaries who commented on an earlier version of this project; to longtime friends from graduate school, especially Dolores Shapiro, my canoeing mate, and Brian Ferguson and the CGAAA gang. Paul Norton helped with editorial support. I would also like to thank Zachary Gresham and Joell Smith-Borne of Vanderbilt University Press who guided me through the last stages of this project. I would like to remember Sharmila Rege of Pune University, Savitribai Phule Women's Center, whose encouragement in the early stages of this project was inspirational; her untimely death left us all bereft.

Over the years many friends have become family. Iris Lopez has been like a sister since grad school and continues with her warmth and affection. Maria-Luisa Achino Loeb and I became friends when our daughters attended the Bank Street School for Children; together we endured the trials and tribulations of graduate school, and in seminars we talked anthropology and power. Above all, I thank Mimma for the laughter we have shared throughout the years. Jessica Scheer Halstead and I became friends when she was a TA for one of my undergraduate anthro class at Columbia. She moved me from fictive kin to godmother (a kin status for Italian-Americans) of her son Alex (an extraordinarily talented DP). Jess is always a phone call away, ever there even for last minute editing; we have travelled through the struggles and joys of a lifetime together—with occasional recuperation at the beach. And thanks, of course, go to her husband, Dr. Lauro Halstead, who routinely, with a gleam in his eye, asks the incisive question; and to Nancy Goldner, for years of support and empathy. And most of all, my weekly dinner companions Gunja SenGupta and Irene Sosa, who have celebrated and suffered with me through the twists and turns of this process. I could not have done this without your consistent and unwavering support. You both are just as the women VHWs describe friendship: *maya* and *prem*.

And to my family—my mother Delia; my accomplished and admired daughter, Sara, who helped at various stages of this project with hugs and editing—sempre amare; my wonderful son-in-law, Ben; and Alex and John, both kind, brilliant, and talented. Without you nothing is possible.

Introduction

Women come together
Let us unite and fight for women's freedom
Dear Venubai, why are you sitting at home being oppressed?
Come, let's go to class
We will go to Jamkhed and learn

In the rural villages of Ahmednagar, an impoverished, drought-prone district in western India, groups of women come together each week to learn, discuss, and plan for the health and well-being of their communities. On my first visit to Jamkhed, as I walked past a one-story corrugated aluminum hospital building, I heard a sound that would become familiar to me—women clapping in time and singing "We Will Go to Jamkhed." Similar to the sacred *bhajans* (hymns), the song is a call-and-response poem that names an imaginary Venubai who represents a burdened village everywoman whose fate the gatherers seek to change. The singers invite women across the district's countryside to learn, to fight for knowledge, and to cast off oppression.

The women are village health workers (VHWs), an official title that reflects their role in the Comprehensive Rural Health Project (CRHP), a community-based health care program that began in the region more than forty years ago. I came to know these women, the innovative program of which they are a part, and the story behind it during seven years of ethnographic research in the town and surrounding villages of Jamkhed *taluka* (block), in the state of Maharashtra.

For the Public Good narrates the role of CRHP, an internationally recognized comprehensive health care approach that offers local solutions to global problems based on a critical premise that identifies everyday injustices as primary social determinants of health. In this part of rural India, the dominant local prejudices are caste and gender inequalities. This book raises the question, How do these social inequalities, as a function of power that is structured through social, political, and economic forces, directly and indirectly affect health and the provision of health care? A corollary question follows: Would the elimination of these embedded inequalities of caste and gender promote health and well-being?

The local women who became village health workers actively participate in ongoing cooperative efforts to reduce mortality, eliminate endemic health problems, and advance social and economic well-being in villages across the region. In turn, the women themselves are able to transform their own lives. In one generation, they progressed from child brides and sequestered wives to valued teachers and community leaders. This book argues that the Comprehensive Rural Health Project created the conditions for village health workers to demonstrate their personal strength, persistence, and resilience to overcome caste and gender inequality, the double problems of local prejudice that the CRHP directly confronts. Hirabai Salve explains how she understood her position in village society: "Before becoming a village health worker, I never thought, who am I? I thought I was less than any animal. I did not know how to live. Because I am from a *Harijan* [an untouchable], a *Dalit* community, nobody respected me. I never thought that this was bad" (Hirabai Salve, personal interview, 2009).

In Maharashtra villages, these deeply felt engrained disparities generate and perpetuate the ideological constructs that historically shape the everyday experiences of women in rural India. In this book, I examine the contested and complex issues that are consequences of the interrelationship of caste, class, and gender by tracing the life histories of VHWs in the context of the CRHP's innovative health care project. Toward that end, I describe the social and material relationships that generate resistance to traditional caste and gender assemblies to explain the shifts and transformations in village life. My challenge is to unravel competing and interacting ideological and cultural constructs within the political and economic structure of India in the context of its history, enduring complexity of caste, contested residual of colonialism, perennial hegemony of patriarchy, and, more recently, growing venture capitalism.

In the early years of CRHP, women's worldviews and personal circumstances often gave them no reference to imagine the dramatic change that becoming a VHW would bring to their lives, families, and communities. Additionally, changes in local and national politics and laws during that period, while controversial, advanced in incremental ways the position of rural women in Indian society. This book examines the relationship between power and resistance when the innovative CRHP model is introduced to promote the public good and directly challenge caste- and gender-based inequality entrenched in village life.

Caste, Class, and Gender: Intersections of Power and Histories

At an anthropology seminar at Columbia University in the City of New York in 1916, B. R. Ambedkar gave a paper on caste in India:

> I am quite alive to the complex intricacies of a hoary institution like Caste, but I am not so pessimistic as to relegate it to the region of the unknowable, for I believe it can be known. The Caste problem is a vast one, both theoretically and practically. Practically, it is an institution that portends tremendous consequences. It is a local problem but one capable of much wider mischief, for as "long as caste in India does exist, Hindus will hardly intermarry or have any social intercourse with outsiders." (qtd. in Rege 2013, 79).

Ambedkar is considered to be the architect of the Indian constitution, ratified in 1949, which established principles of equity and directly prohibits discrimination on the basis of religion, race, caste, sex, or place of birth. Moreover, Ambedkar unsuccessfully advocated that specific measures be included in the 1950 Hindu code bills addressing caste restrictions in marriage, monogamy, and divorce, and advocating for equal shares in property for women. According to Rege (2013), Ambedkar directly confronted the ancient Laws of Manu, which supports gendered restriction and control of women, when he endorsed equality and fraternity, especially the nontraditional allocation or inheritance of property to women. In the late 1950s, as an "untouchable" himself, Ambedkar made the logical yet radical decision to extricate himself from the province of caste by becoming a Buddhist, sparking a social movement and converting thousands of others. To create a sense of cohesion for the lowest groups in the caste hierarchy, Ambedkar introduced the term *Dalit*, meaning "oppressed" or "downtrodden," as a direct contradiction to Gandhi's label *Harijan*, which meant children of God. In the 1970s, in another attempt to end caste oppression, a new social organization and movement adopted the name Dalit Panthers in ideological alignment with other politically radical groups of the time. Today, in cities and towns of Maharashtra, statues of Ambedkar identify his place in the history of the area; the blue flags that signify Buddhist villages are symbols of his legacy.

The Indian constitution of almost seventy years was written as a document of social egalitarianism (Balagopal 1990), yet, today, caste is still a living reality. The disparity of living standards continues unabated even as quotas and allowances for underrepresented caste and tribal groups designated as Scheduled Castes (SCs) and Scheduled Tribes (STs) are legislated (Gang, Sen, and Yun 2011). The Mandal commission (1980) and other attempts by liberal political parties to ameliorate entrenched social structures are relatively ineffective. Ultimately, according to some analysts, these additional categories like Other Backward Classes (OBCs) perpetuate problems of identity politics and confusion over the use of class or caste (Srinivas 1997).

Srinivas (1966, 1997) points out that assumptions attributed to caste, with four *varna* (Sanskrit for "root") based on a clear immutable hierarchical Brahmin, Kshatriyas, Vaishyas, and Shudra reference in the Manusmiriti texts, are ubiquitous in all of India. "Caste is undoubtedly an all-India phenomenon in the sense that there are everywhere hereditary, endogamous groups which form a hierarchy, and that each of these groups has a traditional association with one or two occupations" (Srinivas 1966, 3). Mid-twentieth-century British social anthropologists characterized caste as a fixed system of relationships allotted by birth, highly ritualized, and validated by differential control over productive resources (Bailey 1957). Some scholars like Dumont (1966) assert caste in India as having a structural hierarchical and religious nature. Yet, caste is not immutable, as Lynch (1969) suggests even the lowest caste is able to maximize external scarce resources such as power, prestige, and wealth. Beteille (1996) emphasizes that in spite of these dominant cleavages, "there are powerful forces which lead to loosen the hold of caste in many areas of social life" (5).

Srinivas (1997) and Dirks (1993) point out that the British created a means for certain castes to assume political power. Further, Dirks (1992) advances the argument that the colonial British formulation instead stresses "the social fact that caste structure, ritual form, and political process were all dependent on relations of power" (58). Other scholars identify that the presumption of the theoretical Brahmins and the empirical *shudras* has been held for the last fifty years (Guru 1995). More recently, Gupta (2005) reiterates that caste identity is not necessarily associated with notions of purity and pollution, but with a more recent assessment of caste characteristics as multiple hierarchies against the backdrop of wealth and power.

Even with the changing contemporary analysis of caste, depictions of women in India are traced back to traditional origins and identified with the influence of colonialism and the persistence of patriarchy. Zelliot (2003) notes, "the hegemony of caste translates into a hegemony of gender through codes of pride, privilege, and self-image" (215). In addition, Dube (1997) asserts the sexual asymmetries of boundaries are reproduced by caste through the analytically separate characteristics based on kinship of *jati* (birth group), endogamy, and hierarchy.

Today, mornings in rural villages reveal the lines of gender segregation that varied little during the years of my fieldwork visits. Men gather at the village center uniformly dressed in a white *kurta* (shirt) and white pants and pointed *topi* (cap); some men assemble in small groups near the temple while others sit together at tea stalls. Some men wearing Western clothes sit on motorcycles. Women do not inhabit these public spaces; they are at home, barely visible. For women, mornings are very different: After fetching water in the hours before dawn, women are within confines, squatting over *chula* (stoves) cooking, washing clothes, and tending to animals attached to sheds. Some women in families without property leave the village to work as day laborers in the fields of others' farms. When asked about morning routines, older women evoked even harsher times forty years ago when, as newly married women living in their husbands' village, they were carefully scrutinized, restricted to households, and prevented from associating with other women. For example, one woman remembered that she was admonished daily by her husband, and sometimes her mother-in-law, to cover her face with the *pallu* (veil) of her sari and not to make eye contact with anyone.

These observations may seem stark and essentializing, but they foreground questions regarding gender relations and village life. A central concern of feminist writers and researchers is the notion of the silencing and invisibility of women caused by the absence of a gender-centered argument of women in history and social science (Mathur 2000). Chatterjee (1989) explains, "by assuming a position of sympathy with the unfree and oppressed womanhood of India, the colonial mind was able to transform this figure of the Indian woman into a sign of the inherently oppressive and unfree nature of the entire cultural tradition of a country" (622). For example, feminist historians assert that the idea that Indian women had no voice before colonialism is a false assumption and, in the same way, an additional tactic for silencing women (Forbes 1996).

Ghosh (2007) argues that studies on women's struggles and movements in colonial India emphasize achievements of the "exceptional and educated few," while portraying the rest as passive or ignorant. Further, writing about Indian women as disembodied from caste or religion and without class-based identity appears to be consistent well into the twentieth century. For example, vocal feminists of the 1970s were "middle class and university educated, [and] it was their experience which came to be universalized as 'women's experience'" (Rege 2003a, 90). Further, Rege (1998) argues that middle-class, literate women rarely discussed caste because they falsely believed in an identity of sisterhood among women. Rao (2003) suggests that political empowerment of Dalit and other lower-caste women creates a challenge for Indian feminists.

These critical perspectives provide the basis for a major concern of this work—the assessment of women's local resistance in everyday matters that address gender and class domination in hegemonic societies. Some analysts suggest that "the challenge to disarticulate a unified and monolithic account of patriarchies-in-action" (Rao 2003, 5) requires an analysis of labor and sexual economies. Others emphasize the importance of using women's interpretation of their own histories of resistance and activism by examining women's agency, even as they are participants in an oppressive patriarchal society (Forbes 1996). Still others validate that women use strategic resistance as a means to understand theories of power and withstand and oppose the applications of control (Abu-Lughod 1990).

Some writers locate class relations in the history of social movements in India, especially in Maharashtra and Tamil Nadu, and particularly in the rise of *Dalitbahujan* (people in the majority) history (Ilaiah 2004). John (2000) proposes an alternate notion of social movements, which contrasts "women's rights to rights based on caste, class or minority status in the broader context of a common democratic struggle" (3830). Social movements, especially those of various Dalit groups, are credited with promoting issues of social organization. For example, Rege (2006) uses oral histories of Dalit women to describe everyday experiences within or influenced by social movements of the twentieth century.

Women in Development

Recognition of women's vital role in local economies was virtually absent in the international and global development literature until Boserup's *Women's*

Role in Economic Development (1970). Boserup introduced a definitional shift in the evaluation of domestic labor and agricultural development, pushing national and international organizations to acknowledge the critical role of women as an indispensable and mediating actor in family health and development. While this germinal work is not without its flaws (see below), the recognition of women's role in global economic development was mostly omitted before the second feminist movement of the twentieth century focused on issues of equality.

The Commission on the Status of Women, established by United Nations in 1947, was concerned with rights and gendered aspects of war and peace between 1965 and 1975 (Jain 2005). Subsequently, 1975 was declared the "International Year of the Woman" and 1975 to 1985 was named the United Nations Decade for Women. In 1979, the World Bank created the post of adviser for Women in Development, admitting that economic changes damaged the traditional division of labor to the disadvantage of women. The Convention on the Elimination of All Forms of Discrimination against Women (CEDAW), held in 1979, addressed issues of nondiscrimination and the equality of women, and Development Alternatives with Women for a New Era (DAWN) was established in 1985 to create networks for women of the Third World. However, it was the World Bank publication *Recognizing the "Invisible" Woman in Development: The World Bank's Experience* (World Bank 1979) that permanently altered the perception of women's role in development. As World Bank president McNamara noted, "expanding the social, political, and economic opportunities of women beyond their traditional roles of motherhood and housekeeping enables them to channel their creative abilities" (qtd. in World Bank 1979, iii). Rege (2003b) suggests that global projects and other research launched in the 1980s led to a reconceptualization, often misapplied, and overexposure of women in development and globalization studies, especially with the introduction of the concept of women's empowerment.

Held in Lima, Peru, in 1983, the second *Encuentro Feminista* supported a women-centered focus and was critical of mainstream approaches that assessed unconstructive practices such as "listing women engaged in domestic work as unemployed, unequal wages, discrimination against women in the workplace, women's double burden of work for wages and work at home, and the absence of social security for women who perform unpaid labor at home" (Jain 2005, 79). In *Women's Role in Economic Development* (1970), Boserup's work on women's domestic labor and its direct contribution to economic development was unprecedented. Yet, while feminist economists valued Boserup's rich empirical observations, later considerations framed it as using neoclassical categories that miss the history of colonialism, control of women's sexuality, and asymmetrical gender relations. Benería and Sen (1981) conclude "Boserup's argument remains divorced from any coherent analysis of the interconnections between the social process of accumulation, class formation, and changes in gender relations" (287).

Today, microfinance institutions (MFIs) are targeting women in India with microfinance loans and other financial services initiated by the Grameen Bank in Bangladesh. Muhammad Yunus (2004), who founded the bank, believed these programs to be a panacea for poverty reduction in South Asia and touted microfinance loans and grants for women as a solution for those living in poverty. Nevertheless, economic policies adversely affect women living in precarious economic conditions; as Eisenstein (2009) points out, involving women in financial schemes and the banking system has the potential to introduce additional forms of oppression. Other researchers show that women without experience in money matters are at a distinct disadvantage in negotiating complicated financial instruments, creating new types of gender inequality (Antoniello 2015; Karim 2011; Purushothaman 1998).

In "Missing Women," noted economist Amartya Sen (1992b, 2003) identified the profound connections between social inequality and increased mortality for women expressed as the demographic imbalance of sex ratios in India due to female infanticide or neglect of health and nutrition. Revisiting this assessment of gender imbalance and economics, Klasen and Wink (2003) identified sex selection medical procedures as a growing risk, which could be countered with education and occupational opportunities for women. More recently, Klasen (2018) explains the methodological difficulty of reliably assessing the economic gender gap; however, his analysis does suggest that greater control and decision-making within households benefits the education of children and health of the family. The relationship between gender bias and monetary matters in India is affected by the economy, and financial policies both local and national that can be understood through the framework of a larger understanding of the politics of global health equity.

Neoliberalism and Global Health

Health equity cannot be concerned only with health, seen in isolation. Rather it must come to grips with the larger issue of fairness and justice in social arrangements, including economic allocations, paying appropriate attention to the role of health in human life and freedom. (Sen 2002, 659)

The last four decades of global health are characterized by a worldwide increase in health care spending with fewer and fewer people having access to quality health care, and the inability of neoliberal models to solve even the most basic health problems. Navarro (2007) points out there is a contradiction between the theory and practice of neoliberal policies that produce enormous economic growth and power for dominant classes in the Global South and North while dramatically increasing social inequalities. Mukherjee (2004) criticizes the policies that forced governments of less wealthy countries, usually of the Global South (sometimes called emerging markets or developing economies), to decrease their public service budgets while enriching advanced economies of wealthy countries. More recently, Mukherjee et al. (2019) note that universal health coverage is hampered by demand-side barriers to domestic financing, insufficient staffing and infrastructure, and the lack of attention to both social determinants of health and an achievable plan for implementation.

Neoliberalism maintains that social well-being will be created with a reduction of state intervention in economic activities and the deregulation of labor and financial markets in favor of the unbridled liberation of capital to generate market potential (Harvey 2005; Graeber 2011). Modern clinical medicine, biomedicine, as a platform for neoliberal policies, results in privatized medicine and reductions of public responsibility for the health of populations, which increasingly transforms national health services into less equitable insurance-based health care systems. Paradoxically, in the clinical health sector ill health is often blamed on individuals with an overemphasis on personal responsibility and behavior change as promoting health, and, correspondingly, there is little concern for social factors that intervene in health causality. Thus, internal and external political factors are inextricably linked to issues of both health and quality of life that are driven by global economic policies without adequate consideration of local effects. In addition, other neoliberal projects like structural adjustment programs favored by the World Bank and the International Monetary Fund (IMF) further limit the development of community-based primary health care models to solve global health concerns (Kim et al. 2000). As a result of the neoliberal agenda there is an increase in the influence of international agencies and foundations like the World Health Organization (WHO); Global Fund to Fight AIDS, Tuberculosis and Malaria; the Global Alliance for Vaccines and Immunization (GAVI); the United Nations Population Fund (UNFPA); the World Bank's Human Development Network; United Nations Children's Fund (UNICEF); Joint United Nations Program on HIV/AIDS (UNAIDS); and the Global Health Program at the Bill & Melinda Gates Foundation, to name a few; all of these agencies and foundations have tackled various aspect of global health using advanced neoliberal approaches. Yet, the most pressing global health concerns remain entrenched.

Do We Need a National Polio Eradication Program?

This question may appear absurd or even offensive to anyone interested in global public health concerns, but it was intended to shock listeners by challenging them to reconsider the implications of global health initiatives that preempt the provision of primary care. I first heard Dr. Raj Arole, founder and medical director of Comprehensive Rural Health Project (CRHP), raise this question in 2007 when I attended an open lecture for the three-month Primary Health Care Certificate program offered in Jamkhed. The audience of thirty was made up primarily of students enrolled in the course, with some staff and visitors. When Dr. Arole raised this question midway in the lecture with a long pause, people looked up from their notebooks and there was some muttering in the audience. Of course Dr. Arole advocated the eradication of polio, a disabling degenerative neurological disease, but he asked if this goal should be accomplished in India at the expense of the provision of primary health care. His stated concern was the larger issue of national health policy privileging Western or international projects that divert federal funds to single goals at the expense of providing the comprehensive primary health care that is necessary to deliver basic health. I later learned that part of his criticism was against Indian national policy dictated by the International Monetary Fund (IMF) in the 1990s that made loans contingent on structural adjustment programs (SAPs) that reduced social programs like health and education and funneled limited resources into programs to comply with international health initiatives. In addition, in following Western models of health care, the question was raised, Were the health needs of local villages being served? For example, should a country like India, with a 43 percent rural population, follow the model of highly industrialized nations like the United States?

Drs. Mabelle and Raj Arole founded the Comprehensive Rural Health Project to provide primary health care to rural villages in Jamkhed, Maharashtra. Based on working in a voluntary hospital in Maharashtra State, they point out that children are malnourished and suffer from fevers and diarrheal disease; pregnant woman do not receive prenatal care or skilled care during childbirth; and chronic and endemic diseases are prevalent (Arole and Arole 1975). In particular, unsafe water causes life-threatening waterborne infections. Arole and Arole observed that traditional Western biomedical approaches to health care were not sufficient to cure patients, instead setting up a repetitive pattern of treatment that missed 70 percent of preventable illness. "Since a traditional curative-oriented hospital system does not penetrate the communities and does not see patients as part of a community in relation to the environment . . . it fails to meet the total needs of the community" (70). Thus, CRHP, also known as the Jamkhed Model, was developed to provide promotive primary health care that subscribed to the WHO definition of health—a state of complete physical, mental, and social well-being, and not merely the absence of disease or infirmity. Accordingly, the Jamkhed model has two specific innovations: first, it emphasized illness prevention and health promotion that enable people to begin to get control over their own health and potentially lead to community participation; second, it introduced social and environmental interventions that advance village life. The most revolutionary idea of the model, though, was to develop methods to directly challenge caste and gender inequality in rural communities. One of the innovative and creative aspects of the model is the selection and training of local women to be health practitioners—the village health worker.

For the Public Good: A Gendered Approach to Global Health

This book examines the lives and experiences of the women village health workers of CRHP and suggests that sustainable healthy communities are created when the underlying social, political, and economic processes that mediate the lived inequities—in this case, those of caste and gender—are assessed through everyday experiences. Sen and Östlin (2009) assert that gender inequality and the power relations that perpetuate it are the most influential social factors directly affecting the health of millions of girls and women. Moreover, these conditions are also harmful to men's health and negatively affect communities overall (Sen and Östlin 2009; Iyer, Sen, and Östlin 2008). This book suggests that when local women traditionally marginalized in rural Indian life have the potential to become actors in their villages, it creates visible social change. Thus, I suggest the Comprehensive Rural Health Project's identification of the prevalent gender and caste discrimination and injustices in traditional communities as an underlying element of health contributes to the success of the model in changing social and environmental factors to create a positive health profile for rural villages.

Orientations: Theories and Methods

My long-term relationship with CRHP began in 2008 when Dr. Raj Arole invited me to design a research project, which I conducted during sabbatical semesters in 2009 and 2010. Since then, I have made almost yearly visits to Jamkhed to both conduct research and teach a study abroad program at the site.

ETHNOGRAPHIC METHODOLOGY

Anthropological qualitative methods are designed to develop a compendium of ethnographic information from which to conduct wide-ranging analysis. To collect ethnographic data for my research, especially my research in India, I used qualitative research methods including participant observation, focus groups, and life history interviews. Participant observation is the primary tool for data collection in sociocultural anthropology that includes the day-to-day study of social life, along with the researcher's active involvement in everyday activities of daily life. For example, in nine years of fieldwork and visits, I attended births, marriages, festivals, religious services, housewarmings, and funerals throughout most of fifty CRHP project villages. I enjoyed local *caha* (tea) in the homes of VHWs almost every day and at harvest time I happily ate charcoal-cooked *jowar* (sorghum) under a mango tree. In order to understand the educational and training process for village health workers, I observed classes, presentations, meals, informal meetings, evening chats, tea intervals, group discussions, and song performances. At the CRHP medical center, I observed outpatient clinics, in-patient care, and scheduled and emergency surgical procedures. Travelling by Jeep I accompanied the mobile health team comprised of a physician, nurse, social worker, and elected village leaders to provide health care and services in remote villages where VHWs were resident practitioners. On several occasions I attended clinics and classes offered for VHWs and the CRHP community by physicians and public health researchers from Australia, Italy, Japan, Korea, Belgium, the United Kingdom, the United States, and many states of India. In addition, I participated in seminars and conferences with local and statewide elected officials and financial leaders. I am referred to by VHWs and staff as Dr. Pat, Patbai, and Pattai (-*bai* is an honorific of respect added to women's names in this part of India and -*tai* means "like a sister").

One of my key ethnographic fieldwork tools was the broad-ranging life history interview, which I developed after two separate research visits and months of participant observation. The interview questions were based on the culmination of a preliminary analysis of the structure and organization of the social life and work practices of VHWs. The short and open-ended questions were translated into the local Marathi language and incorporated specific questions in several categories to capture the everyday routines, knowledge, traditional practices, beliefs, and behaviors reported by VHW study participants. These categories included early life, marriage, reproductive history, selection and training as a health practitioner, income-generating projects, and understanding of local and national political and economic processes. During the interview sessions each woman was encouraged to make the interview her own by answering questions with unconstrained and often long narratives of remembrances. These interviews often lasted more than two hours and subsequently generated later informal discussions raised by study participants. While formal interviews generated specific data, continuing participant observation was essential to generate additional materials through conversations that might add or verify information and relevant observed behaviors.

The informed consent and life history interview questions were translated into Marathi by local speakers. Since most village women had no formal early schooling, informed consent was read aloud in Marathi to each study participant before each interview. Informed consent forms included permission for both audio and video recording. For the purposes of translation, speakers of local Marathi with university degrees, who collaborated with me in assessing subject-matter-specific interview questions, were present at all life history interviews. Study participants were selected based on an original list of over eighty names from which every third name was asked to participate. The final sample contained thirty-three life history interviews. The granting of informed consent was witnessed, and women study participants signed or placed a thumbprint on informed consent forms.

THEORETICAL MODELS

My research approach is grounded in a perspective commonly employed in medical anthropology that examines power and privilege using a historical perspective to assess how larger social, political, and economic processes constrain and enable women in their everyday lives. While casteism and racism are both components of systems of oppression and subordination, both are based on history and locality; consequently, it is the analysis of lived experience that shows commonalities of discriminations, expressed as social relations, that create and perpetuate inequalities. My research adopts an approach grounded in ethnographic methods and based on a theoretical model that was used to examine the meaning of inequality in everyday lives and to assess the political, economic, and social context of gender and pregnancy outcomes and morbidity and mortality in Harlem, New York (Mullings and Wali 2000; Mullings et al. 2001). Expanding the model to examine women's health in the United States more broadly, these theorists are critical of biomedical research protocols that consider gender, race, and class as characteristics of individuals; rather, the historical, social, and political processes that create present-day inequalities are assessed as a function of embedded social relations (Mullings 2014; Schultz and Mullings 2006). This medical anthropological approach considers that beliefs and behaviors, sometimes narrowly called "lifestyles," are not fixed ideas that are independent of social and historical contexts. For example, in India caste is not equivalent to the social concept of race and racism in the United States; yet, there are countless parallels in how social and economic inequities are expressed in health outcomes, especially those for women and children.

Crenshaw (1989, 1990) coined the term intersectionality to explain that black women in the US experience discrimination differently—not just as women or as African Americans but as result of the interrelationship of underlying aspects of society, such as racism, sexism, heterosexism, ableism, and classism, which directly and indirectly affect black women. She asserts, "Feminists thus ignore how their own race functions to mitigate some aspects of sexism and moreover, how it often privileges them over and contributes to the domination of other women" (154). This perspective based on a critique of the American legal system is useful in assessing difference in systems of discrimination and oppression; however, there remains the question of its usefulness as an analytical tool and its adaptability to understanding feminisms in South Asia. Some South Asian feminists question the value of importing Western models or Eurocentric views for the study of equality for women in Asia or Africa (Jayawardena 2016). Agnes (2012), a feminist legal scholar, in writing about legislation affecting Muslims, raises concerns about how both Dalit and high-caste women are addressed, suggesting that "covenants of equality and equal protection may unfold in diagonally opposite trajectories for the mainstream and the marginalized" (51). She suggests that questions regarding gender and community benefit from an intersectional focus.

In *Gender in South Asia: Social Imagination and Constructed Realities*, Channa (2013) writes, "to create monolithic constructions of women, of any time period or spatial location, is not academically a sound procedure; yet, in everyday conversations and in the collective mind, the archetypes of womanhood not only exist but they inform actions and practices, albeit most often erroneously" (1). Theorists like Rege (2000, 2006) reinforce the necessity of a comparative reading of the lives of leaders of national and anti-caste movements in Colonial India to understand the "processes that defined the personal and the public sphere in diverse social locations" (27). Rege warns against the use of caste, class, and gender without a guide for method and theory, suggesting the use of the Ambedkarite's theoretical legacy.

As a white working-class Western anthropologist, I am informed by anthropological approaches over the last thirty years. These provide a background to avoid pitfalls of essentializing women, namely, articulating reductionist views framed by biology and evolutionary psychology and formulaic postmodern (re)definition. I draw on the work of feminists who explain the decisions and actions of women and explore the persistence of individual agency within the ever-present limitations of race, class, caste, and gender. Thus, as Lopez (2008) suggests, women are not victims of life choices; rather, decisions are based on purposeful agency within societal constraints. My book adds to other approaches that examine the explanatory potential of the concept of gender and its limitations as an analytical category, not as a gloss for "women," but to understand how political and economic factors are mediated by power, agency, and structure. I acknowledge the lasting impact of Chandra Mohanty's 1984 work, in which her intention was to analyze the production of the "Third World Woman" as a singular monolithic subject, while at the same time calling on "Western feminists" to avoid limiting "the possibility of coalitions among (usually White) Western feminists and working class and feminists of color around the world" (333). More than twenty years later the challenge and question persists: "what are the concrete effects of global restructuring on the 'real' raced, classed, national, sexual bodies of women in the academy, in workplaces, streets, households, cyberspaces, neighborhoods, prisons, and in social movements" (245). My research adopts an approach that examines power and privilege using gender-centered models and a historical perspective to assess how larger social, political, and economic processes constrain and enable women in their everyday lives.

This book is able to employ a unique historical perspective due to published work by the Aroles and others about the Jamkhed Model. I used the 1994 publication by Drs. Mabelle and Rajanikant Arole, *Jamkhed: A Comprehensive Rural Health Project*, as a backdrop and historical record of the project. Additionally, I interviewed many of the CRHP staff and VHWs who are named in this work (using pseudonyms) to compare and contrast their own perspective of the ongoing project of CRHP and its effect on community health and development. My longitudinal fieldwork and the already published work on Jamkhed contributed to the writing of this book, which unpacks a complex process of creating, structuring, and implementing a community participatory primary health care model in a rural setting.

Plan of the Book

This book is organized by constituent and interconnected parts to construct an ethnography about village health workers and the history and practices of the CRHP organization. First, the analysis is based on longitudinal contemporary fieldwork over a nine-year period. Second, the more than forty-year history of CRHP forms the scaffolding for the analysis documented through published work and unpublished documents. Thus, Chapter 1 describes the Jamkhed Model—the creation and development of the Comprehensive Rural Health Project—and Chapter 7 details the legacy and sustainability of the Jamkhed Model, focusing on its survival over more than forty years in the context of the changing goals of global health and the pressures of top-down international neoliberalism. The ethnographic-rich chapters 3 through 6 examine stories of the lives of the village health workers and their experiences, education, and training. Using ethnographic life histories, interviews, and participant observation, I detail the everyday work and organizing of VHWs and their contribution to the well-being of villages. This work identifies the resilience and the resistance of VHWs and their transformative experience at CRHP.

Chapter 1, "Two Hundred and Fifty Miles East of Bombay," introduces the life story of Latabai Kadam. The chapter discusses the conditions that were created to introduce local village women to their new status as village health workers at the Comprehensive Rural Health Project. "The Jamkhed Model: Comprehensive Rural Health Project" details the history and ongoing progress of wide-ranging innovations for community health and development. Based on CRHP's fundamental principles of equity, integration, and empowerment, the Jamkhed Model maintains a unique place in the history of international health and community-based primary health care. This chapter depicts the development of an inclusive model of health care delivery with a multidisciplinary team that emphasizes a prevention and health-promotion model in local villages. The organization itself is located within the history of global health and the initiatives of the World Health Organization, especially the Alma Ata (1978) conference. Underlying theoretical arguments in anthropology, public health, and human rights frame an analysis of current global health perspectives within the constraints of emerging national and international policies.

Chapter 2, "The Endemic Problem of Caste and Gender Inequality," assesses the problems of caste discrimination, gender oppression, and class exploitation as affected by the history of the locality and how recent changes in political and economic factors locally and nationally directly impact the health and wellness of villagers. It explains how CRHP created the conditions for VHWs to directly negotiate changes in the social relationships of caste and gender as part of a forty-year sustainable project. It portrays the fundamental changes in VHWs' ideas of themselves and their relationships with other women, upheavals in family life, and the potential for social change. It begins the description of the collaboration, changing consciousness, and continuing friendships described in Marathi as *maya* (affection) and *prem* (love) that are the key processes that sustain the mutual learning and long-term relationships of VHWs. The chapter examines interventions to untangle the traditional and ingrained caste practices in rural villages that lead to intolerance, unfairness, and ill health.

Chapter 3, "Health Is What Women Do: Transitions and Transformations," explains the CRHP's unique approach to education and learning by addressing inequality through health advocacy and self-actualization. It focuses on how women conquered personal insecurities, family impediments, and societal restrictions to become independent actors and public figures in communities that actively endorse gender segregation. The chapter describes how VHWs learn to be part of a professional team that changes the health profile in rural villages by eliminating local endemic diseases and reducing infant and maternal mortality. A central feature of this program is the kinetic and often serendipitous measures employed to reduce caste prejudice and to diminish gender inequality. VHWs from different generations, religions, and castes, as well as Dalits (formerly, untouchables or *Harijan*), describe their mentoring process and individual paths to acceptance as practitioners in their home villages. Finally, the CRHP approach to adult learning is compared to other models that emphasize consciousness and political empowerment.

Chapter 4, "Why Are You Sitting at Home Being Oppressed?" describes how VHWs participate in health care delivery with a multidisciplinary team that maintains and advances CRHP's model of primary health care for local villages. The chapter begins the development of the central narrative of *For the Public Good*—in one generation local women accomplished the transition from subjugated wives to respected community organizers instrumental in radically improving health, creating economic life for women, and advancing caste and gender equity in impoverished rural Indian villages. Through their own words and life stories, village health workers explain their journeys toward becoming the center of a dynamic process of social change and public good. For example, VHWs make clear how they work against caste and gender discrimination by learning about and actively changing multiple local factors that affect daily village life. This chapter describes how local women establish themselves in their home villages. It details a program of cooperative classes and biomedical seminars that use memorizing songs, adapting local adages, and imaginative drama in an ongoing creative process for illiterate women to learn and teach each other.

Chapter 5, "Woman and Child Health: You Will Give Birth to a Beautiful Baby," examines VHWs' patterns and practice of providing health care, especially to women and children. It describes the value of VHWs' use of a primary health care model for infant care and reproductive health by communicating accurate and current health education for villagers. Among the many advantages for village health is the ability of VHWs to diagnose and access appropriate care for pregnancy, birth, and postpartum concerns. VHWs explain the ongoing challenges of their everyday work in villages and the importance of being available as village residents. The transition from high infant and maternal mortality to reduced family size is detailed through the experiences of thousands of safe at-home births managed by VHWs.

Chapter 6, "Money in Her Hand," explains how women's development clubs (*mahila vikas mandals*) teach village women about positive health practices and eliminate traditional negative prohibitions. Ultimately, these clubs became vehicles for social change to help women contribute to the well-being of families and eventually entire communities. The successful women's clubs led to self-help groups (SHGs) that modified the economic status of women and families. For example, SHGs adopted an informal self-financing credit plan to develop income-generating microcredit projects known as *bhishi*. This chapter describes the process of organizing, naming, and conducting self-help groups and the successes and failures of groups and cooperatives. It traces VHWs' role in economic education and in helping women's income-generating clubs access government programs for grants and local bank loans. The discussion raises concerns about whether women's income-generating projects—like raising goats, tailoring, selling produce and dried fish, and even running upscale dairy communes—are sustainable and will lead to lasting economic change.

Chapter 7, "Standing on My Own: Women and Equity," addresses a central question: Is the CRHP Jamkhed Model transformative and able to establish caste and gender equity for women? This chapter analyzes resistance to common reality and everyday struggles against inequality as it is lived, discussed, and deconstructed by VHWs. It explains why local women in patriarchal rural villages were willing to accept this change and assesses how their consciousness was transformed by understanding the relationship between one's position in a local community and larger political and economic processes.

The Conclusion, "Local Solutions to Global Problems," evaluates the role of the CRHP and the Jamkhed Model as an example of a comprehensive primary health approach. This chapter recapitulates the notion of community participation and the authenticity of local solutions to solve global health and development problems. It explains how attention to social disparities and a rejection of neoliberal-motivated medical systems and treatment regimens changed health care for thousands of villages. The joy and commitment of the CRHP women who meet weekly in Jamkhed for continuing education is living proof of the possibility for creating healthy communities and social change for the public good.

CHAPTER 1

Two Hundred and Fifty Miles East of Bombay

My name is Latabai Kadam. My village is Pimpalgaon-Unda. I am giving service to my village since 1973. Before, I swept the cowshed and streets for food. The mayor's wife would throw the leftover bread (*bhakri*) to me that I caught with my sari. . . . Now, I am standing on my own. The village children are well nourished and immunized. Women use family planning. I have many saris on my back. In my village, people call me doctor.

VILLAGE HEALTH WORKER LATABAI KADAM, personal interview, 2009

Latabai Kadam describes a life of resilience and joy unimagined by women of her age and caste in rural drought-prone Jamkhed two hundred and fifty miles east of Mumbai. I met Latabai Kadam on my first trip to the Comprehensive Rural Health Project (CRHP). Arriving at Chhatrapati Shivaji International Airport on the drive through the outskirts of Mumbai (Bombay), one can barely take in all the sights, sounds, and smells of the City of Dreams. Sleek modern hotels and apartment buildings rise alongside the elegant remains of the mansions of the British Raj in contrast to the one-story makeshift corrugated metal dwellings with blue tarp roofs that stand along sidewalks, alleys, and highways, the homes of workers. At once, the paradoxes of a city with its growing population of billionaires and sprawling poverty are framed in a snapshot. Traveling over the Western Ghats toward the Deccan Plateau, recent-model cars are replaced by old trucks painted with colorful flowers, birds, geometric designs, and the white, ochre, and green Indian flag. Without road signs either in English or the Marathi language, or traffic lights, car horns become the ubiquitous and only arbiter of traffic. Eight hours later our Jeep reaches Jamkhed, a bustling town like many we passed along the way with a population of less than thirty thousand (52 percent men and 48 percent women) (India Census 2014). At a mosque with a bright green dome, we turn off the main road into unregulated throngs of motorcycles with blaring horns and motorized three-wheel rickshaws

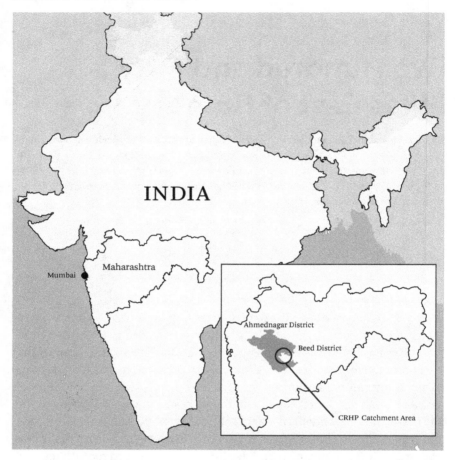

FIGURE 1: Ahmednagar and Beed Districts. CRHP catchment area in circle: Jamkhed, Karjat, and Ashti talukas

alongside cows, small herds of goats, and wild pigs. Just out of town, we turn on to a one-lane dirt road. Barely noticeable is an inconspicuous one-square-meter sign—The Comprehensive Rural Health Project.

On the compound we drive past a modest one-story corrugated alumi-num structure that I later learned is the hospital. As we approach a long rectangular building called the White House, I see forty very worn pairs of sandals and flip-flops haphazardly scattered at the entrance. Inside, on a synthetic woven carpet, Dr. Rajanikant Arole, in a Western shirt and pants, sits shoeless in a circle with forty women in saris of different vivid colors and patterns. Dr. Arole welcomes me, asks about my journey, and says, "The women are eager to meet and talk with you. What questions do you have for them today?" Surprised in my first minutes at CRHP by this gentle on-the-spot style, which I learn is typical, I ask a general question about the day's program; Dr. Arole translates the question into the village dialect of Marathi.

Latabai Kadam is the first to speak. With the attention of everyone in the room, she stands, drapes her *pallu* (sari veil) over her head, makes eye contact with me, smiles, and answers in the Marathi dialect. "We talked about fever caused by a mosquito bite, chikungunya fever. People get very sick with fever and headaches. Sometimes there is bone pain." Another woman begins speaking without standing about possible symptoms of an elderly man in her village. Latabai Kadam retakes her seat on the floor. Preeti Sadaphule, in a perfectly pleated sari without head cover, raises her hand to ask about mosquitos and soak pits as a local solution to mosquito control. Another woman makes a barely audible comment, probably a quick joke, that sets the entire room laughing. Dr. Arole speaks about the recent chikungunya (CHIKV virus) outbreak in Kerala, a state in the south of India. He responds to the many questions raised by the women, filtering out off-topic comments. Finally, the women form small groups of six and eight to discuss the issues and raise new questions.

For women without formal education, reciting new bits of knowledge and sharing their experiences with each other are part of the CRHP method, an all-consuming process of learning, sharing, and collaboration. Telling and retelling allegories, singing songs, and creating performances about health care and social issues are ways to learn and retain complicated new ideas about medicine, health, and wellness. Latabai Kadam's perpetual smile and her connection to the women in the room made by eye contact and silent gestures foreshadowed the profound connection the women felt for each other that I later learned is described by words like *maya* (friendship) and *prem* (love). This was my introduction to CRHP, the Jamkhed Model, and the women village health workers; more importantly, it was the beginning of the women's acceptance of me.

Latabai Kadam's Story

At my first formal meeting with a group of thirty village health workers, I talked about my proposed research, especially the life history interview, which I intended to use to collect personal information and formative experiences. This sparked a discussion among the women and several asked me for details about the process. When I proposed this methodology, I was unaware that CRHP uses personal histories of the VHWs as teaching and learning tools to break down traditional barriers that isolate women. Most typical village women adhere to time-honored hierarchical rules and barely make contact or speak with strangers. As part of the CRHP team, village health workers learn and practice various methods of communication with villagers, health professionals, staff, and visitors to the health center campus.

With her smile and confidence Latabai Kadam was the first VHW to agree to be a participant in my study. She told me that she was proud of her devotion to CRHP and her service as the village health worker for Pimpalgaon-Unda since 1972. In her sixties at the time of the first interview, Latabai Kadam represents the first generation of village health workers. Her life experiences are typical for a woman of her age and caste; married at age twelve or thirteen, she immediately moved to her husband's village. Latabai Kadam began having sexual relations with her husband only when her mother-in-law noticed that she had reached menarche. Within a few months Latabai Kadam was pregnant. Even before her pregnancy was apparent, her movements in the village as a young newly married woman were restricted by her husband: "I was told never to speak to others, even other women at the well. I had to wear my sari *pallu* covering my face, walk with my head down, and not make eye contact with anyone" (personal interview, 2009). As we sat together, she demonstrated the posture, with a laugh.

Latabai Kadam's husband decided to move away from their home village to Goregaon, a suburb of Mumbai, to take a job at a factory. Latabai Kadam found work on a rock crew for road construction for ₹30 a day (less than $1) breaking rocks into gravel for a roadbed. Each day she brought her infant son to work and placed him in a makeshift cloth hammock as she worked continuously without breaks or rest periods. She lived with her husband in a rented room; a few acquaintances and some of her husband's other family members lived nearby. Latabai Kadam remembers that life away from the village was hard and that her husband became cruel, accusing her of talking to young men. Soon after, family life started to fall apart. On one occasion, her husband became exceptionally aggressive, threatening her by sitting next to her bed all night, clasping a knife in his hand. Soon after, her husband took Latabai Kadam to a nearby lake with the intention of drowning her. Whether they were aware of the plan or heard her screams, her husband's brother and his wife intervened and were able to save her. Ultimately, her husband sent her back to the village, but he refused to let her take her son with her and kept him in Bombay.

Three months later, Latabai Kadam's son was sent back to Pimpalgaon-Unda village. At this point in the interview, she lowers her eyes and her rapid talk abruptly stops. After a pause, she surreptitiously wipes tears from her eyes with her sari *pallu*. Her voice shaking, she says, "When he arrived, I did not recognize him . . . my own son. . . . He was sick and filthy, with measles and diarrhea." Within a few days, Latabai Kadam's son died.

Such personal tragedy, a pattern of early adolescent marriage and pregnancy, hard manual labor, domestic work, and physical abuse, typifies the lives of some women who became village health workers in the early years of CRHP. In Jamkhed villages, most girls of her generation received less than the third standard (three years) of formal education; it would have been almost impossible for them to dream of a different life. How could she have imagined that one day she would be a respected health practitioner in her village? How could she conceive of a program like CRHP that enlists village women from their destined place at home as only wives and mothers? Would it ever be possible for a Dalit like Latabai Kadam to be more than a menial farm worker and animal tender? How could she begin to think that she would be a part of helping her village get safe drinking water, eliminate constant health problems like scabies and waterborne diseases, and end food shortages?

Latabai Kadam speaks with pride of six hundred safe births in her village and of helping women stay healthy with appropriate birth spacing. She weighs infants to monitor their growth and development and keeps charts of children's health progress. She explains that social and environmental factors affect health, so she initiates women's clubs that start income-generating projects. Finally, she learned how politics both local and national affects her village, and while she has no desire to run for office, eventually she helps lay the groundwork to elect a woman village *sarpanch* (mayor). All of these accomplishments are a result of the model and the process designed by Drs. Mabelle and Rajanikant Arole that created the category of village health worker and generated the conditions for dynamic changes in health, wellness, and agricultural development in the Jamkhed region.

The Comprehensive Rural Health Project:
The Jamkhed Model

What we want to do is make knowledge available to everybody and in doing so create new manpower, who will be able to understand this knowledge in a simple way and apply this knowledge to the people on a massive scale, because few doctors or a few health professionals scattered here and there will not do.

DR. RAJANIKANT AROLE, (BBC 1984)

What medical science is today is a pool of the experiences of many people, it is a common pool of knowledge. . . . I do not believe that this pool of knowledge should belong to one particular sect of people, that is, the doctor. I do not think that the doctor should have a monopoly of that and then use that common knowledge to make money for himself.

DR. MABELLE AROLE, (BBC 1984)

In 1970, Drs. Mabelle and Rajanikant Arole launched their project in Jamkhed, (Ahmednagar district), Maharashtra, where the majority of villagers live below the nationally designated poverty line (BPL). What came to be known as the Comprehensive Rural Health Project or the Jamkhed Model was designed by the Aroles as a processual methodology to create healthy sustainable communities. The greater Jamkhed area including Ashti, Karjat, and Jamkhed *talukas* (land blocks) was selected as the site for the project because it represents one of the poorest rural areas without a government health system or private doctors, but also because of an invitation and agreement of support from local leaders (Arole and Arole 1994). Selecting an appropriate location was a major concern because the Aroles knew the approval of elected officials and village leaders was essential to build the type of support needed to introduce innovative ideas and radical changes required for the success of the model. While the goal was to eliminate preventable and endemic diseases that threaten morbidity and mortality, the model was constructed on the premise that health and development are two sides of the same coin. In order to raise the health profile, it was necessary to improve social conditions and boost the level of economic well-being.

The Aroles graduated first and second in their class at Vellore Christian Medical College in Tamil Nadu. They were Fulbright scholars who completed residencies at Case Western Reserve University and earned MPH. (Master of Public Health) degrees at Johns Hopkins School of Hygiene (now

Bloomberg School of Public Health). It was at Johns Hopkins that they formally developed the participatory approach that they hoped would eliminate preventable and endemic diseases and dramatically improve the health profile and well-being of the local population.

Principles of the Jamkhed Model

Based on three encompassing principles—equity, integration, and empowerment—the CRHP mission statement reads:

> Health is a universal human right. Eliminating injustices, which deny all people access to this right, underlies the very essence of our work and our approach. Using the combined talents and energy of our staff and the families we work with, we strive to develop communities through a grassroots movement. By mobilizing and building the capacity of communities all can achieve access to health care and freedom from poverty, hunger and violence. (CRHP 2009)

The Aroles translated their observation of the social processes in rural India into the progressive idea that people have the right and the duty to participate in initiating, planning, and implementing health care in their own localities. The idea of individual rights and equity is part of Drs. Mabelle and Raj Arole's own experience, having lived through the rejection of British colonialism and the creation of India as an independent nation. The Aroles' views were framed by the historical trends of the latter part of the twentieth century of grassroots civil rights movements, the second wave feminism in the United States, antiwar student movements in Western Europe, and social movements in India.

However, the clarity of purpose of the Jamkhed Model can be traced back to their extensive experience as medical students in India, residencies in the United States, and collaborations during public health studies in Baltimore. The Aroles' Christian faith, in large measure, is responsible for the formation of the underlying principles of the CRHP. Since the program's inception the Aroles connected their Christian faith to their mission, yet CRHP was not an organization interested in converting villagers to Christianity and made no attempts to do so apart from having prayer services each morning. Rather, their profound beliefs were the source of understanding and implementing principles of equity focused on the social origins of disease and the idea of health for villagers given by villagers.

For the Aroles, the integration of local knowledge and experience into complex health and development projects created a foundation from which to introduce a human rights perspective that challenges the status quo in rural villages. Raj Arole's personal perspective was gained as a boy growing up Christian in a largely Hindu village in Rahuri, Ahmednagar, Maharashtra, not far from Jamkhed, where both his parents were schoolteachers. In contrast, Mabelle Arole's father, Rajappan D. Immanuel, received a degree in theology from Boston University, taught at Duke University, and was a professor of New Testament Greek at the Theological Seminary in Jabalpur, Madhya Pradesh. Her family name Emmanuel is part of a long history of Christianity in South India.

After working in a rural voluntary hospital in Vadala, Maharashtra, from 1962 to 1966, the Aroles decided to undertake clinical training in the United States on a Fulbright scholarship that took them to the Midwest, a month on a Navaho reservation, and eventually to Baltimore. At Johns Hopkins School of Hygiene and Public Health they began graduate work in public health with Dr. Carl Taylor, initiator of the International Health Program. But as Carl Taylor, who became a longtime colleague and friend, notes, their ideas for a comprehensive primary health care program were their own and completely original (Taylor 1992). The model that the Aroles created was based on their common interest in communities with underserved health needs. They made a promise to each other upon graduating from Vellore Medical College to reject the commercialization of biomedicine and to work with local communities and for promotion of health and security.

Community Participation

The cornerstone of the CRHP Jamkhed Model is community participation and capacity building. The Aroles believe that fulfilling their mission depends on the entire community for its knowledge, cooperation, support, and ability to plan and maintain health and development.

> We did not want the health center to be a stereotypical hospital, and it did not necessarily have to meet the standards set by the urban elite. Because it was supporting the health activities in the villages, it should be a place where ordinary villagers felt comfortable. In order to reduce patient costs, we hoped to encourage relatives to participate in the care of patients, and so we wanted to provide enough facilities and space for relatives to stay and cook. (Arole and Arole 1994, 97)

The Jamkhed Model for community participation and involvement is innovative and compelling in two ways: first, local knowledge from the bottom up informed health interventions, development projects, and medical treatment; and second, the introduction of every new program and practice was based on and directly addressed the identified basic inequalities within villages and communities, namely caste and gender discrimination.

The goal of community participation pursued by Drs. Mabelle and Rajanikant Arole respected the potential of all village members to learn about health and health care and to reflect on the social pressures that inhibit cooperation and mutual aid for the well-being of all. In the early days of CRHP, when the Aroles gave a class on any medical topic, everyone interested in learning was invited, from the bus drivers to the nurses and physicians. For example, a class that explained the functioning of the eye and surgical procedures to address cataracts, a common problem, would draw more than twenty participants when held in the courtyard or garden. The Aroles deduced that villagers who were uncomfortable interacting with physicians and health professionals were more likely to talk to workers, like the CRHP van drivers. By opening classes to all, accurate information about health and medical procedures became more accessible to villagers and visitors, reinforcing the conviction of equity and integration.

Project Villages and Local Heterogeneity

Project villages, a term used to describe those villages that are active with CRHP, generally have a population of approximately 1,500 to 2,000 and are located in two districts in Maharashtra. In Ahmednagar district there are two *talukas* (blocks or sections): Jamkhed, which is the name of both a town and *taluka*, and Karjat. In Beed district the only *taluka* represented in the project is Ashti. These distinctions are significant especially regarding health and sanitation projects since district administration may handle funding allocations differently. Notably, not all villages in a particular locale are members of the CRHP but join based on village consensus through elected officials.

The internal heterogeneity of Indian villages as previously assessed has been described in the 1950s as being characterized by a social structure system and a "structural nexus" in relation to other communities (Gough, Srinivas, and Marriott in Marriott 1955). In the early 1970s, village life centered on individual and joint families and was stratified by caste and religion in the Jamkhed area. Typically, villages were comprised of 20 percent to 40 percent Maratha and other castes; 20 percent to 30 percent Dalit; 10 percent Brahmin; and 5 percent to 15 percent Muslim (if Muslims were present). Each village or *vasti* (neighborhood) flies a triangular solid-colored flag indicating its religious affiliation—ochre for Hindu, green for Muslim, and blue for Buddhist, which in this region generally also means Dalit.

The Mobile Health Team

To meet the diverse needs of villages in the Jamkhed locality, CRHP created the mobile health team (MHT), a group of integrated professionals who travelled daily by Jeep directly to villages to administer health care tailored to the community. Implementing a primary health care model in rural villages in an area with poor roads and villages spread out miles from the health center in Jamkhed required this special innovation. In the early days, public buses and oxen carts were the primary means of transportation. Today, wooden carts are still used by farmers to transport goods, especially sugarcane, and very few Jamkhed villagers own their own cars, although there are an increasing number of motorcycles on the roads.

The mobile health team acts as a bridge between the CRHP health center and the villages. The team is comprised of a nurse, social workers, a paramedical worker, and sometimes a physician or an Ayurvedic doctor. The team makes rounds in the project villages with morning and evening visits. A major function of the MHT is to support and promote the work of the VHWs. On a typical morning visit the team, accompanied by the VHW, walks around the village visiting homes with pregnant women, newborn babies, and those with illness. Evening visits take on a different character, with team members attending village meetings or talking to groups of villagers. The team members, each with a different specialty, provide a particular type of care. For example, in the days before treatment and a cure for leprosy, those infected were shunned by the community. The MHT leprosy specialist played a crucial role in helping to identify and treat the medical and social issues and stigma of the disease.

Antecedents of Primary Health Care

In 1970, the secretary general of the World Health Organization, Halfdan Mahler, expressed concern that since the 1950s many developing countries focused on specialized mass campaigns to eradicate disease at the expense of advancing basic health services (Djukanovic, Mach, and WHO 1975). Mahler asserted that the underlying causes of illness and lack of well-being are social and economic disparities, which exist both within and between countries.

Mahler commissioned a WHO report in early 1970, *Alternative Approaches to Meeting Basic Health Needs in Developing Countries* (Djukanovic and Mach 1975). This report highlights the work of projects in various regions of the Global South which demonstrated significant changes in the provision of health care using innovative alternative approaches to solve basic health concerns. Mahler wrote, "The strategy adopted for this purpose by many developing countries had been modeled on that of the industrialized countries, but as a strategy it had been a failure" (qtd. in Djukanovic and Mach 1975, 8). The WHO report included China's "barefoot doctor" model and other grassroots community health worker programs of the 1960s in Cuba, Tanzania, India, Mexico, and the Philippines. One project singled out for its success in the 1975 report was the Jamkhed Model: "One of the most important aspects is that the project is based on the recognition, particularly by the project leaders, of the priorities determined by the community. To the community, health is not a number one priority; agriculture, water supplies and housing are more important" (Arole and Arole, qtd. in Newell 1975, 77).

Health for All: Alma-Ata

Subsequently, in 1978, a World Health Organization UNICEF conference was convened in Alma-Ata (Almaty), Kazakhstan, (formerly in the USSR) to endorse a proposal for universal global health based on the premise that health is a fundamental human right. The conference document ratified by the 134 countries declared *Health for All by the Year 2000*. The Alma-Ata conference's chief accomplishment was the iteration of a primary health care (PHC) model described as "essential health care based on practical, scientifically sound and socially acceptable methods and technology made universally accessible to individuals and families in the community" (WHO 2002, 2). Conference participants using examples of established programs articulated this community-based model; antecedents of the idea were the product of collaboration between Halfdan Mahler and Carl Taylor, originator of the International Health program at Johns Hopkins. These basic principles detail a comprehensive and integrated PHC approach for

education concerning prevailing health problems and the methods of pre-
venting and controlling them; promotion of food supply and proper nutrition;
an adequate supply of safe water and basic sanitation; maternal and child
health care, including family planning; immunization against the major infectious diseases; prevention and control of locally endemic diseases; appropriate treatment of common diseases and injuries; and provision of essential
drugs. (WHO 2002, 2)

Major principles advanced at the Alma Ata conference support the original WHO definition of health as a human right and a potential social goal,
and the existing gross inequality in the health status of people was identified as a common concern. Importantly, an essential contribution of this
perspective was the idea that health care be "made universally accessible
to individuals and families in the community through their full participation and at a cost that the community and country can afford to maintain at every stage of their development in the spirit of self-reliance and
self-determination" (WHO 2008).

Selective Primary Health Care—Maintaining the Status Quo

Before the ink was dry on the Alma-Ata document, a 1979 conference in
Bellagio, Italy, produced a paper by Walsh and Warren published in both
the *New England Journal of Medicine* and *Social Science and Medicine* that
aimed to transform the idea of primary health care, mollify biomedical
institutions, and eventually set the stage to redress the ratified Alma-Ata
declaration. According to Walsh and Warren (1979), "The goal set at Alma-
Ata is above reproach, yet its large and laudable scope makes it unattain-
able in terms of its prohibitive cost and the numbers of trained personnel
required" (145). Shifting the focus primarily to infectious diseases in what
they termed "less developed countries," the authors put forward a modification to selectively target specific diseases.

This approach intentionally reduced and limited the scope of primary
health care with a set of goals, such as growth monitoring, oral rehydration
techniques, breastfeeding, and immunizations (GOBI), that fit neatly into a
biomedical individual-focused model. In and of themselves these measures
are clearly important, even essential, but they ignore the more pressing and
long-term effectiveness of a comprehensive health program. In fact, after

the introduction of GOBI it was apparent that this selective focus missed essential aspects of reproductive and child health, so food supplementation, female literacy, and family planning (FFF) was added. Many international financial institutions (IFIs) and UNICEF adopted selective primary health care as ostensibly more compatible with a neoliberal biomedical approach, especially its elimination of community participation as too difficult and cumbersome for short-term interventions. Hong (2004) points out that the selective approach was an instant hit with donors because of its relatively limited scope and technology-based focus, and money poured in from the World Bank, USAID, the Vatican, and many NGOs.

Notably, the selective approach favors more easily measurable biomedical features and eliminates the social- and community-based components of PHC (Cueto 2004). In addition, health and human rights activists suggest that the substitution of a neoliberal top-down model would short-circuit the community action and participation aspect of the Alma-Ata model, which would prevent positive long-term health effects for both local communities and global populations (Hong 2004; Gish 2004). While some claim that "vertical" or "top-down" programs are as good as the comprehensive Alma-Ata PHC model, Hong (2004) disagrees, asserting that selective models reinforce notions of free choice and competition, and implies that "health is not an absolute human right but rather a private good" (30).

Primary Health Care: An Alternative Model?

In 1984, Heggenhougen framed a crucial issue regarding primary health care with the following question: Will PHC efforts be allowed to succeed? The history, process, and value of primary health care is controversial (Brown, Cueto, and Fee 2006; Cueto 2004), yet proponents of the model confirm its usefulness and efficacy for comprehensive, community-based care (Solheim, McElmurry, and Kim 2007; Fritzen 2007). In addition, PHC based on a participatory model requires an approach that starts at the community level rather than generalizing from the top down with broad policy initiatives that miss embedded inequality. PHC is not only a matter of changing the equation of curative medicine in favor of health promotion but an alternative expansion to identify and incorporate development activities (Heggenhougen 1984). From an anthropological perspective, Coreil (1990) suggests that ethnographic methodologies and research perspectives contribute to an understanding of PHC implementation. Mull (1990) points out that "it has been difficult to integrate primary health care programs with existing government agencies, to ensure meaningful community participation, and to achieve true coordination of health care activities from bottom to top" (37). Others identify finer-grained distinctions that enable a comparison between normative utilitarian perspectives versus notions of empowerment (Morgan 2001). Nichter (2008) demonstrates the importance of informed communities through familiar images and analogies as a way to develop community involvement to introduce biotechnology, such as vaccines. Other researchers suggest that there is a need for internal change agents to promote human potential that leads to human rights outcomes (Werner and Bower 2005). While anthropologists were early adopters of PHC, the enthusiasm in the discipline waned, as it did in many public health interventions, when major funding sources accepted and preferred neoliberal approaches, especially for funding NGOs. More recently, anthropologists have identified the importance of ethnographic research to understand health financing in India (Ahlin, Nichter, and Pillai 2016), the necessity for public health interventions to address teamwork and community needs (Nichter 1996, 2008), and the need for community participatory involvement (Whiteford and Vindrola-Padros 2016).

Other anthropologists agree that the goal of anthropological work "in global health is to reduce health inequalities and contribute to the development of sustainable and salutogenic sociocultural, political and economic systems" (Janes and Corbett 2009, 169). Based on his work in Mongolia, Janes (2004) is critical of neoliberal economic models that negatively affect health care and suggests that we advocate "for a universal system of global health values that challenges the narrow and inhumane economic paradigm that now governs global health development" (468). Clearly, since the Alma-Ata Declaration, community participation as a major component of PHC has been an elusive concept to define and, more pragmatically, to implement as part of a public health intervention or research project.

Primary Health Care: Challenging Neoliberalism

Neoliberal shifts in the economy over the last forty years, driven by international economic development activities among IFIs like the World Bank that emphasized stakeholders rather than identifying health needs at the community level, have left large sectors of nations and states, especially in the Global South, with unrecognized and unfulfilled health and social requirements and promoted the continuation of existing conditions that benefit dominant groups and overlook those most in need of care. As Green (1989) points out, in the 1970s, after the WHO Alma-Ata conference, the United Nations International Children's Emergency Fund (UNICEF) and bilateral agencies like the United States Agency for International Development (USAID) actively began promoting and financing comprehensive primary health care (PHC), but by the mid-1980s PHC programs had been abandoned. Others suggest that the neoliberal emphasis on privatization and international aid programs has left existing primary health care approaches channeled through non-governmental organizations understudied (Pfeiffer 2003). In addition, Pfeiffer and Chapman (2010) assess how structural adjustment programs used by IFIs like the IMF and the World Bank to promote market fundamentalism further inhibits possibilities of primary health care models. These austerity policy decisions have a history of promoting negative consequences. For example, in India a 1990 memorandum sponsored by the World Bank recommended cuts in social-sector spending to reduce the fiscal deficit by devaluing the rupee by 23 percent, providing fewer government interventions and introducing market-friendly approaches ("The Bank and Structural Adjustment" 1996); this policy recommendation directly affected funding for education and health care. Further, Navarro et al. (2006) disparages the influence of neoliberalism on health outcomes asserting that policies addressing social inequalities, such as public expenditures on medical care and unemployment, seem to have a beneficial and sustainable effect on selected key indicators, especially infant mortality.

Krieger et al. (2016) connect reproductive justice and preventable maternal and infant deaths to public funding for health care. However, the reduction in public health financing caused by austerity measures generated by neoliberal policies directly influences national health systems and adversely affects local populations without adequate resources, especially for women and children living in poverty. Analysis of empirical epidemiological and population-based data quantify and summarize information that becomes benchmarks or targets to understand general patterns of health, morbidity and mortality (see for example WHO 2015; World Bank 2015, 2018; CDC 1989; IIPS and ICF 2017). Thus, one major indicator of a nation's health profile is the infant mortality rate (IMR), which describes the number of deaths under age one per one thousand live births for a specific time period, usually a given year (Skolnik 2016). This indicator reveals a stark comparison between an under-resourced country with a primary health care system,

Cuba, and one of the wealthiest nations with an advanced biomedical fee-for-service system, the United States. While some researchers are critical of the reliability of Cuba's national statistics regarding health and population data (Gonzalez 2015), the infant mortality rate in Cuba has consistently declined over the last forty years, from twenty-two deaths per one thousand live births to four in 2018, due to the introduction of a dedicated program to improve the health of women of child-bearing age and their children, the Maternal–Child Program (Programa Nacional de Atencion in Materno-Infantil [PAMI]) (Espinosa et al. 2018; Whiteford and Branch 2008). In contrast, the United States IMR has been intransigent; the rate in 1980 was thirteen per one thousand, and in 2018 it lingers at six, making the US the lowest-ranking country in the Organisation for Economic Cooperation and Development (OECD) (World Bank 2018). Set side-by-side with an integrated primary health care model like Cuba's, the United States insurance-based health financing that relies on highly technological top-down biomedical interventions appears to be hampered with gaps, imbalances, and asymmetries in medical care delivery that contributes to health inequalities in particular communities (see Chambers et al. 2018; Krieger 2020). The question remains: Is the reduction of major health markers like infant mortality inextricably tied to health financing structures that are systematically unable to solve health disparities generated by social inequalities?

Accessing adequate funding from government sponsored or private philanthropies unencumbered by neoliberal guidelines has remained a constant challenge for CRHP, especially when financing is attached to research methods or interventions that might compromise the basic principles of the Jamkhed comprehensive primary health care model. Instead, the Aroles worked closely with Christian philanthropic institutions who appreciated the basic tenets of the CRHP model. For example, a 1972 report submitted by Dr. Rajanikant Arole to the Christian Medical Commission and World Council of Churches was instrumental in shifting funding priorities from primarily curative hospitals to local community health care projects (Litsios 2004). Thus, CRHP established a long-term relationship with funding institutes like Lutheran World Relief. Further, the Aroles were cautious about accepting grants from agencies that attempted to directly dictate methods, interventions, and projects that undermined desired outcomes, especially for community participation. For example, CRHP applied for funding for the breakfast program (see Chapter 2) from a European NGO that funded nutrition projects for mothers and children under five. Many mothers from

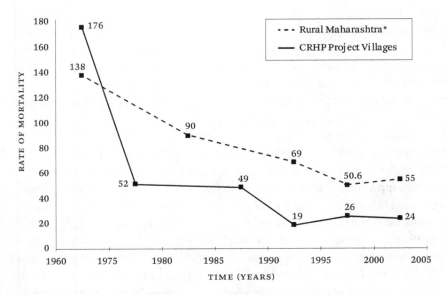

FIGURE 2: Infant Mortality Rate: CRHP Compared to Rural Maharashtra
*SOURCES: Census of India 1971, 1981, 1991, and 2001; IIPS National Family Survey II: 1998–99.
Compiled by R. S. Premkumar, PhD

Jamkhed families living in the most urgent poverty conditions were not able to participate in the program because they were working as day laborers on local farms and sending instead older sisters who were routinely child minders to accompany siblings to the breakfast program. The NGO would not accept the addition of older siblings as part of the project. Funding was crucial to continue the nutrition program, yet, Drs. Mabelle and Raj Arole rejected the grant due to the unacceptable NGO restrictions that would change the purpose and goals of the project. Fortunately, other sources were secured to continue the work as planned.

Despite funding constraints, one of the greatest successes of the Comprehensive Rural Health Program was the dramatic reduction in infant mortality within five years of implementing the Jamkhed model. The infant mortality rate of 176 deaths per one thousand live births in 1971 was decreased to fifty-two deaths per one thousand live births in 1976. This unprecedented 70 percent reduction in the mortality of neonates and infants prevented the unspeakable pain and horror of witnessing the illness and death of a child.

The successful decrease of infant mortality, a global indicator thought to be intractable, was not based on high-tech biomedicine but instead was the result of the everyday labor-intensive efforts to promote health and prevent illness by the newly trained village health workers who were able to offer antenatal care and safe home deliveries with the support of the CRHP medical center, as necessary. As Table 1 shows, infant mortality rates for CRHP villages are compared to other rural villages in the Jamkhed region to demonstrate the magnitude of the decrease and the sustainability of the reduction overtime. For example, in 2016 the infant mortality rate for CRHP project villages was eighteen deaths per one thousand live births and the Indian national rate was forty-one (IIPS and ICF 2017). As the following chapters will show, the CRHP comprehensive primary care approach demonstrates the value of equity and advocacy for village health by rejecting neoliberal top-down research protocols in favor of implementing on-the-ground evaluations of health needs to generate local solutions for villagers.

The value of the Jamkhed Model is that these innovations produced positive long-lasting effects. Through the more than forty years that CRHP served the Jamkhed community with its innovative change-model, dramatic solutions for many maladies were achieved in a short period of time. Today, CRHP innovations have reduced the incidence of major infectious diseases that are causes of death in other rural areas. In project villages, formerly endemic diseases like scabies were eradicated using local remedies; leprosy and its stigma is virtually eliminated; and tuberculosis rates are almost negligible. Basic health care was introduced and sustained over time, and the project met its desired goal: community participation and mobilization that led villagers to become involved for positive change.

These transformations in the health status of the community, sustained over time, demonstrate the efficacy of the model and the underlying mission for social justice and economic development. By selectively choosing appropriate funders, the Aroles kept true to the original purpose of their mission: to work with those living in poverty in the spirit of equity by integrating local knowledge and experience into complex health and development projects. Using methods and programs developed for a specific community in a discrete period of time, the Jamkhed Model creatively introduced local solutions to solve an intractable global problem.

CHAPTER 2

The Endemic Problem of Caste and Gender Inequality

"Health does not exist in a vacuum . . . it depends upon sociocultural and economic factors. In most societies, women are the keepers of health in their households and therefore their status, knowledge and attitudes influence health."

MABELLE AROLE AND RAJANIKANT AROLE, *Jamkhed: A Comprehensive Rural Health Project*, 182

The health and wellness of Jamkhed is shaped by the overt and hidden cleavages embedded in caste discrimination, gender oppression, and class exploitation set by entrenched historical patterns and modified by recent changes in political and economic factors locally and nationally. The comprehensive approach developed by Drs. Mabelle and Raj Arole established principles of equity, integration, and empowerment and focused on human rights and social justice to mitigate the impact of the existing inequalities that they believe directly affected the well-being of the people of Jamkhed. Based on their experiences as physicians in rural India, the project's public health design required specific modifications and flexibility for its introduction in Jamkhed. Selecting local women for instruction as health specialists, although not their first choice, created the official category of village health worker that placed women at the nexus of providing village-based health care as part of the CRHP team, and moved women to a new and unfamiliar place in village life. Establishing women as health practitioners in rural areas helped to tackle a critical global public health concern—the health of women and children—yet, the diversity within villages and the endemic problem of caste and gender inequality posed challenges that tested the mastery of the Aroles' strategy and the ingenuity of the Jamkhed Model itself.

While villages in this largely rural region of eastern Maharashtra appear to be homogeneous, there are differences in caste, class, and religion that shape and conceal the intricacies of daily life. More than two hundred women village health workers representing the diversity of caste and religion were selected through self-governing decisions made in each participating village. For the purposes of this study, based on the chronology of their education at CRHP, I divide the women into two groups: the first generation, from 1970 to 1994, and the second generation, from 1995 to 2007. (There is a third generation that started in 2007 who are not included in this volume.) There are village health workers of all three generations currently practicing in their home villages. As noted above, the population of CRHP participant villages varies from approximately one thousand to two thousand and is stratified by caste (Maratha, the area's dominant caste, to Dalits), religion (Hindu, Muslim, and Buddhist, with Jain, Christian, and a number of tribal groups living on the outskirts of Jamkhed town), and class differences (80 percent of the population is BPL). As the CRHP mission statement affirms, the sources of poor health and lack of development characteristic of the region is directly connected to the underlying causes of caste and gender inequality and injustice. In discussing gender equity in health, Sen and Östlin (2008) assert that the elimination of bias in health care systems by improving the relationship between community action and health inequalities can guarantee health care as a human right for civil society.

Women and Equity

In *Voices of South Asian Women* (1995), a UNICEF study, Dr. Mabelle Arole writes:

> There is a tenacity, inner strength, wisdom and infinite capacity to give. Conceived in violence, unwanted from birth, discriminated against throughout life, they [women] must struggle for their very existence. They are stripped of their rights and treated as property. They work, they serve, they please. Yet, they are raped, they are abused, they are even burned. Paradoxically, these same abused South Asian women are also revered as wives and mothers, and even worshipped in traditional rituals. (2)

While this view may appear to broadly characterize or to essentialize South Asian women, rather, it delineates the vast continuum on which different castes and classes of women are placed and place themselves. For example, in Jamkhed when young Hindu girls talk about marriage choices and rules in everyday conversations, their words normalize conventional ideas and reference the "laws of Manu" (Manusmiriti). These early Hindu scriptural writings command that a girl as a daughter must give complete obedience to the father, a wife should honor her husband as a god, and a mother should relinquish independence to her husband.

Mathur (2000) points out that the interpretations of Indian women continue to have ideological consequences of colonialism in Indian law, tradition, and morality that create oppositions such as "home/world, material/spiritual, and traditional/modern," (99) which categorize rather than explain women's position in society. Others suggest that the range of descriptions of South Asian women mark every point along a spectrum that describes women's activities and dynamic strategies, from subjectivity to agency (Ghosh 2007). Still others who specifically examine British colonialism in India note that the juxtaposition of abuse and reverence toward Indian women attaches to ideas of social reform and nationalism (Chatterjee 1989). C. Mohanty (2003) and other postcolonial scholars caution against accepting and repeating assumptions made about subaltern women; in Jamkhed these assertions are based on the meanings of caste, class, and gender, especially for rural women living in poverty.

To explain the deep-seated caste and gender inequalities embedded in Indian society, feminist scholars have generated numerous and significant theoretical and methodological approaches to gauge the historical antecedents and contemporary concerns. For example, Channa (2013) asserts gender constructions are linked with patriarchy as one aspect of inequality and maintains "gender is not uniformly constructed across society and internal differences intersect on axes of race, class, ethnicity and caste" (185). Ghosh (2007) points out that women's struggles and women's movements have privileged educated women from colonial times until the twentieth century, often without accounting for the hold of caste, religion, and class-based identities. More recently, Menon (2015) initiated a debate about the usefulness of the concept of intersectionality as conceived by an American legal scholar (Crenshaw 1989) and cautions that "feminism requires us to recognize that 'women' is neither a stable nor a homogeneous category" (Menon 2015, 37). Menon is concerned that the use of the concept of intersectionality may be too narrow to understand the "Indian experience" and may suffer from its origins in the Global North and the inadvertent use of imperialist classifications, stating, "When we in the non-West theorize on the basis of our experiences, we rarely assume that these are generalizable everywhere, unlike theory arising in the West" (37). Further, given the outsized influence of large-scale political and economic interventions, Menon voices concerns about the interpretation and adoption of the concept by international funders like the United Nations. In contrast, John (2015) contends that given the historical role of colonialism and nationalism and the uniqueness of feminism and the women's question regarding the Indian context, intersectionality may have "genuinely liberatory potential . . . to building solidarity across subjects that are recognized as otherwise getting lost between movements and agendas" (76). Some feminist scholars assess the relationship between knowledge production and feminist agendas and point out that it raises questions of who produces theory, from what location, and for what purpose, especially in the context of colonialism and Western theories (Loomba and Lukose 2012). Others consider intersectionality as a corrective to critique feminist orthodoxy and recognize the hegemony of mainstream women's movements to reject upper-caste Hinduism as the norm in creating theoretical knowledge and gender binaries, making it difficult for other women's perspectives to gain ground even within a political and economic analysis (Kapilashrami, Bisht, and Ravindran 2016).

The debate about the application of the concept of intersectionality may be useful in developing feminist positions or advancing knowledge about the complexity of women's issues in India. Does it rise to the level of a theoretical direction? Or as John (2015) suggests, is it an additive framework that contributes to a holistic analysis to decipher gender, caste, religion, and community? For example, as a feminist advocating for women's rights I have learned the importance of understanding current conflicts in the US against privilege from an antiracist perspective. This level of analysis furnishes insights that helped me decipher the intercaste discord I observed in the Jamkhed area between two Dalit groups, Mang and Mahar, that potentially impacted community and personal interactions. Thus, my anthropological viewpoint uses a holistic approach based on the systematic study of a specific community at a specific time to understand the circumstances of everyday life through the examination of people's perspectives, values, practices, and social organization. This approach emphasizes the value of underlying multivocal relationships between gender and caste inequality in the context of power and privilege using a historical perspective to assess how larger social, political, and economic processes constrain and enable women in their everyday lives. Based on my ethnographic study, I suggest that the influences and methods to challenge caste and gender inequality, and the recognition of class exploitation developed by CRHP, recast the lives of women village health workers and Jamkhed villagers. These transformations were primarily successful because the underlying and elementary points of prejudice and discrimination are accurately recognized and made accessible for interpretation by local women through the various components of the Jamkhed Model.

Interventions and Transformations: Agents for Change

Historian Rao (2003) raises the question of how the complex history of caste as a "form of identification and as a structure of disfranchisement and exploitation" (3) affects women. Challenging ideas about caste structure among individual women and ensuring their cooperation and collaboration in the complex process of becoming village health workers required the invention of a compendium of strategies. These creative interventions integrated local knowledge and practical techniques, through often time-consuming processes, to introduce positive change to village life. As part of the CRHP process and philosophy, Drs. Mabelle and Rajanikant Arole affirmed in both actions and words that in every aspect of the project, from the surgical theater to the classroom and in villages, the elimination of local prejudices that affected health and well-being was the objective.

Based on the life history interviews I conducted with village health workers, the notion of caste was fixed and central to the woman's understanding of her own identity and position in the community. Aware of the need to alter deep-seated beliefs and long-established attitudes, these interventions raised questions about the nature of caste and gender in both everyday village life and in the broader social and political context. If local women were to be the primary health providers in villages, then helping each woman to understand her position in her family, village and civil society became a central goal. Whether the VHW was a Brahmin or a Dalit, the problems of identifying and accommodating the different needs of diverse village populations necessitated ongoing discussions about village diversity that could affect the provision of health care. In addition, Dr. Mabelle Arole and the entire CRHP staff modeled interactions with each other to avoid the appearance of bias. Information that facilitates understanding of the basic factors that perpetuate poverty, especially local and national economic structures, was made accessible to women through the CRHP teaching process (see

Chapter 4). Inequities embedded in village life took on new and compelling meaning when women were confronted with the process of sharing experiences and learning in an environment that rejected the everyday status quo.

Initiating Relationships: *Prem* and *Maya*—Love and Long-Lasting Affection

I met Dr. Mabelle Arole here [in Jamkhed] when I came for training. I refused to look at Dr. Mabellebai. I was afraid. In my village when government health workers came everyone would go and hide. I was afraid of everybody, all the [CRHP] staff. No matter what they did they looked different and dressed different. I thought we don't know what they are going to do. They might do something to me. . . . One thing Dr. Mabellebai did was sit next to me. She would touch my arm or pat me on the back. Those are the things that made the fear gradually go away. I started feeling like a human being. (Ushabai Bangar, personal interview, 2010)

What each woman remembers from their first acquaintance with Dr. Mabelle Arole are the genuine feelings of caring and concern. "It feels like going to one's mother's house," was a common response when asked what women thought of going to weekly meetings at CRHP. Most women portrayed the stays as a time and place of caring. As Ushabai Bangar notes, women began sensing a different environment of feelings, a beginning of a changing understanding of themselves, and a new way to interact with others. As with so many women in rural villages, Ushabai Bangar never forgot the loneliness and isolation she felt in her early marriage moving to her husband's household and being a daughter-in-law. Another woman recalled questions Dr. Mabelle Arole asked: "'How are you? How are your children?' No one ever asked such questions or seemed concerned about me."

Coming to CRHP propelled local women into a new situation previously unavailable to women living in rural villages in which most women lived below the poverty line (BPL). The first generation of VHWs, women born in the middle of the twentieth century, typically few had more than three years of formal schooling. Over the course of my fieldwork in both interviews and informal interactions I was struck by the consistency of women's explanations of unconditional understanding of the role of a daughter, wife, and mother, but the consequences of these societal expectations and societal pressures, like early marriage and patrilocal residence, left indelible marks. Kaushalya Gaikwad describes her childhood memories of rejection because of not giving birth to a son:

My mother became a widow when my brother and I were small. Because we were Harijan [Dalits] she had no other way of getting food except cleaning cowsheds and scavenging. When I was twelve my uncle got me married. Soon after menarche I got pregnant with a girl who soon died. I became pregnant again with another girl, but the baby was a stillborn. Two weeks later my mother-in-law threw me out of the house; I had no place to go.

Manjula Gite, a second generation VHW, describes the consequences of being born the third girl in a family without a son:

I was the third girl. I was born in my mother's [natal] village. When my father found out that I was a girl, he disowned me. He said, "Take that child and throw her in the river." So, I was left in that place in my grandmother's care. My father disowned me, but my grandmother's neighbors helped care for me and gave me clothes. When it was time for me to go to school my father would not sign. My father wanted to get me married as soon as possible. When I was eleven, he found a husband for me. The man was disabled [from polio]. He did not have use of one leg. I did not like him, and I didn't want to marry. My father told me that he would kill me if I did not agree. We got married and my husband's father supported us. But my father-in-law got TB and died. We had no one to support us. It was left to me.

By confronting injuries of the past, women began to see themselves as individuals, not just as wives or mothers. As women thought about providing health services for villagers, practical concerns of restrictions on women and castes became an obstacle. Would the internalized notion of a woman's place in rural society be an impediment to becoming a village health worker?

As a Muslim woman, Rukhsanabee Shaikh remembers that in the early days of her education at CRHP, she felt like a stranger until Sunita Sadaphule extended her kindness and concern: "I felt like Dr. Mabellebai was a loving Auntie." Rukhsanabee Shaikh observed that both Dr. Raj and Dr. Mabelle showed this same regard and respect for everyone in their interactions with villagers, village leaders, government officials, and especially for the VHWs and their families. Rukhsanabee Shaikh explains that learning to care for others became one of the most essential and memorable first lessons at CRHP: "Dr. Mabelle Arole would begin each class by asking us how we were. Then she would inquire about the events of the week in the village, especially the deaths of children. She asked, "Why did that child die? Why did this child die?" It was Dr. Mabelle asking and asking. It was her concern for each child that caused the change" (Rukhsanabee Shaikh, personal interview, 2009).

In my interviews with VHWs, they spoke of the value they place on learning about how to care for others and respect each other as individuals. They each gave examples of how Dr. Mabelle showed genuine concern and kindness for all the women equally without regard to caste or religion. In addition, at the daily morning organizational meetings at CRHP which began with prayer and meditation, the VHWs observed the relationship of both Dr. Mabelle and Raj with the entire staff—medical, office administration, and auxiliary, who were Buddhists, Christians, Hindus, and Muslims. The women saw how the staff came together to exchange ideas and concerns as they planned for the work of the day. The consistency of Dr. Mabelle's caring for others was clear to the VHWs who began to model her behavior in their own interactions. Most women described learning about caring and overcoming fears of difference as one of the most intense aspects of their early days of training. Through these experiences, the VHWs were beginning to understand what it meant to be part of a team and the role of an individual in a community. In addition, as women started to think of themselves as independent health practitioners, they also began to reevaluate their own place in the family, community, and nation.

When I asked Ushabai Bangar about the first things she learned when she began training at CRHP, she responded, "On my first day I was shown the flash cards that told the story of the bridge of life and I learned about food and immunizations. But then I learned about humanity. I learned about love [prem] and long-lasting affection [maya] and today this I still know" (personal interview, 2010). By women's own reports, this type and quality of human interaction, especially the level of communication and collaboration, was foreign to them. When recounting their own individual histories most women felt they personally had few resources or protections. However, conversation in the classroom and during evenings when women were alone together was the first time anyone could remember talking about or questioning traditional patterns of village life that was not just superficial complaining about the everyday difficulties. What women began to confront were internalized notions of village life. Questioning traditional and long-held worldviews challenged notions of personal well-being and was the beginning of individual awakening. Women developed changing notions of self and subjectivities and reexamined their roles and status as wives, mothers, and daughters-in-law. Consequently, the new and chang-ing relationships that developed from learning within the CRHP framework and its principles led to a basic awareness of issues of gender inequality as part of the lived experiences of caste hierarchy that so insidiously affect the daily lives of village women.

Young Farmers' Club: The Value of Local Knowledge

With the goal of community participation and direct involvement, the Aroles developed methods and practices to incorporate the values of indi-vidual contributions and authentic involvement. They believe this method enables villagers to eventually take health into their own hands and incorpo-rate new information into the knowledge of their own local environment.

Raj Arole describes in vivid detail how caste appeared to be a deciding influence on every aspect of village life and how differences were so evident when he was a child, especially the everyday plight of Dalits (then called Harijan). For example, he remembers watching Dalits walking through his village shoeless with shrubbery branches tied to their backs to erase their footprints in the dirt and tiny clay pots tied to their necks with string so that even spit would not touch the ground, all to avoid real or potential contact with villagers. Using these critical observations of the social organization and stratification of Jamkhed area villages, Mabelle and Raj Arole mounted a campaign to incrementally reverse what they perceived as centuries old trends of poverty and discrimination.

The first attempt at community organizing by Mabelle and Raj Arole began with village visits and informal meetings to engage men of all castes and religions to discuss health matters. Most villages were initially welcom-ing of the two new area physicians and set up official meetings with elected officials, elders, and village men. Through these encounters the Aroles learned that health per se was not the most pressing issue; instead, men identified their major concerns as livestock, crops, and access to water. As I've been told countless times by village women, men care more about their animals than their wives; women lament, "if an animal gets sick attention is given immediately; if I get sick nothing is done." When the Aroles canvassed local Jamkhed villages they observed stark divisions; the notion of "untouch-ability" was apparent in everyday life and caste was a major factor in village organization, with Dalits segregated from the rest. For example, in Ghode-gaon Village, typical of many villages, dwellings occupied by higher-caste families were within the ancient walls, while the Dalits lived on the periphery, completely outside village boundaries. To promote integration and generate cross-caste conversations among villagers, events were designed to stimulate community interest, including intervillage volleyball games, drama clubs, and singing groups (Arole and Arole 1994).

Ironically, it was the well-to-do farmers who first engaged in the process while the landless poor were suspicious of these changes. Nevertheless, these discussions initiated a situation for men to communicate with each other, eventually leading to informal meetings and encouraging the potential for mutual aid, and the Young Farmers' Clubs (FCs) became an official organization.

Based on many discussions in villages with Drs. Mabelle and Raj Arole and the mobile health team facilitated by farmers' clubs members, two major problems were mutually identified for immediate action: the need for clean, potable water and the persistence of malnutrition among children. The implementation of the projects addressing these needs required more organizing to overcome entrenched local politics. For example, *panchayat* (village ruling councils), in the early 1970s, were controlled by the dominant castes, who exercised unchecked power over village resources. In contrast, those living in the most extreme poverty (mostly landless people who earned less than $1 USD per day) had no representation in village governance and consequently had little access to government projects for those living below the poverty line. While village meetings continued, the Young Farmers' Club met on the CRHP compound in Jamkhed for seminars approximately every third month to discuss improvements in methods of farming, the process of getting credit through banks, and access to seeds and fertilizers. In addition, experts from agricultural universities were engaged by the Aroles to demonstrate methods of farming suited to drought-prone areas. Landless villagers and farmers with uncultivated plots benefited from the seminars by learning from specialists innovative farming techniques and animal husbandry for cows, goats, and chickens.

Arole and Arole (1994) credit these seminars as the first opportunity for men of different castes and different villages to interact. Farmers' clubs were formalized as part of the village organization with membership fees, but to include all community members, fees were paid on a sliding scale based on ability to pay. These approaches proved very successful in some villages; for example, in Ghodegaon village, the Young Farmers' Club helped develop sixty uncultivated hectares of land belonging to Dalit farmers using newly introduced irrigation methods. Some village clubs became a catalyst for local village development by pooling resources to buy farm implements such as ploughs, spray pumps, and winnowing machines. In some cases, CRHP helped individuals or groups of men by providing capital in the form of loans to directly stimulate new ways of farming.

The farmers' club was instrumental in assisting the mobile health team and the village health workers to develop village mapping and to identify the hierarchy of village leaders. The FCs were part of a participatory rural appraisal (PRA), defined as a method to enable rural communities to share and analyze knowledge and information of life, the environment, and conditions for planning and acting on local initiative (Chambers 1994). Each year, the farmers' club, along with the VHWs, created a village plan map that included all of the dwellings, temples, wells, bore pumps, government buildings, and other structures. These maps and charts are crucial for VHWs who conduct door-to-door health care assessments; maps assign a number and color code to each dwelling based on religion, caste, and type of health problem (the use of these categories on village maps will be discussed later). Drawn on large brown newsprint poster paper, a chart of the twelve Hindu months cites the festival cycles; this is also used to identify seasonal illnesses. For example, during the monsoon months there is a higher incidence of diarrhea and an increase in the number of mosquito-borne diseases. Another table created by the FCs, a *chapati* chart, named for the round, unleavened flat bread, uses a circular design to identify the leaders of the village including elected officials, government workers, and tax collectors. Prominent on this chart is the VHW, who maintains a position on the second level of the chart immediately after elected leaders, indicating her importance in the village organizational structure.

Community organizing as a way to introduce new ideas into village life shows the strength of a participatory model and the insight of the Aroles into village matters. Yet changing generations of caste and class practices was fraught with pitfalls both anticipated and hidden. For example, Dalit farmers reported that early crop growth was destroyed when wealthy farmers surreptitiously sent cattle to eat and trample early plantings; others found that access to water was cut off after fields were planted (Arole and Arole 1994).

Nevertheless, the small successes of the farmers' clubs began to grow and became the vehicle to promote incremental steps that led to prolonged improvements in both health and development. Today, CRHP continues to introduce pioneering farming and development methods and maintains a model experimental farm currently managed by women in Karjat *taluka*. This innovative farming project introduces ecologically appropriate agriculture and irrigation techniques and experiments with variations in livestock types and animal husbandry methods. One successful model farm project is the creation of vermicomposting production using sheds with concrete containers for worms to transform farm waste and cow dung into rich organic fertilizer. The Young Farmers' Clubs continue to contribute projects like a recent program to construct individual household water supplies and latrines for sanitation. These time-tested farmers' clubs comprise men of all caste groups, including Dalits, and in some villages Muslims; they continue to be a framework for addressing inequality and promoting economic development, showing the definitive and continuing connection between village and CRHP.

Food and Caste

One of the first agreed-upon large-scale CRHP projects was to reduce malnutrition and related poor health among children. The Aroles adopted a simple yet elegant idea of public communal village meals, known as the Breakfast Program, especially necessary in a time of drought. The Young Farmers' Club members mobilized everyone in the community to participate and set up communal cooking pots in the village center with external financial support from Oxfam. The children were called each morning to the village center to sit in a large circle around the oversized common cooking vessels while the men prepared the porridge. Every child, regardless of caste or religion, helped by contributing a cup of water taken from their individual home water vessels to prepare the meal. While this activity may seem like a simple method of inclusion for a participatory model, it also had another more important function—it addressed caste and related food taboos that are pervasive and destructive in area villages.

As the breakfast program began to get underway, Dr. Mabelle Arole observed that the children sat in clusters divided by caste and were served food by fathers who were members of the same caste groups. Aware of these cleavages, Dr. Mabelle Arole devised a plan to begin breaking down these traditional barriers by actively rearranging seating patterns of the girls and boys. Ushabai Bangar, one of the first generation of VHWs, remembers that Dr. Mabelle used the breakfast clubs as a way to interrupt the pattern to stop men from serving the breakfast to their own caste groups only: "I saw what Dr. Mabellebai was doing. She mixed up the seating of children in the circle. She put the girls with braids together. Then she sat girls with red hair ribbons together. And like that she mixed up the different [caste] groups" (personal interview, 2009).

This simple yet extraordinary act is an example of the creative and intuitive methods implemented by Dr. Mabelle Arole to integrate children of different castes; preparing, sharing, and eating a meal together began to break generations of caste segregation and exclusiveness that reinforced divisions and hierarchies in village life. "Once the children started eating together, and high caste groups and Dalit men participated in serving food, the process of breaking caste barriers was initiated throughout the whole community" (Arole and Arole 1994, 128). Castes in these rural villages are most clearly identified by occupational groups, with food-sharing prohibitions and endogamy being the most obvious and pervasive signatures. Although the Indian constitution of 1949 bans discrimination based on religion, race, caste, gender, or place of birth, de facto caste prejudice was the arbiter of village life. Food- and drink-sharing prohibitions were a facet of daily village life, even for drinks like the omnipresent *caha* (sweetened tea with milk), drunk many times each day. In the villages of Jamkhed, Karjat, and Ashti *talukas*, the dominant caste is Maratha, with a range other castes, many Dalits and some Muslim households. In this one innovation, using a public event to recognize and disrupt traditional patterns, the Aroles made a significant inroad into the deep-rooted segregation of caste. Although the children were, of course, still seated by gender, this small inroad of food sharing fractured one of the prominent prohibitions of caste and began an ongoing process of integrating castes in villages.

Women and Water: The Divining Deception

Potable water is an essential public health requisite to reduce or eliminate many endemic health problems in this region, especially cyclical diarrhea outbreaks. Drs. Mabelle and Raj Arole called for a meeting in Rajuri Village, Jamkhed taluka, in the early 1970s to discuss implementation of a tube (bore) well project. In villages stratified by caste, the most pressing question raised was the location and placement of the well. Of course, the *sarpanch* (mayor), a member of the dominant caste, recommended a site next to his office in the center of the village. During the meeting the high caste villagers enthusiastically supported the *sarpanch*, and the Dalits tacitly agreed with the rest.

After the village meeting, a group of Dalit men requested a private meeting with the Aroles in the outskirts of the village. The Dalit leaders voiced their concerns of potential exclusion from operating this new and vital technology. They explained that although they followed protocol by negotiating with the dominant-caste elected village leaders during the meeting, they feared that high caste villagers might object to Dalits physically touching the well handle when pumping water. This restriction is based on a traditional caste bias—if a Dalit touched an object, or even if the garment of a Dalit brushed against something, it would be considered polluted. They pointed out what every villager knew: that if even one high caste family protested, all of the Dalits would be prohibited from using the tube well. While this incident shows the respect, trust, and confidence of the Dalit men in Rajuri village for Drs. Mabelle and Raj, it reinforced concerns about concealed and pervasive caste discrimination in the villages and its ultimate negative effect on the introduction of new ideas about health and development. Mindful of the concerns of the Dalit elders and well aware of the range, depth, and sometimes arbitrary nature of traditional restrictions that were often relaxed at the behest of the dominant or high castes, the Aroles devised a plan.

The location of tube wells became the center of an elegant deception to manage two central concerns of CRHP: the necessities for healthy, clean, and potable water and the central, underlying, and unassailable social concerns of caste discrimination. To craft this plot a geologist was engaged by CRHP to find locations for the 250-foot pump bore wells to access underground water. He traveled to more than forty villages and identified forty sites for tube wells. With few exceptions, sites were located exclusively in the Dalit areas of villages that were often outside the village walls or confines. This intentional manipulation went undiscovered until much of the drilling had begun, because the sites were located in villages throughout the Jamkhed *talukas* (Arole and Arole 1994).

The customary quotidian village patterns of caste segregation were profoundly changed by this new technology. Traditionally, water was obtained by women who walked to open wells usually located outside the village; in some cases, women walked as much as a mile with one or two twenty-pound silver metal water jugs balanced on their heads.

At these traditional wells, because of notions of purity and contamination, prohibitions were placed on touching a bucket or pulley ropes, forcing Dalit women to wait until an upper-caste woman would agree to pour some water into her vessel. Once a village pump well was activated, the arduous daily task of obtaining water for drinking, cooking, and bathing instantly became less grueling. With the placement of the bore pumps in the Dalits' *vasti* (areas), Dalit women now had easy access. Because of the tube well location and concerns of pollution, upper-caste women continued to use traditional open wells. Upper-caste VHW Shilabai Amte describes the changes brought on by the installation of bore pump wells:

> When I first started at CRHP there was the open government well here [in Halgaon village] and women had to carry water from the well. It was a one-hour walk to go to the well. So, in the early morning before sunrise we went and made a queue and waited in turn at the well. . . . There are three wells that the women in the village used for Harijan [Dalit], Maratha, and for others. Muslims used the high-caste Maratha well. If there was not enough water in the Harijan well, they used to come to ours. We [Maratha women] would pour some water in their bucket, a very small amount. . . . Then, Dr. Arole put a bore pump in the Dalit area. Then everything changed. Maratha women had to go the Harijan area bore well. . . . I was already changed—I often went there so I did not care about going through the Dalit area of the village. But Maratha women used to go to the bore well in the dark, so no one would see them. . . . All the Dalit women used to say, "Why are you coming to our area?" After that we would say, "Now we are the same. We all are one." (Shilabai Amte, personal interview, 2015)

With this change in everyday technology, village life was altered irrevocably. Upper-caste women were forced to make a choice to either walk long distances, sometimes balancing water vessels atop their head in the traditional way, or break the caste embargo by using a communal tube pump well. As Shilabai Amte tells us, attempts by dominant-caste and other women to secretly take water in the darkness failed. VHWs of all castes used these occasions as an opportunity to teach village women that there are many more similarities in the needs and work of women than differences.

These well water events crystalized the importance of understanding how eliminating caste practices makes a village more equitable and creates the conditions for learning and teaching about health and social factors affecting well-being. Additionally, this circumstance was transformative in helping VHWs to comprehend the ramifications of an intervention to reduce the traditional grip of caste ideology on village life. Each VHW, in her own way, seized the moment to share this perspective with other village women to express newly learned and felt understanding about gender inequality and the damages of centuries-old prohibitions of caste that prevented women from making their own lives easier and healthier. It confirms the value of actively studying new ideas that help VHWs diminish their own residual prejudices. Finally, these rejections of caste embargos as explained to local women by VHWs promoted village solidarity and encouraged community participation.

The introduction of pump bore wells, and the elegant deception, brought easier access to safe water, eliminated some of the drudgery of women's work, and, more importantly, changed relations among women. It paved the way for positive health outcomes and improved community relationships. The Aroles set out to solve two major problems identified by villagers—malnutrition in children and access to potable water. The success of addressing caste discrimination in a nutrition project and gender inequality with water development shows the value of the CRHP approach. Seeing the benefits that the innovation brought to their communities, village women and men began to petition the local government to install more bore pump wells, thus promoting community self-determination.

Conclusion: The Hidden Context

Issues of gender and caste hidden in the context of daily life were writ large when women found themselves outside their everyday experiences. The endemic double problems of caste and gender inequality required Mabelle and Raj Arole and the CRHP team to design ingenious techniques to transform the social fabric of the villages and change the health profile of rural villages. In doing so, they untangled centuries-long contradictions of village life dictated by traditional, conventional, and habitual patterns that limited and controlled rural communities. The Aroles used their understanding of local social, political, and economic factors and the conditions of daily village life to develop a so-called grassroots approach that relied heavily on social science and public health perspectives. Accordingly, a fundamental organizing principle of the Jamkhed Model is to develop working solutions to defeat detrimental caste conduct, address a woman's position in a community, and acknowledge the interpretations of her own life in the context of village society.

The evaluation of women within an ethnographic context is informed by anthropologists and feminist writers who examine women, work, and hierarchy in the social, political, economic, and historic context. Anthropologists suggest that ideas about human rights can be made accessible when translated into local terms and placed into a context of power and meaning (Merry 2006). Mullings (2005) emphasizes the methodological value of assessing the direct and indirect ways that larger social processes constrain and enable women in their everyday lives. The actions of VHW to engage women in a dialogue about gender inequality and new tube well technology shows an understanding of local resistance and activism in everyday matters that ultimately recognizes gender and class repression in hegemonic societies. Thus, the double dilemma of the lived inequalities of women in a caste society is addressed directly by the CRHP model when village health workers located in communities learn about health from a rights-based perspective and communicate those ideas to others.

CHAPTER 3

Health Is What Women Do

Transitions and Transformations

These Old Traditions (*Kay sangu bai bai*)

(Chorus)
What can I tell you about these old traditions?
I conceived at age fourteen

The girl came into age at twelve
She married at thirteen
Now I feel bad about it

Chorus

Now I tell you to a new generation
Let the girl live with pride
Let her stand on her own

Chorus

Each week for more than forty years, the village health workers of the Comprehensive Rural Health Project have met for class in Jamkhed. The women make the journey to attend topical classes, report on village health and development, and visit with friends. On this day, they wear brightly colored patterned saris of turquoise, red, lime green, and fuchsia, and few wear the *pallu* (loose end of the sari) covering their heads. One or two of the older women dress in the nine-yard sari that is drawn around the legs, giving the appearance of billowing pants; the old-style tattered cotton sari with patches and stains is gone. Most VHWs arrive on local noisy, ramshackle buses, in motor rickshaws, or on the backs of motorcycles. They carry notebooks with information about the health and wellness of villages, though most of them never learned to read or write. As I watch the fifty women effortlessly gather in groups of fours and fives and stand in the intense sun or under trees, talking, smiling, laughing, it is hard to imagine the personal struggles and persistence that each woman brings with her. Slowly the women file into the classroom, leaving their *chappel* (sandals)— some leather, some worn plastic—at the door; they continue their conversations even as they arrange themselves in one close-knit semicircle on the red, synthetic, woven mats. While not all VHWs attend every weekly meeting, many women have maintained an unbroken relationship with CRHP since they began studying in the early 1970s, despite personal and family obligations and opposition from spouses.

The song "These Old Traditions" ("Kay sangu bai bai") that begins this chapter is an example of the songs that VHWs write about a woman's life experience as a means to learn about health and social well-being and to teach and advocate for village women. The songs offer layers of meaning about everyday lives, the position of women in society, and the potential for change. What is meant here by "Old Traditions" is the recognition of the need to resist patterns of a woman's life that appear natural but are a means of control and domination. Using the customary practices of songs and narratives is a way of communicating ideas and memories from one generation to another. Oral storytelling makes a connection between the talker or singer and the listeners that preserves customs, legends, ritual, lore, and myths. From the Sanskrit epic poems of ancient India to the work songs of the fields, songs preserve religious, philosophical, and popular beliefs. Singing is common in every aspect of a woman's life, from the sacred *bhajans* to lullabies, and commonly accompanies arduous labor, such as singing while making *jowar* (sorghum) into flour for flat bread using manual stone grinding wheels. Chapter 4 shows in detail the importance of songs and songwriting in the education and learning process of VHWs, especially for the first generation of women who were without formal schooling.

In a society in which gender discrimination is an ever-present force of daily life, why are women selected exclusively to be trained as local health workers? As advocates of human rights and reproductive justice know, formulating social change requires an activist framework that explicitly incorporates an understanding of social problems and reassesses hegemonic neoliberal thinking (Zavella 2016). In the Jamkhed case, the intersection of gender and caste, with an increasing emphasis on class, is an aspect of local society that requires analysis. Drs. Raj and Mabelle Arole constructed the Jamkhed model to directly address human rights and social justice, based on the fundamental CRHP principles of equity, empowerment, and integration, and the myriad ways that inequalities of gender and caste negatively affect health. Selecting women to be the primary local actors in villages, although not the first choice, created the official category of village health worker, placing women at the nexus of providing health care, initiating development projects, and eventually moving women to the center of village life. As Sen and Östlin (2008) assert, the elimination of bias in health-care systems by improving the relationship between community action and health inequalities can guarantee health care as a human right for civil society.

According to the WHO (2015), India represents almost one quarter of the world's maternal mortality due to pregnancy and delivery complications. Births are commonly conducted at home by *dias* (traditional midwives) or family members. In the early days of CRHP the infant-mortality rate, maternal-mortality ratio, and death rate of children under five were unchecked and uncontrolled by local or national structured policies, exacerbating death and disability. In Jamkhed, selecting women as part of the health care team directly addresses the health problems of women and children and has the potential of incorporating local knowledge and increasing community participation. The exclusive selection of village women representing a diversity of caste, class, religion, and social standing raises fundamental questions about the potential for change and advancement: Is the idealism and practical application of the CRHP process transformative? How can the transition of the women of Jamkhed be explained? How are the VHWs able to mount resistance in the face of hegemonic social formations? Is there something exceptional about the women of Jamkhed? Are they examples of a modern Indian "Everywoman"?

Local Health Workers

Health for all requires an effective health care system and comprehensive primary health care as an essential aspect of preventive and promotive care, and this is enhanced by an effective community health worker (CHW) workforce. While the category of community health workers for global health initiatives was recognized more than fifty years ago, there remain unresolved questions about the selection, training, and efficacy of these individuals as health practitioners within medical systems. In the years since the Alma-Ata Declaration, the anthropological and public health literature has assessed community health workers in the context of national health systems and at the local level. The 1989 World Health Organization CHW Study Group definition emphasized the importance of appropriate professional training, being selected by and answerable to the community, and supporting the health system (WHO 1989). A later review of community health workers pointed out that the term "community health worker" is an umbrella term due to variation among people selected "men or women, young or old, literate or illiterate" to conform to societal "norms and customs." A subsequent report found that 70 percent of community health worker programs were women only, 12 percent men only, and 18 percent both; however, it noted an uneven reporting by programs of their workers' gender designations. In addition, the review showed that in India many community projects had a life span of twenty years or less; by the late 1980s, few programs functioned effectively (Lehmann and Sanders 2007).

More recently, the 2018 WHO guidelines on health policy and systems support review of published literature "identified state-of-the-art evidence on what is required to facilitate the proper integration of community health workers in health systems and communities" (6). The report detailed fifteen programmatic recommendation categories: selection, duration of pre-service training, modalities of pre-service training, competences and curriculum, certification, supportive supervision, remuneration, contracts, career ladder, target populations, data collection and use, type of worker, community engagement, mobilization of community resources, and availability of supplies. In evaluating the strength of the evidence, the review committee considered that most of the fifteen categories had a "very low certainty of evidence and the strength of recommendation was considered conditional." The outlier was recommendation thirteen, community engagement, which was "described as a key community health intervention that should be part of CHW practicum and activities" (58). The guidelines acknowledged, however, that there is variability in defining the concept of community, especially for urban environments.

How do guidelines and models for CHWs account for the complexity of social science constructs, especially a rigorous definition of community that includes all groups, particularly the nondominant? How can the intricacies of social institutions and social relations in specific communities be assessed? Are assumptions about the apparent organization of people living in communities dictated by the dominant or powerful segments of society missing peripheral groups? Without identifying these social factors, is comprehensive primary health care and health equity possible? From an anthropological perspective, social relations on the local level are distinctly particular to each community and are directly and indirectly affected by embedded historical, political, and economic circumstances that contribute to everyday life. Thus, recognizing the hierarchical nature of community or village life and untangling the social hegemony of civil and political society can help identify differences and prejudices affecting everyday life. However, these underlying levels of inequalities found in contemporary society, if not acknowledged and addressed, contribute to the status quo and will likely prevent effective provision of health care to all members of a community working to create health equity.

As Mishra (2014) points out, caste and class status of the health worker affects service delivery in multi-caste and multi-tribal villages. In Jamkhed, social interactions, both overt and concealed, mark instances when lurking social prejudices produce behaviors that betray underlying social discrimination. For example, in the early days of CRHP a Brahmin VHW refused to enter the house of a Dalit family, even after attending classes and participating in open discussions on the necessity to avoid such actions. Instead, without entering the dwelling, the VHW called out directions to family members in attendance to assist in a difficult childbirth. In another incident, a Dalit VHW remembers accompanying the mobile health team headed by Dr. Raj Arole for a visit to the house of the *sarpanch* who was from a high local caste. When tea was served, the VHW was given a chipped and cracked cup and saucer. Noticing this, Dr. Arole exchanged dishware with her and drank from the cracked saucer, to the dismay of the *sarpanch*. These examples of intangible social interactions foreground the need to understand the implications of social hegemony and its underlying power relations that potentially limit health equity and perpetuate health problems for certain unidentified groups in a community.

The Social Determinants of Health commission supports engaging intersectoral action in order to improve health equity. Intersectoral action for health, which uses the acronym ISH or ISA, is defined as actions affecting health outcomes undertaken by sectors outside the health affiliations to improve quality of life (WHO 2008b). The target audience for the WHO 2018 guidelines for CHWs is policymakers, planners, and managers responsible for health workforce policy and planning at national and local levels. Using case studies to promote comprehensive primary health care, Labonté et al. (2017) connect improved health equity to changes in policies both governmental and nonstate (private). For example, a model of comprehensive primary health-care reform linked to Brazil is Estratégia Saude da Familia (Family Health Strategies), which was used to integrate health systems; in an Ethiopian model connections were created between the educational and agricultural sectors. However, in "Ingkintja: The Congress Male Health Program, Alice Springs, Australia," in the same volume, Rosewarne, Wilson, and Liddle (2017) describe an organization for men self-identified as Aboriginal that used a social health framework to promote health. Approaches like the Ingkintja congress that act as advocacy organizations for groups outside the mainstream can effect change, even policy alterations, from the bottom up. While health care systems in specific nation-states legislate policy, these systems can also reinforce and bolster existing political and economic institutions that prevent establishing health equity by excluding certain groups or insufficiently addressing specific needs. In addition, programs that fail to challenge the status quo can mask injustice by accepting dominant beliefs and top-down concepts that reinforce cleavages in a society and likely perpetuate underlying bias, such as class exploitation, caste prejudice, racial discrimination, gender subordination, religious persecution, sexual normativity, or ableism, which potentially demean certain members of a community, ultimately interrupting health care and blocking or limiting social well-being.

Though some type of discrimination of a particular group or groups is present in every society and varies by degree globally, one is omnipresent: gender inequality, with the most pressing effect being on the health and well-being of girls and women. Yet, 2018 WHO recommendations for community health workers emphasized support for health sector employment for women, calling for "gender equity appropriate to the context (considering affirmative action to preferentially select women to empower them and, where culturally relevant, to ensure acceptability of services by the population or target group)" (14). Statements like these ignore the intricacies of social processes and the inherent hierarchical nature of gender relations in contemporary society. Obviously, the report is based on a distillation of more than one hundred research articles, but this only reinforces the lack of emphasis on all forms of gender bias that directly affect health and health equity for communities.

Worldwide maternal mortality has been steadily declining in the last twenty-five years. Many WHO-sponsored global interventions focus on gender issues, such as the Millennium Development Goals (2000–2015) to promote gender equality and empower women and to improve maternal health, and one of the 2015 Sustainable Development Goals is gender equity. These goals have not been universally successful; for example, the maternal mortality ratio in India is 174 deaths per 100,000 live births, ranking India 128th of 183 countries in 2015 survey (World Bank 2015). In India, sex predetermination, gender hierarchies in education and health care, early marriage, early childbirth, dowry and arranged marriages, and lack of employment opportunities vary based on caste and social class and in their impact on a woman's health and life expectancy. However, as this chapter will show, the complexity of social and cultural patterns and behaviors influenced by centuries-long traditions further complicates health issues for women. In communities in which women are not held in high regard and have unfavorable and even antagonistic status, community health workers have an additional social hurdle.

Women Are a Natural Choice: Selecting Practitioners

Given the complexity of women's roles in caste, class, and gendered society, Arole and Arole (1994) assert that local women are the natural choice as local health practitioners and promoters of village participation. In early 1971 the health profile of the Jamkhed area showed an infant mortality of 176 death per one thousand live births; only 0.5 percent of pregnant women received prenatal care, fewer than 0.5 percent of deliveries could be considered safe, and 40 percent of children were malnourished (see Table. 1). The health needs of women and children were clearly an urgent problem. Arole and Arole (2007) identify eight primary characteristics as necessary and sufficient for the selection of a village health worker: preferably a woman, a representative of the poor, accepted by the poor, roots in the community, residency in the community, literacy level on par with the community, motivation and commitment to work as a vocation, and the desire to learn. Establishing these characteristics for the selection and education of VHWs fit the many requirements of the Jamkhed model and is consistent with a comprehensive primary health-care approach.

The recommendation to choose local women as primary village practitioners was made by a village leader and Young Farmers' Club member and supported the CRHP process of village self-determination. As a child Dr. Raj Arole lived in Maharashtran district adjacent to Jamkhed district; he used his knowledge of the intricacies of local governance to promote village participation as a means to gain trust and acceptance. Elections of the *raj panchayat*, the village governing body in the Jamkhed block of Maharashtra, take place every five years; eleven members from each village are elected, and as a body they vote for the village *sarpanch*. In most villages, 80 percent of the population over the age of eighteen is eligible to vote. The selection of the first generation of village health workers was negotiated at village meetings, *gam sabha*, headed by the *sarpanch*. Second-generation VHWs were selected by a similar process with the approval of village leaders, and often with the recommendation and consensus of older VHWs and the mobile health team.

In the original VHW selection plan, one woman from each project village was selected to take on the responsibility of identifying and addressing the health needs of residents and village environmental problems while continuing to live in the village. The first groups to begin classes at CRHP had approximately nine women from different villages. While some local leaders realized the potential inherent in having a health worker to provide care, there were misconceptions about the extent, type, and purpose of VHW training. Some village leaders assumed that the work would be menial and hard, for example, working at unclean jobs such as washing floors, sweeping, or hand laundering for the patients. These villages selected women who were Dalits and widowed or abandoned by their husbands. In another village, a woman of the dominant caste (Maratha) was selected because her father had leprosy. In those days, people with leprosy were forced to live solitary lives, cast out of their home villages, causing additional hardship and stigma for the family. In contrast, one village whose elected official understood the potential for collaborating with CRHP for health and agricultural economic opportunity chose a Brahmin woman. The Aroles were careful to avoid the appearance of favoritism, especially when a *sarpanch* or other elected officials selected his wife or a close relative. Yet one woman approved for training was the *sarpanch*'s wife, who was accepted by the Aroles because she fit the preferred VHW profile. Some women had a previous connection to CRHP—one had helped work on an earlier project, while another was treated at the CRHP clinic for tuberculosis. Like most women in the Jamkhed area, all were married in their early teenage years.

At the time CRHP classes began, only five of the first nine were living with their husbands, while others were widows or abandoned.

Understanding the local political processes and working with elected officials to achieve consensus in villages underscores the CRHP principles of integration and participation that assure that all caste, social, economic, and religious factions were included in the selection. The misconceptions of village leaders about the position of VHWs contributed to the diversity of the initial first generation of VHWs. Nevertheless, in the creating of this new and untested role for women, these village-centered decisions preserved the notion of village self-determination and, it was hoped, each VHW would have a mandate from her community. The process itself, however, was not always accomplished without controversy, especially when powerful leaders promoted unsuitable candidates, and in some cases, meetings were closed diplomatically without resolution because of village factionalism (Arole and Arole 1994). However, the Aroles knew that providing care for all could not be accomplished without taking on the challenges of the hidden and wide-spread practices of caste-based traditions common in the area. Based on the innovation of the Jamkhed model, the VHW selection process proved an unqualified success, creating the first group of nine women of different castes and religions who would be trained to administer care to all villagers equally.

Women's Consciousness: Remembering and Learning

In the course of my data collection, using ethnographic life history inter-views, I documented women's hope and optimism against the backdrop of living in a rural community that is inhospitable to the ideas of individual woman's rights. Each interview revealed formative experiences of a girl and woman's duties as a wife, mother, daughter-in-law, cook, laundress, tender of animals, worker in the fields, caretaker of the sick, childbirth assistant, builder of houses, road worker, upholder of religious rituals, and water carrier that reveal the indignities of the gender-separated world of rural villages. The CRHP educational process transforms these complex life trajectories into teaching and learning strategies to help women make the common connections necessary to become a member of a collabora-tive team. In addition, the process incorporates women's local knowledge of the social dynamics of each village to support the VHW to become an independent practitioner able to make connections between village needs and the promotion of health and wellness.

Latabai Kadam vividly recalls her introduction to the idea of becoming a Village Health Worker:

> The *sarpanch*, the person who was in charge of order in the village, sent for me. But I did not go because I thought that I had done something wrong. . . . It was my time to do farm work and I did not want to lose my wages. Again, the *sarpanch* sent a call. So, I went. He said to me come ahead. I would go one step and stop. Again, he said come ahead. People from the CRHP mobile health team were standing there. The *sarpanch* said, "You are selected. These are doctors and nurses from Jamkhed. You will go and learn from them." [I thought] I cannot read and write, what can I do? If I do not do well, they will beat me. I am not going to do it. . . . The *sarpanch* told me there is one other woman whose name is Sunita Sadaphule from another nearby village, go spend time with her and see if you like it. Then, I went. (personal interview, 2009)

Latabai Kadam was not alone in her obvious reticence. Many of the women selected had difficulties understanding how another task could be added to their already overburdened lives. In personal interviews, women recall some of their first concerns about becoming a VHW: How will we overcome the severe restrictions on our activities and movements? Will we able to move freely in our village? Will our husbands and mothers-in-law permit us to leave our homes alone without permission? Will we be permitted to or expressly forbidden from freely communicating with other women? Will our husbands allow us to take care of village men who are ill? Will we continue to be allowed to travel to Jamkhed without restriction?

For example, Hirabai Salve, as a young, newly married woman, felt controlled by her husband and mother-in-law, which she experienced as imposed isolation that kept her apart from other women. Hirabai Salve explains how changes in her own consciousness helped her understand women's position in rural society.

> In my village, my experience was that women did not speak to each other. Your mother-in-law and husband tell you, "do not speak to others." There was no talking even when a woman went to the well for water. If my husband ever saw me talking to another woman that was enough of an excuse to beat me. . . . A husband values his animals more than his wife. . . . Basically, there was no communication [among women]. If there was communication it was fighting, there was only fighting and bickering over little things or things children did.

There was no sense of community. The only time that women got together was twice a year and both were for festivals. . . . A woman was not a person. There was never equality or anything close to equality. We didn't understand what a woman was. We did not understand ourselves as people. Now, attitudes have changed. Now, we have a lot more power. Now, we are smarter. We know how to make our own living. We know how to keep our money and spend our money. (personal interview, 2009)

Overcoming fears and finding ways to learn was a protracted process for many women who had to rise above their own personal trials, family pressures, and in this case, a high-caste perspective about villagers. Gangabai Kulkarni, a Brahmin woman and first-generation VHW, remembers the dread of her first days at CRHP campus and the difficulty of making the transition from an at-home wife to a VHW. Gangabai Kulkarni explains:

I never left my home village before. The first time was to come to CRHP [learning center]. I had never seen men dressed in Western shirts and pants. I had never seen the different type of people other than those of my own village. So, the first time I ran away. I sat under a tree all day until it was time to go. The next time, one of the village elders took me to the classroom. But I stayed for the day and went home that night. For the first year, I would not stay overnight with the others. I came once a week only. After that first year when everyone got to know each other I stayed for a month of training. But what I remember most from those first days was that I was taught to learn, taught how to live with other women, how to get along with others and love each other. (personal interview, 2009)

The concealed issue of caste for Gangabai Kulkarni, a Brahmin, was shown in her reluctance to stay, sleep, and eat with the other women, especially Dalits. What made her change her views, not only about staying at the CRHP learning center with other women, but about entering the houses of Dalits? Gangabai Kulkarni reported that slowly, over time, due to the atmosphere of trust and mutual support for learning created in the classroom and through personal interactions with VHWs, she was persuaded to care for lower-caste and Dalit villagers.

Each woman's past reveals a different story of the lives of women in a rural community where the majority of households live below the official poverty line. For example, Sunita Sadaphule, a Dalit woman and first-generation

VHW was in her late sixties at the time of her life history interview. At age thirteen she was abandoned by her husband after the birth of a stillborn. She was left alone in her husband's village with no means of support; her only living relative was a brother who lived in a village more than a day's walk away. Sunita Sadaphule reflects on her early experiences and how her education at CRHP taught more than medical facts. Sunita Sadaphule learned about societal issues and local and national political concerns that allowed her to make connections about the consequence of gender and caste repression in her own life. Using local language imagery, she states:

> My mother and her generation never had any opportunity. But I had the opportunity and I was able to live my life story. The good we do will remain forever and everywhere in India, and throughout the world they will remember my story. You need to show people kindness and love, that is the only way to solve their problems. Even if they get angry at you. You still show love. Dr. Mabelle taught us even no matter if my body rots, my knowledge will be there forever. . . . In the beginning [of training], the people in my village used to beat me up with brooms. They used to say, "Who do you think you are? You think you are a great doctor? What do you think you can teach us?" They thought I couldn't do anything because of what I was [Dalit and alone]. I worked hard. CRHP solved my poverty. I wrote a song [she sings the first line]: "Women, why are you sitting at home oppressed. Let's go to the Jamkhed project and learn. . . ." My dream for the next generation of young girls today is that they should learn a lot, use their opportunity to become doctors, engineers. (personal interview, 2009)

Rambhau Dalvi, a Maratha woman, recalls the early days at Jamkhed and her difficulties associating with women of other castes, especially Dalits. She recalls her fear of others and how it framed her first interactions:

> Latabai Kadam and Sunita Sadaphule were there. So, I could tell that two of the women were Dalits, so I did not want to sit with them or eat with them. I'm a Maratha, which is a high caste. The Dalits used to come to my house to buy buttermilk. If they wanted milk I would give from a distance without coming into contact with them. If they wanted water in their pot I would pour it from a distance from my pot to theirs without touching. So, I also had that idea [about caste]. For two–three months I was coming frequently to CRHP, Dr. Mabelle Arole was sitting with them and eating with them. I would sit together but I was keeping a distance away. (personal interview, 2009)

The five women quoted here each in their own way describe underlying concerns they faced as first-generation village health workers and the necessity to surmount issues generated by caste, class, and gender. As Latabai Kadam, Hirabai Salve, Gangabai Kulkarni, Sunita Sadaphule, and Rambhau Dalvi testify, CRHP created a new social situation that irrevocably changed each of their lives and the fabric of their villages. These reflections and insights of first experiences create a baseline of common patterns and the beginnings of an evaluation of the position of rural women in hegemonic patriarchal society.

The challenge for CRHP was to help women make the transition from being restricted by circumstance and education to becoming active members of a professional health team. Creating the conditions in which village women would learn about health and health care, have the freedom to move unrestricted within villages and to the training center in Jamkhed, and negotiate caste diversity in villages were primary tasks. In addition, incorporating classroom learning into their already over-packed days and evenings required ingenuity and cooperation that only a participatory effort can surmount. The CRHP's basic curriculum and continuing-education classes were developed collaboratively with the women themselves and with a great deal of creativity and invention (see Chapter 4). Over time and always through an understanding of the dialectic between theory and practice, the Jamkhed Model of VHW education and training focused on the restrictions of traditional Indian rural society, and the many and varied needs of local women who embarked on this new endeavor. Each training session had a dual purpose: first, of teaching practical applications of medical and health care to prepare VHWs for working as health practitioners; and second, of identifying consequences of prejudice in everyday life, especially regarding women's inequality and caste discrimination, that were silent impediments to promoting health and social well-being.

Introducing Social Transformation through Personal Change

The ingenuity of the CRHP model is that it centers on community participation and collaboration, creating the conditions to support women's individual learning and preparing competent health care practitioners to further social change. While the method and practice of VHW education will be discussed in detail in the next chapter, it is useful to note here that a corollary goal of the model focuses on using the accomplishments and knowledge of

VHWs to foster social change in villages. The success of VHWs demonstrated the great personal strength and determination of everyday women. Establishing oneself as a VHW in one's home village meant essentially creating a new position that would be virtually the only public activity for a woman.

Once established, village health workers organized informal women's groups to teach villagers what they had learned about health care at CRHP and lay the groundwork for change. These village groups were modeled on the same principles of caring and collaboration the VHWs experienced in their own classes. As is typical of any of these innovations, the process began slowly. For example, some village women were already aware of the changes and benefits that VHWs brought to village life, and they were eager to take advantage of new ideas. On the other hand, some women shied away from outwardly endorsing VHW activities due to fear of potential reprimands from husbands for socializing with other women.

Women's assemblies and associations of this type had been unheard of in the Jamkhed area before CRHP instituted women's clubs (*mahila vikas mandal*). Initially, some village men misunderstood the purpose of the meeting or objected to women socializing outside of the confines of the household. For example, Hirabai Salve, a VHW from Jawalke, reported an incident at one of these early informal meetings where "one woman's husband came with a stick ready to beat his wife. I pleaded with him, 'Why do you object to your wife learning how to take care of your own son?'" (Arole and Arole 1994, 186). Nevertheless, trust, confidence, and appreciation grew for an increasing number of women and men villagers who connected the work of village health workers to children's survival and the elimination of incapacitating endemic health problems (M. Arole 1998).

The Soak Pits of Jawalke Village

One of the early successes of the women's club in Jawalke village was a coordinated effort to control mosquitos and prevent malaria. Hirabai Salve began organizing a women's club as a way to communicate new ideas and to make the village healthy and safe. The club activities took on a new dimension when she introduced the idea of a construction project to create soak pits for mosquito control during the rainy season. The purpose of the project was to prevent stagnant water from forming breeding grounds for mosquitos. Seeing the value of these changes, the women's club asked the village men to begin constructing soak pits in front of houses throughout the village.

The idea was resoundingly rejected by the men of Jawalke. Undaunted and with the encouragement of the VHW, the women embarked on an unprecedented action. The women's club members were willing to circumvent the men's opposition in order to participate in a project to benefit health and prevent malaria, an especially dangerous illness for infants and children.

The village women hatched a plan to surreptitiously construct the soak pit. During late morning, after the men left the village to work in the field or ride their motorcycles away from the village, the women used a children's trick of banging a rock on the village flagpole. Constructing a soak pit requires digging a trench and installing rocks and gravel of graduated size from large to small to allow water to filter through and not remain stagnant on the surface. The women would gather and work together to dig a one-meter-deep pit, carry bricks and rocks, and assemble the graduated sizes of stones necessary. This type of task was not difficult for women who frequently were employed in day jobs on farms or road crews. With enthusiasm for making their own village better, over time soak pits were dug in front of the homes of cooperating women. Then other women began to participate. Experience like this helped to reinforce the importance of cooperation and gave women a sense of independence and accomplishment. For women who were reluctant to go against traditional village patterns, this action helped them to recognize that the value of soak pits for the health of the village was worth risking family conflict. By using her own ingenuity to devise and execute a workable plan, Hirabai Salve gained the trust of the women of her village and laid the groundwork for more projects and programs.

Clearly, this one activity demonstrated how the VHWs absorbed the spirit and letter of what they had learned at CRHP. Unprecedented a generation before, these accomplishments mark the transformation of VHWs into social actors, agents of change, and the motor behind the transition of villages into healthy communities. Ultimately, an awareness about gender inequality begins when women advocate for others and form associations to address the structural processes that produce gender stratification and exacerbate disparities in health.

Conclusion

While anthropologist and feminist writers have been examining women, work, and hierarchy in the social, political, economic, and historic context, this perspective adds to an evaluation of women community health workers even within an ethnographic context. As one of the first analysts of gender inequality in anthropology, Leacock (1983) asserts that women's oppression requires a historical process and an interpretation of cultures within capitalist society. Using a Gramscian framework, others assert in an examination of resistance and power that "not all resistance produces improved outcomes for subaltern classes" (Whitehead 2015, 669). In addition, Chandra (2015) questions the Foucauldian precept that where there is power there is resistance, and instead asserts that hegemony and resistance are encased in context-specific ambiguities in which power and resistance are "entangled" rather than simply opposed. Clearly, the global, national, and local setting embedded in the wider historical, social, and political economy complicates the valuations of the realities and situated lives of VHWs as women and workers in a health system. Among the VHWs of CRHP, resistance to the powerful traditions of caste and patriarchy and the social relations it engendered was made possible when the CRHP created the conditions for women to recognize their position in society and the possibility for change.

Early assessments by anthropologists of CHW education and practice identified some of the interstitial social community factors that might affect CHW training (Nichter 1980). An earlier anthropological analysis of community participation as both desirable and necessary foregrounds the distinctions between normative utilitarian perspectives versus notions of empowerment (Morgan 2001). More recent anthropological analysis of CHWs in Ethiopia emphasizes the importance of the political and economic factors affecting training and practice (Maes et al. 2015) and the lived experience in the local and global contexts to assess the potential for change in South Africa (Colvin and Swartz 2015). Whiteford and Vindrola-Padros (2016) demonstrate the value of a medical ecology framework to assess the role of capacity building and leadership using a community participatory involvement (CPI) model. In addition, Mishra (2014) emphasizes the importance of an ethnographic approach over statistical evidence to assess the value of integrated service and teamwork by CHWs in India.

In their own way, the CRHP principles underlie the ability to organize for equity and the actualization of human rights as the CRHP fights oppression in the form of caste and gender inequality. In a similar approach from the same era, Freire (1970) used education to help the people of Brazil and Chile identify political and economic oppression. The work of Freire in

Pedagogy of the Oppressed describes two distinct stages. "In the first, the oppressed unveil the world of oppression and through the praxis commit themselves to its transformation. In the second stage, in which the reality of oppression has already been transformed, this pedagogy ceases to belong to the oppressed and becomes a pedagogy of all people in the process of permanent liberation" (54). The CRHP methods might be compared to the Freire (1970) approach that defines learning as a process of action and reflection leading to transformation. Freire (1998a) uses the concept of *conscientizaoção* (awareness), sometimes described as critical consciousness, to explain a method that helps individuals identify and examine the social, political, and economic contradictions of society that lead to oppression. The Freirean model of adult education identifies external political and economic oppressors, as well as local patterns of inequality. In Jamkhed, this notion of consciousness is incorporated into the participatory process to help women make connections between their experiences and the inequities of caste and gender so common in rural village life.

From a Gramscian perspective, in the case of patriarchal caste society, rural women who accept unchallenged the structure of village life might be considered to have submitted to "intellectual subordination [and] adopted a conception which is not its own but borrowed from another group" (Gramsci 1971, 327). Further, in this case, VHWs who are part of a collaborative learning experience are exposed to new ideas that contradict rooted beliefs; this process might conform to what Gramsci describes as inculcating an "organic totality" that sustains a transformation of women in rural society. As local health practitioners, village health workers promote health and wellness as they work with other women to create the social conditions necessary for changing the material world: women are no longer objects but subjects of their own invention. Accordingly, as Freire (1970), Gramsci (1971), and C. Mohanty (2003) suggest, women's consciousness was changed by living and learning within a condition that allows ideas to be formed through understanding the relationship between one's position in a local community and the larger political and economic processes. In India, understanding the position of women requires disentangling social, political, and economic factors embedded in the context of history, the enduring complexity of caste, the contested residual of colonialism, the perennial hegemony of patriarchy, religious antagonism, and, more recently, growing venture capitalism. Thus, it is a gender-centered approach that explains the broader importance of individual and community rights and relations that form the basis for women VHWs' transformation from housebound wives to health workers and village leaders.

CHAPTER 4

"Why Are You Sitting at Home Being Oppressed?"

Becoming a Village Health Worker

Women Come Together (*Chalaa warga wari*)

(Chorus)
Women come together. Let us
unite and fight for women's freedom
Dear Venubai, why are you sitting
at home being oppressed?

Come, let's go to class.
No longer will you be chained to
cooking and housework
And lead a bonded life

Chorus

Come, come you only have
to take the initiative.
We will go to the Jamkhed Project and learn.
No longer will we remain oppressed.

Chorus

Until now you were kicked and beaten
And remained in servitude
Now you will not remain demoralized
you will be fearless.

Chorus

We will participate in politics
And fight for leadership
We need to have power in the
hands of women.

Chorus

Composed in the 1970s, this song written by Sunita Sadaphule, one of the first generation of village health workers, encapsulates a range of meanings about the way women understand the value of learning, take the initiative of self-development, and become conscious of societal inequities. Each stanza identifies a central personal challenge faced by village women who aspire to gain control, power, and authority over their lives and offers solutions through education, collaboration, and mutual struggle.

"Venubai chalaa warga wari" has become the equivalent of an anthem for the VHWs, joining other *bhajans* (sacred songs) that women value. It's sung at the beginning of every meeting and appeals to an imaginary woman named Venubai, a general metaphor for all village women. She is entreated to join together with other women to learn. This and other songs, often sung as spontaneous call-and-response, composed by the women themselves, are part of the cannon of VHW education.

"Venubai chalaa warga wari" enjoins women to use individual initiative and self-actualization to relieve their oppression, burden, or bondage—*gulama*, the word translated as "oppressed" in the chorus of the song, is often translated as slavery. The notion of abuse, or fear of abuse, whether physical, verbal, is introduced to make the connection between each woman's demoralization and the solution of gaining knowledge as a key to autonomy. The song describes women's aspirations to play roles in village life and local politics, and, most forcefully, to become leaders and attain the power that should be placed "in the hands of women." But more than just gaining knowledge and training, the idea of women's exclusion and silence is exposed and identified as everyday oppression. Sunita Sadaphule's anthem captures the essence of the resilience necessary for the transformative experience of becoming a village health worker.

In a precise way this theme song articulates the sentiments of the CRHP collaborative educational process for VHWs, which centers on women and the value of others, respect for individuals, and a realistic appraisal of political and economic conditions. Principles of equity, integration, and empowerment are bolstered by the view that it is not hard technology but often social actions that improve health. Drs. Mabelle and Raj Arole assert that medicine needs to be demystified, knowledge should be shared freely with people, and above all that rural communities are capable of planning and maintaining their own health (Arole and Arole 1994). This criticism of neoliberal biomedical tactics rejects a top-down, cookie-cutter approach resulting from external programs imposed on national health systems, especially for rural communities in India. At CRHP, the education and training of VHWs is tailored to fit into the lives of villagers, and it is consistent with a primary health care (PHC) approach of a balance among curative, promotive, and preventive health services. Nevertheless, the strength of this participatory model and the collaboration of village leaders proves effective for the intervention of using local women to work as health workers, each in her home village. The Aroles were confident that women's life experience and local knowledge would be translated into a training program to "preserve the traditions that promote good health and remove the superstitions and practices that are detrimental to health" (Arole and Arole 1994, 153). Thus, methods and procedures were designed and redesigned, invented and reinvented to use the talents and experience of village women to help them learn the complex biomedical, social, and environmental issues necessary to be a part of a team promoting health and well-being. Their Jamkhed model required developing an innovative teaching design for women with limited experience who could neither read nor write, and were confined to households, bound to family and caste, and constrained from traveling outside of their home village. Another consideration was to respect a woman as a member of a family and community who has her own innate intelligence and life experience.

"I Am My Own Person"

The mindfulness of Jamkhed women is the product of their memory, experience, judgment, and morality. Dr. Mabelle Arole spent many hours talking with women about their own self-worth, which most women were unable to realize and express (Arole and Arole 1994). Local women firmly rooted in traditional notions of family and duty never formally questioned their identities and their positions in rural society. How do these subjectivities articulate with this new and exclusive role for local women? Basic notions of self were compounded by early marriage, sometimes before menarche, and patrilocal residence, which separated women from natal families and childhood friends, leaving them, in most cases, controlled by a husband and mother-in-law. Both women and men in rural villages followed separate paths and clearly defined roles of conduct that were maintained through social pressure. Consequently, challenging the traditional values of a woman as a daughter, wife, or mother required an innovative approach to prepare her for the formidable and complex task of becoming a local practitioner for all of the families in a village.

A first step was to start encouraging the women's own sense of self to reverse the received idea of a woman as someone's daughter, someone's wife, or someone's mother. Even saying one's name aloud became a sign of growing individual identity and practical healing. The exercise was simple: Take a hand mirror. Walk outside behind the training center building to a quiet place where you are alone. Hold the mirror to your face. Look at yourself in the eye and say, "I have a name. I am a woman. I am my own person. My name is _____." The process may seem naïve, but for a woman struggling to understand herself in a unique way and find a new place in a very closed society, the result was substantial, especially when gaining a sense of independence that was never before desired, supported, or even permissible.

Dr. Mabelle Arole points out that learning rote procedures and practices occupied only half of women's training time: "The other half was reserved for their own growth and understanding unjust social structures, the prevalent value system, and their effect on health" (Arole and Arole 1994, 173). Consequently, before any real learning could begin, a lifetime of treatment as a woman in a gender- and caste-segregated society needed to be addressed and decoded. An ever-present obstacle to developing group cohesiveness was the perennial distrust among the women themselves. As Janabai Pol reports, "Women who lived in the same village never spoke to each other. If they did speak it was to argue" (personal interview, 2009). Shantabai Sathe states, "Before there was really no communication. No unity. They [women] got along but at the same time they really didn't. Because they were talking to each other but lightly [duplicitously]" (personal interview, 2009). How can women from different villages, castes, and religions be integrated into a new whole? How can everyday avoidances and traditional prohibitions of being in the same room, sitting, eating, or even taking tea together be chipped away to build a new reality for the public good?

Under One Blanket

One idea for defeating the obvious and ubiquitous demarcations of caste, class, gender, and religion was at once symbolic and practical, when the first group of VHWs in training spent the night at the CRHP center—all the women would sleep together in a common room, under one large quilt. A blanket was stitched together from several individual single-mattress-sized quilts to cover eight women. In Jamkhed, winter nights can be chilly and for a few weeks, sweaters, woolen scarves, hats, and blankets are used when the temperature falls to 15°C (59°F), which is considered cold in this region. The homemade quilts were originally a gift to the CRHP from American Lutheran women as a spiritual commitment to service. The stitching together of the quilts acts as a symbolic connection of the values of working for the public good at home and abroad. It is not clear to me if the first eight women in training knew this connection to foreign faith-based communities. Nevertheless, this constructed quilt blanket itself became an icon of newly formed connection, promoting a sense of solidarity, especially for women from varied backgrounds who refused social interaction.

This drawing by a local artist (see Fig. 2 0, delivery kit drawing), like so many other teaching aides, helped women to see a new way of understanding their position within their communities and CRHP. Village health workers of all generations point to the requirement of staying overnight in the initial phase of their education as a time when they began to see themselves as a member of a group of women with common concerns and interests for family, community, and health.

Learning Strategies

Creative approaches are needed to involve adults in a process that promotes learning and the exchange of ideas, especially when introducing complex biomedical concepts and treatment regimens. In the 1970s, many physicians and public health professionals who worked in international health saw the need to develop alternative models of health practices (Newell 1975). *Where There Is No Doctor* (Werner and Sathyamala 1977) and *Helping Health Workers Learn* (Werner and Bower 2005) were some of the teaching and learning approaches developed for global audiences. These published works show that people's own talents and abilities are legitimate contributions and just as valuable as advanced technology: "a health worker's most important job is to teach—to encourage the sharing of knowledge, skills, experiences, and ideas" (Werner and Bower 2005, 1).

In addition to skills and experience, the CRHP process introduces mutual learning and critical consciousness to the process that helps women make connections among these political, economic, and societal factors to instill a growing understanding of caste and gender oppression. Dr. Raj Arole saw medical knowledge and training in health as collaboration for all; when formal content classes were given, all personnel were invited: medical staff,

Ayurvedic physicians, social workers, leprosy specialists, artificial limb technicians, and even transportation staff. In this way, opportunities for meeting their needs for specialized learning were designed and introduced to help them gain and retain complex medical knowledge that was easily operationalized for novice learners. One of the hallmarks of the Jamkhed Model is the multidimensional and often time-consuming processes of listening to the women themselves discuss how to learn and to teach each other (Arole and Arole 1994). Both the Aroles' Jamkhed Model and Freire's (1970, 1998b) construct of *conscientizaoção* elucidate the imperative to identify and teach the economic conditions of individuals within one's own political and social experience, to support resistance to authoritative power, and to affirm personal validation.

COLLABORATIVE LEARNING: MAKING *LIMBU PANE*

How making *limbu pane* (lemon water) is taught, learned, discussed, and implemented is an example of the collaborative education process at CRHP that incorporates essential medical treatment into effective primary health care and values women's local knowledge. In the late 1960s, biomedical research considered oral rehydration therapy (ORT) the "magic bullet" to save lives in South Asia threatened by dehydration, especially from cholera. According to the WHO, diarrheal disease is the second leading cause of death worldwide in children under five years old, with approximately 525,000 deaths each year; it is both preventable and treatable (WHO 2017; Ruxin 1994). In the Jamkhed region, diarrhea is a symptom of various diseases including microbial and viral infections that for young children, particularly infants, can cause dehydration leading quickly to death. The preparation of *limbu pane* as a form of oral rehydration therapy is a first line of defense and an essential tool used by VHWs to prevent and treat dehydration.

The basic practical remedy of making *limbu pane* is one of the first procedures each VHW learns because of its valuable contribution to infant and child health. When Dr. Mabelle Arole began teaching the first-generation of VHWs how to assemble *limbu pane*, she used traditional kitchen tools and measurements to convey the precise formula. Observing the cumbersomeness of the method and recognizing that none of this kitchen equipment was available in most village households, Latabai Kadam confidently offered an alternative.

We are used to measuring with our hands and fingers. We have definite measures with our hands that everyone understands. There is *moot bhar*, which
means fistful, *pasa bhar* means a palm full, *onjal* is the cupping of two hands
together. . . . *Chimut bhar* is a three-finger pinch, *nakh bhar* means a minute
quantity. Almost every house has a water jug called a *tambya* measuring approximately 1/2 litre. (Arole and Arole 1994, 167)

Clearly, this explanation gives a well-defined, easy-to-access message that
all VHWs can replicate and can teach village women to implement in their
own kitchens. This example of the collaborative learning process shows
respect for individual talent and local knowledge and produces sustainable
practices for promoting health.

WEEKLY SEMINARS: AFTERNOON SESSIONS

Village health worker initial training and education is conducted weekly
at the CRHP health center for a two-day seminar beginning on Wednesday
afternoon and continuing the next day with two sessions, morning and
afternoon. The VHWs spend the evening and overnight eating together and
sleeping on campus. This pattern has been consistent for almost forty years
with occasional breaks. For example, in 1993 women left the Jamkhed area
to travel more than one hundred miles (163 kilometers) to Latur to help
with the victims of an earthquake.

Nonetheless, this continuing educational process is one of the many
strengths of the model, both for learning purposes and establishing social
relationships with and among VHWs. Afternoon meetings are generally held
in the CRHP Training and Research Center in the thirty-two-foot by sixty-
five-foot (ten by twenty meters) ground level classroom with six windows
on the outside of the building and six windows on an internal courtyard.
Florescent lights and ceiling fans dot the twelve-foot (3.6 meters) ceiling;
the glossy yellow paint has lost some of its luster. There are air condition-
ers in two of the windows that have not functioned in years. Yet, the exuber-
ance of the women, even on the hottest days, is palpable as they take their
places on red woven floor mats. After the singing of the call-and-response
theme song, women report and discuss weekly events, difficult cases, and
incidents that occurred in their villages, as well as progress on village environmental interventions. Another function of the afternoon meeting is to
identify potential topics for the next day's recitation in the morning session.

MORNING SESSIONS

Women sit on woven mats in a semicircle two or three deep in the CRHP main classroom waiting for the morning educational seminars to begin, shoes and *chappels* have been left at the door. Older, more experienced women generally sit at the back, with the front row reserved for new trainees to sit front and center. Slowly the women stop their conversations as they begin to pay attention to those who sit on the floor in the front of the room. This day Dr. Raj Arole, Dr. Shobha Arole, and two members of the mobile health team—Ratna Kamble, a social worker, and Mr. Pundit, a health specialist—join the women on the floor mat facing the group.

The complete curriculum of the program is extensive. For example, during 2012 the topics included maternal child health (nutrition during and after pregnancy, immunizations, infant and child nutrition, care of the newborn, care during pregnancy, care during labor and delivery, growth and development, and family planning); chronic diseases (hypertension, diabetes, heart disease, diseases of the eye / cataracts, and oral health); communicable diseases (tuberculosis, leprosy, pneumonia, HIV/AIDS, and sexually transmitted infections); protozoal disease (malaria); nutrition (adolescent and adult); and mental health (depression and domestic abuse); as well as kitchen gardens and local remedies. Class topics vary as the need arises based on curricular needs or VHW requests. Each topic is presented using a variety of educational and didactic techniques to accommodate women without formal education and to make sure that different levels of learning are addressed. Of the thirteen women in the first generation of VHWs I interviewed, eight had no formal schooling, four had four years, and one had seven years. In the second generation of eighteen VHWs the education level improves: eight women had no formal school, and the remaining ten had an average of six years of school. Yet the structure of training and classroom work developed in the early days of CRHP has been shown to be so effective that it is has changed little over time, with only some additions like the use of videos or PowerPoint.

The topic for the next day's morning session is either chosen the afternoon before or selected by the teaching team to introduce a new training module. For example, when HIV/AIDS became a public health emergency, a new module was developed to teach appropriate practices and procedure, such as how to avoid stigma. In additions, researchers from Pune, a large city four hours from Jamkhed, were invited to make presentations regarding potential for VHWs to participate in a research protocol. Over the eight years of my ethnographic fieldwork observing the formal classes, I have found a consistent pattern in both small and large groups. In each class meeting, women paid close attention to the class leader, respected each woman's comments, and kept side conversations to a minimum. Attention to the flow of the seminar is decidedly active; women nod their heads in agreement, shake their heads in disagreement, or raise their hands to offer points of clarification. The atmosphere in the classroom is collaborative and friendly, with women eager to help each other and show the knowledge and experience they have acquired. Of course, there is often a side conversation or joke that sets off pockets of conversation or laughter.

The topic of the day is reinforced through the questions and responses of the women. For example, the class on the H1N1 virus is based on a fundamental understanding of mechanisms and prevention of person-to-person transfer of viruses. Thus new information is introduced and basic concepts are reinforced. First-generation VHWs, some from the first original group, participate in classes to renew foundation concepts and keep up to date with new health concerns affecting villagers. In most classroom sessions, older VHWs wait to offer their thoughts and opinions, deferring to the younger generation who actively participate in answering questions and asking for clarification of class content. In general, older and more experienced VHWs listen carefully to the questioning and discussion by the younger women, only offering their analysis if a major point or concept is overlooked.

VHW INNOVATIVE PEER EDUCATION THROUGH PERFORMANCE

In the morning session, after the formal lecture or presentation and a tea interval, the women organized into groups of six to eight to discuss the lecture, raise questions, and develop a presentation for the class to demonstrate what they view as the major learning points of the seminar session. Sufficient time is allotted to assemble performances that are creative and content-driven. In the group work, women agree on content and manner of presentation amid excited exchanges and laughter. If there are discrepancies understanding class content, during group activities women are able to ask questions, correct information, and refine concepts. Often older first-generation women illustrate concepts with practical examples from years of experience and suggest songs or drama from past performances that were considered useful for learning.

Presentations begin with the recitation of specific facts by each woman in turn followed by the group performance which can include a combination of drawings, drama, and songs. Often women working in groups of two or three create drawings with colorful markers on large poster paper to illustrate take-away points from the seminar. Later these drawings will be displayed as teaching tools to explain valuable concepts to the entire class. Sometimes standard songs that all VHWs know by heart are used to emphasize the lecture material. Short impromptu songs are occasionally written, which have the potential to be refined and added to the repertoire. At the end of the group work period, each small group, in turn, gives its recitation or performance.

The following two scenarios are typical of these types of performances.

SCENARIO 1: Avoiding Heavy Work in the Last Trimester of Pregnancy
With a sweater stuffed under her sari, an extraordinarily pregnant woman lumbers comically to the front of the room carrying a bucket, holding her hand on her back as she is very pregnant and past ready to deliver. Another woman hands her a broom (Typical brooms are made of bristles with a short handle attached requiring the user to bend forward while sweeping). Stooping over the broom with one hand on her back and an exaggerated pained expression on her face, she pretends to sweep the room. The audience erupts with laughter at her comedic acting. Another woman, portraying her mother-in-law, walks up to her, asking "Why aren't you working harder?" and pushes her slightly. There are negative noises from some in the audience. The mother-in-law starts complaining and accusing the daughter-in-law that she is not doing her share of the work. The mother-in-law admonishers the pregnant woman to work harder and faster. The young pregnant woman makes no comments or protests and, head down, continues sweeping. Another village woman who questions the mother-in-law for troubling the pregnant daughter-in-law is ignored. Finally, the village health worker arrives and begins talking to the mother-in law, who at first refuses to listen. The players over-act this part of the drama with excessive clowning trying to control their own laughter; the audience is clearly identifying with and enjoying the performance. The VHW character tries to explain to the mother-in-law the importance of good nutrition, relief from work, and the importance of rest during the last months of pregnancy. The mother-in-law is rude to the VHW, turning her back and walking away. Undaunted the VHW continues to reinforce her recommendations, now more forcefully, telling the mother-in-law and the audience that working too hard and lifting heavy loads is dangerous

and can lead to death. The mother-in-law begins to listen only when the VHW reminds her that the fetus the daughter-in-law is carrying will be her grandchild.

SCENARIO 2: Feed Your Daughter-in-Law

Another group worked on the topic of nutrition during pregnancy. In this scene, the mother-in-law seems to be preparing plates of food. The pregnant daughter-in-law is nearby, but she is being ignored. Wearing a fake mustache, a VHW acting as the son sits down and is immediately given a plate that we are told is heaped full of pretend food. The pregnant daughter-in-law is given what looks like an empty plate. Another woman acting as the VHW asks why the daughter-in-law is not given enough food. The mother-in-law ignores the VHWs questions. After another short speech the VHW takes the plate from the mustached son, who looks bewildered and gives it to the pregnant women sitting alone. The mother-in-law exchanges the plates again, giving her son the plate of food. In response and with a grand gesture the VHW exchanges the plates again to the laughter of the audience. The exaggerated exchange of plates continues several times to embellish the dramatized argument among the characters. The audience responds with smiles, laughter, and applause. This presentation ends with a song about proper nutrition for pregnant women. The refrain repeats "I am weak and fainting. She does not give me bread. She does not allow me to eat papaya and banana."

The lyrics raise the issues of mistreatment by mothers-in-law (*sasubai*) and proper nutrition in contradiction of local food prohibitions against eating yellow food during pregnancy. While these presentations are conducted in the lightest of spirits with laughter and joking, the commitment of women to present factual content demonstrates the apparent value of performances as part of the learning process. Learning together in circles emphasizes self-esteem while demystifying the technological aspects of biomedicine to make information accessible for the management of health problems. These types of classroom performances were introduced in the early days of CRHP when there were few visual aids for women without formal education, and these presentations have remained a customary part of the learning activities.

SINGING TO LEARN

In the lives of village women, songs and singing occupy many roles both secular and religious; "Women like to sing *bhajans* (religious songs). They also remembered lyrics they sang while grinding the grain by hand" (Arole and Arole 1994, 185). Expressly, Sunita Sadaphule's anthem "Dear Venubai," "Venubai chalaa warga wari," implores women to desire learning, develop a mindful consciousness, and confront oppression. The songs generally are performed as a call-and-response with hand clapping to keep time. When "Dear Venubai" is sung, women take on a serious tone; it seems almost like a traditional *bhajan* or sacred song. Other songs make women laugh as they sing, and sometimes they improvise joking lyrics. Some of the women have beautiful voices and sing solo songs and enjoy leading songs

Most instructional songs are composed by VHWs as mnemonic devices to help them remember complicated facts and procedures. Other songs written for classroom presentations by impromptu groups highlight and emphasize important class content. Some songs written for a class presentation become staple songs; for example, "Women's Traditions," "Kay sangu bai," that began Chapter 3 was originally written as a classroom performance song and later developed by friends Sundarbai Paudmal and Preeti Sadaphule.

Older women report that work songs were common for a variety of different tasks. An example always mentioned is the work song heard every morning formerly sung by women grinding sorghum into flour to make *bhakri* and *chapati*, the staple flat bread served at every meal. Preparing flour required grinding the grain between two stones approximately eighteen inches in diameter with a central hole in the top stone to insert grain that spills out between the two circular stones. The top stone is turned with an upright stick handle at least eighteen inches long. The process of grinding requires two women with both hands on the handle to exert enough force to move the top stone. A continuous work song accompanied this labor-intensive predawn task, which takes at least one hour of grinding to amass enough flour to make *bhakri* for a family meal. One woman reported if she and another daughter-in-law assigned to the grinding chore stopped singing, the male head of household would shout out for the women to continue.

The songs I was able to collect in the course of this project cover a variety of topics, from reproductive health, "Mahine tujhe saran jatil" ("You Will Give Birth to a Beautiful Child"), to income-generating projects, "Dhani adwu naka mala naduwu nak" ("O Husband Don't Be in My Way"). Other songs are against female infanticide, selective abortion, food prohibitions during pregnancy, early marriage, and dowry. And still others promote adequate nutrition and reduced work during pregnancy or convey practical information like how to make *limbu pane* to prevent diarrhea. For the most part, whether compared to work songs or sacred anthems, music and sing-ing maintain an essential role in the CRHP teaching and learning for VHWs. Particularly, VHWs introduced learning songs at village women's clubs meet-ings to teach about the health of children and women.

FLASHCARDS: APHORISMS AND PRACTICAL APPLICATIONS

VHWs developed "flashcards" as teaching tools and learning devices to reinforce their own learning and to use as a visual teaching aide. The page's stories explain aphorisms, allegories, and local common lore that convey necessary and intricate aspects of health and health care to villagers. The flashcards were developed because audio-visual materials designed for stan-dard training for nurses or paramedics purchased by CRHP had both topics and images that proved inadequate for teaching VHWs. The women them-selves devised the idea of what came to be known as flashcards—a bound set of twenty-four eleven-by-eight-inch laminated sheets that cover every-thing from making *limbu pane* to emergency care for snake bites and how to organize a women's club. Working with a local artist named Kachuru, the women helped develop the series of pictures, making sure these hand drawings were able to communicate complex ideas and concepts while serving as a practical and easily understood tool (see Figure 2).

Local sayings, maxims, and sometimes clichés translated by the women became the sketches for the flashcards. These depictions of local village life explain material learned in recitation of symptoms, diagnosis, and treat-ment of illness in the context of local customs. Tailoring the message based on common visuals and concepts makes complex medical knowledge acces-sible to villagers. Flashcards, like other teaching tools developed at CRHP, preserved traditional practices that promoted good health and rejected com-monly practiced behaviors that negatively affected health and well-being.

For example, one local aphorism says a child must cross twelve rivers before reaching his or her third birthday. This flashcard portrays a large sturdy stone bridge traversing a river in the foreground. The upper right is an oversized mother breastfeeding a baby but looking at the other end of the bridge where a small child is playing with a ball. In the metaphor the mother is described as the architect of the bridge helping her child move from infancy to a healthy child at play and avoiding the river, which repre-sents a common cause of death. The flashcards portray symbols of health and nutrition—the sturdy bridge signifies the healthy building blocks of breastfeeding; various fruits and vegetables represent supplemental nutrition after six months; a syringe indicates immunization, early treatment of illness, and home remedies.

In rural communities many aphorisms and stories use examples from the agriculture cycles of planting and irrigation and the production and care of farm animals. The following is an example of a story that accompanies a flashcard that explains the dangers of traditional beliefs about delaying breastfeeding:

> We feed the cows well in order to get plenty of good rich milk. Then why do we starve the breastfeeding mother? We don't allow the baby to breastfeed the first three days of life, believing the mother's colostrum to be harmful, but babies drink the colostrum of cows with relish. The goat's kid is forced to suckle right after birth and the kid immediately starts prancing around. (Arole and Arole 1994)

These explanations require creativity as they are adapted to fit specific situations. For example, one VHW describes her explanation for birth spacing to a woman with a three-week-old baby:

> I said, just as we give plants enough room to grow, we need to give children space to grow and thrive before we have a second child. Which will grow better—a plant [that] is shaded by other plants and has to fight for space and water, or a plant that has enough space to grow and spread its roots? (Latabai Kadam, fieldnotes 2012)

Using the flashcard as a visual tool allows the audience to make their own interpretation, leading to more questions and dialog to help people understand the dangers of local unhealthful practices. Out of the imagination and creativity of VHWs and supporting the CRHP educational modules, flashcard images become a central teaching and learning device that is easily adapted for health promotion and social awareness.

CHALKBOARDS AND NOTEBOOKS: TRANSFER OF DATA

The Aroles created the village chalkboard as a major tool to improve village conditions through the regular collection and monitoring of health and disease statistics and information about development and sanitary projects and community organizing. Each CRHP village has its own board that is kept in a central location either near the temple or in a community room. At three feet wide and five feet high, it is taller than most VHWs. The thirty categories are painted on the board with permanent white paint, information is added with chalk for each category as the condition or project warrants and eventually the chalk numbers are written into the VHW's statistics notebook that is brought to the CRHP to be transferred for record keeping and analysis.

The village chalkboard identifies thirty categories beginning with typical demographics like total population, recorded as the number of males and females and the number of boys and girls in primary school. Illness among children under five is recorded for the number of cases of malnutrition, especially important in the early days of CRHP but negligible today, and the number of fevers in a month, important during seasonal diseases and sickness. Several headings relate to reproductive health and childbirth: infants weighing less than 2 kg (4.5 lb.), infant deaths, maternal deaths, safe deliveries (without complications, usually attended by the VHW) and nonsafe deliveries (with complications that might require medical treatment); birth control statistics are recorded as the number of couples using condoms, taking oral contraceptives, and using a copper T intrauterine device, as well as the numbers of tubectomies (since 1974) and vasectomies (since 1974). Other health statistics are also kept, including the numbers of patients with TB (cured and in treatment), leprosy (cured and in treatment), and, since 1980, with HIV/AIDS (deceased). The immunizations are recorded as the total numbers vaccinated for polio and those who received BCG vaccines for tuberculosis. Development projects are recorded for the watershed program, including check dams, land leveling, water absorption trenches, and pipelines, and for a large-scale agricultural initiative for planting saplings. Sanitary programs in each village are also counted as the number of soak pits and latrines. Social organizations within each village are also tallied: *mahila mandals* (women's clubs), farmers' clubs, youth clubs, and self-help groups (SHGs).

Each VHW keeps a hardcover notebook that contains all of the health and development information of the chalkboard categories. Since most cannot write in the Marathi language of Jamkhed, village men (most have at least an eight standard education) or children in school assist by writing chalkboard figures in the VHW's notebook. This communication and transfer of information is yet another aspect of the integration from the

village level to the community block level that is subsequently used to analyze the health and well-being of each village.

MENTORING THE SECOND GENERATION

For second-generation VHWs the indispensable mentoring program amplifies the inventive classroom organization and kinetic patterns of teaching
and learning. As CRHP expanded to include new project villages, the first
generation of VHWs became the mentors and trainers of newly selected village women. As mentioned earlier, the personal transition of women from
young wives to effective practitioners was accomplished under the careful
eye of Dr. Mabelle Arole, who modeled the type of relationships that VHWs
now share. While the complicated VHW selection process is endorsed by
elected village officials and supported by the farmers' club, women were
chosen for the second generation based on the preferences of established
VHWs who chose co-workers or successors with an aptitude and desire for
training. First-generation VHWs became mentors in both education and
village life, helping a beginner make the critical transition to health practitioners and social agents, especially regarding changes in consciousness
about gender and caste inequality.

When second-generation women were asked about their own education,
they uniformly described supportive, collaborative learning interactions.
Most VHWs spoke of the mentoring relationship as a crucial way of learning how to interact with villagers, establish rapport among members of
the mobile health team, and manage time. As Sundarbai Paudmal recalled,
"When we started learning, much of the hard work was done already by the
older women." The mentoring process itself, which could last for several
months or longer, helps those in training gain support and confidence by
establishing strong relationships that are often referred through kinship
terms: most mentors are called "auntie." Second-generation women found
their mentor relationships to be transformative and suited to their specific
needs, helping them conquer personal challenges about gaining and retain-
ing information and manage fraught relationships and family pressures.

Family Opposition

VHWs of every generation express concern about family opposition, especially breaking the pattern of family life by staying overnight at CRHP. One

elderly man reported in an interview that his position on his wife's participation in the project changed over time: "I am happy about it now. . . . She
does good work, people respect her" (fieldnotes, 2012). In the early days of
the program, suspicious husbands would peer into classroom windows;
they were concerned that women might be in the company of other men
or convert to Christianity. In some cases, men actively tried to make their
wives return home. Shilabai Amte, a Maratha who has been a VHW for more
than thirty years, reported that her father opposed her desire to become a
VHW and refused to speak to her for two years.

Salma Pathan tells a different story of opposition from her family because
she is a Muslim and her community, especially her husband, frowned on
women working outside of the home.

> In 1974 there was a famine in the whole state. So when I returned to my hus-
> band's village after a visit to my father's village, we had no food to eat. And
> because of our religion [Muslim], my husband would not allow me outside of
> the house to work. I was a victim of false pride of the community. Then I broke
> all the customs. When I came to CRHP and became a health worker, my own
> people were angry and would say things to me because I had to go from house
> to house. I decided that this is one way to feed my family and I decided to con-
> tinue. So when I came here for training every week my husband would come
> and peek through the window to see what was going on, but fortunately my
> father-in-law was a good man and he protected me. Even with all of the opposi-
> tion that my society put on me, I was able to do my work. I did very well with
> the village people and I was elected a deputy mayor. Through it all, my hus-
> band was very suspicious, and he troubled me a lot. If I was not bold and did
> not have courage no one would have survived in my family. (fieldnotes, 2012)

On a visit to Salma Pathan's home I asked her husband how he felt about
Salma Pathan becoming a VHW. He responded, "In the beginning I was very
opposed to what she was trying to do. I did not like her being away from
home. Now I see the value of her work for the family" (Salma Pathan, fieldnotes, 2012). Unfortunately, these issues of distrust and potentially abusive
verbal and physical behavior by spouses have not changed significantly over
time. Women reported that sometimes they would stop coming to class
and drop out of the programs because of physical beating and abuse by
husbands. For example, among the class of women selected in 2009, one

woman who dropped out of the program reported that her husband refused to let her continue at CRHP under threat of physical harm.

Patrilocal Residence

The conditions of women and their life struggles also might preclude the training of village women. The patterns of early marriage that are now illegal in India (laws mandate marriage after age eighteen) are less common, but girls are still married in their late teen years. In rural villages patrilocal residence after marriage continues to be practiced by both Hindus and Muslims. A side effect, or possibly a purpose, is to separate young women from their families and integrate them into their new villages with little opportunity to maintain relationships with childhood friends and relatives. Women still report that as young wives they are closely guarded and subject to strict rules about leaving the house. Often young wives are sequestered in dark and dank mud-floor houses that have poor ventilation, especially during menstrual cycles. Older women report that Dalit women had a greater burden within the confines of the village, even of removing their own footprints from the paths as they walked. Daughters-in-law still appear to have the greatest burden, working from dawn until dusk on housework—fetching water, cleaning the house, tending animals, cooking meals, and working in the fields. There is never any monetary compensation for this work. If a woman works outside of the home on a landowner's field or on roadwork, it is unclear who receives the money. When a young bride became pregnant the workload was never reduced, inadvertently placing the health of women in danger and creating the potential for fetal loss.

These residence patterns continue to have a profound effect on young women. Preeti Sadaphule, a VHW who was married at eighteen, said that when she began living in her husband's family house, "I felt lonely, fearful, and isolated. I had no one." In contrast, becoming a VHW added a new connection and created a space and place for women to congregate. Women describe their relationships with other women as friendships and describe the weekly meetings as going to "my mother's house," using the same language as describing visiting their natal homes for the birth of a first child or a religious festival. Today, head and face covering for travel within and even between villages is no longer commonplace, although some Muslim women force their daughters-in-law to wear a garment covering their head and shoulders. Generally, in CRHP classrooms the *pallu* is rarely used as a head covering by Hindu or Muslim women except for older first generation VHWs.

Tea Intervals and Meals

The morning class is punctuated by a tea interval when *caha* (sweet tea) prepared by the local method of boiling with sugar and milk is brought to the classroom in small cups carried on a large tray by CRHP kitchen staff. Meals are always communal; the lunch break gives women time to rest and socialize. The CRHP kitchen staff prepares a vegetarian meal and some VHWs help by making *bhakri* (sorghum chapati), the staple bread of every meal. Women sit on woven mats in the garden outside the classroom in small groups of four or five eating their lunch.

These informal lunch meetings provide a setting to observe patterns of group interactions of inclusion or exclusion, especially regarding caste. During my participant observation I used these occasions to monitor the configuration of informal clusters as an example of friendship preferences and group dynamics. Based on these observations and after reviewing photos and videos, it seems that some women are clearly personal friends, but they are not inseparable, either in informal groups or formal classroom settings. For example, two women who are exceptionally close are both Dalits, but when in a focus group on caste each made sure that I was aware that they are friends but from different Dalit sects who traditionally quarrel; one is Mahar while the other is Mung, the two lowest groups. In addition, I have never seen a group of exclusively Muslim women sitting together. Similarly, specific age groups or first-generation VHWs never congregate without others sitting with them. Sometimes older women who still wear the *sari pallu* as a head covering sit together, but these patterns are based on convenience of space. In these lunchtime observations, I especially paid attention to Maratha women who admitted having difficulty integrating into a group without caste distinction, and it appears that these original notions of caste superiority are no longer evident. Clearly, these women demonstrated a different consciousness and actively performed caste integration in formal and informal settings. Although VHWs model this behavior in their everyday interactions with villagers, evidence of a rejection of caste hierarchy is not always so apparent in villages.

Social Overnights

Evenings at CRHP during the overnights between classes are devoted to socializing. Women walk around the CRHP campus talking with staff and visitors. Time is spent primarily in the communal classroom where they eat, sleep, talk, and laugh together. Women report that being away from their villages is a rare situation that affords them opportunities to be on their own and free from home and family responsibilities. When asked about the relationships that have been developed over time by the first generation, the women freely acknowledge their continuing affection for each other and consider their generation mates to be closer than biological sisters. The younger women consider the older women aunties. In the several years that I have observed women together, especially in casual conversation during free time or arriving and leaving the CRHP campus, there appear to be no consistent patterns regarding relationships or cleavages based on age, caste, or religion. This is especially notable since not all women attend every weekly session. So, although there are thirty to forty women at each weekly meeting, the attendance patterns vary, as do the numbers in groups who are socializing.

Challenging Traditional Healers

In the1970s, there were various types of undocumented health practitioners, faith healers, god men, and trancers common in the Jamkhed area. In addition, some practitioners who were unlicensed and without formal training gained the trust of many by prescribing medications that were appropriate to solve the basic conditions (Arole and Arole 1994). The Aroles describe such an incident reported by a farmers' club member:

> I saw a crowd gathered in my village. A man was pretending to be a divine healer having extraordinary powers. Village people had brought their sick relatives to him for healing. Among the many things placed before him was an egg that was jiggling about. He was moving a flame around the egg and chanting meaningless words. I picked up the egg and the shell broke and a beetle came out. The trickster had placed the beetle and carefully glued the eggshell back together. With the heat of the flame the beetle moved inside, causing the egg to move. The man was exposed, and we asked him to leave the village. We identified many tricks like this and showed them to people, not only in our own village but in others as well. (Arole and Arole 1994, 116)

Shri Gulabro Mandlik was a traditional healer who held large meetings that purported to cure sickness and disease. During these performances, Mandlik, with a theatrical flair, would consult his "venerable book" of mystical cures to announce a guaranteed remedy that would require a monetary sum and some animal sacrifice. However, when his father was cured of leprosy by the CRHP health team, Mandlik agreed to become a worker for CRHP (Arole and Arole 1994). He renounced his charlatan past to use his ability as a performer to help CRHP to teach people about the tricks and gimmicks of those who claim to be faith healers.

In one such performance for CRHP, Shri Gulabro Mandlik dressed in the extravagant robes of a healer and pretended to diagnose a young man who had red skin patches on his forearm that have no feelings or sensations (a classic symptom of leprosy). Ceremoniously, he consulted his "book" and pronounced that the young man would die in six months unless he performed certain rituals and paid money. Suddenly a VHW, carrying her metal medical case, interrupted the proceedings, observed the young man's skin patches, and tested the area using a pin to judge sensitivity to pain. Rejecting the faith healer's claims, the VHW emphatically announced that the young man has leprosy that can be cured with medications. She declared that leprosy is a disease, not a punishment from the spirits or gods, and there was no need for him to be a social outcast. Additionally, for people with leprosy, damage and deformities due to insensitivity to heat and cold can be avoided with good health care and attention to protecting the affected areas. In these performances, frequently held in project and nonproject villages, Mandlik helps expose the techniques of charlatan healers to challenge the commonly held ideas of villagers, and the VHW demonstrates her medical knowledge and ability to solve health and social problems.

VHWs reject traditional healing, which they claim has no therapeutic value. They expose ritual trancing and such practices as pretend and false, and they reject the idea that common objects like coconut, turmeric, betel nuts, and lemons have magical properties. These views are frequently the subject of classroom performances; for example, in one skit, Rukhsanabee Shaikh pretended to be a healer who used trancing as a method of curing a young woman's health problems. A young woman who struggled with an exaggerated limp, barely able to walk, was brought to her and laid on the ground before her. Rukhsanabee Shaikh, playing a trance healer, began to examine the young woman and announced that she can heal her for a small donation. Then Rukhsanabee Shaikh knelt next to the young woman. Slowly she began to writhe up and down. Her writhing motion grew in its intensity. As she thrashed about she made a rhythmical breathing noise that almost sounded like barking. In constant motion, she shook her head fiercely until her long black hair fell out of its tie, dangling as she hung her head over the young woman's body. Finally, after several minutes, the writhing and barking reached a crescendo and Rukhsanabee Shaikh keeled over. These performance ridicule strongly held local beliefs that a cure occurs when a goddess visits the healer during the trance state.

Some VHWs reported that they decided to investigate whether the trancing was an act or a real state. It was commonly believed that if a menstruating woman is present the spirits would not enter the body of the trance curer or faith healer. In addition, it was believed that during trancing, the visit by the goddess spirits makes her impervious to worldly surroundings and external stimuli and, thus, unable to feel physical pain. Two VHWs who were menstruating attended a trance healing. Notably, when the trancing began, Hirabai Salve decided to take the test one step further. Hirabai Salve deliberately poked the trancer with a needle. Stunned, the healer immediately stopped, cursed, and turned to look at Hirabai Salve. This was considered proof that the trance healer was a fake.

Testing new information about ritual healing gave VHWs confidence in their ideas and tools to use in teaching other villagers the difference between a traditional healer and the new model of health they were learning. As Arole and Arole (1994) point out, "the village health worker needed a long time to internalize these new concepts. Each incident was discussed in detail by women as they shared their experiences, yet each woman had her own doubts" (172).

Compensation

Drs. Mabelle and Raj were aware that village health workers needed some type of compensation for service to the villages. The two initial alternatives were that either CRHP or the village *panchayat* would pay the VHWs a salary; however, neither had sufficient funds to pay an adequate salary. For the nine women who participated in the first training program at CRHP, a decision was made to pay them for their time and transportation for the day and overnight they attended classes in Jamkhed. Of course, food and lodging were provided for the overnight at the CRHP center. One of the social workers helped the women improve earnings with small income-generating projects. In addition, VHWs accepted the typical compensation given to *dias* after a childbirth—usually grain, cloth to make a blouse that is worn with a sari, and glass bangles typically worn by all women. As will be discussed in Chapter 6, women participate in financial arrangements that were more lucrative and appropriate for their position in the community.

Conclusion: Ways of Learning

Based on the underlying CRHP principles of equity, integration, and empowerment, an educational process specific to the need of the women of Jamkhed was developed. This model, conceived by Drs. Mabelle and Rajanikant Arole in collaboration with other staff VHWs, is an example of how community participation can create a collaborative teaching process that becomes a dialogue of learning. The success of the Jamkhed Model for learning is mirrored in the long-lasting social relationships among the women. However, do these learning approaches and collective processes have the potential for universal applications for community health workers?

Firmly anchored in community participation, respect for others, and the urgency of communicating essential demystified biomedical information for the well-being of the community, it enables those who were taught to become teachers in the same collaborative and mutually respectful way. Research conducted in Jamkhed by Ketan Chitnis was the basis for his dissertation, "Communication for Empowerment and Participatory Development: A Social Model of Health in Jamkhed, India" (2005), which emphasizes that communication enables what he called participatory learners to gain self-confidence and raise their consciousness, which can permit them to prevail over oppression. As the song queries at the beginning of this chapter, "Why are you sitting at home being oppressed?" Women had many reasons for becoming health workers, but few imagined that they would be part of the process of creating new ways of knowing and learning. Few of the women would have thought the process of becoming a health worker itself would irrevocably change their perceptions of self and the way they understood their families, villages, and the larger society. The longevity of the model and its ability to establish a comprehensive approach to primary health care that adapts and develops to meet health challenges in a remote rural area with limited access to advanced services is evidence of the creativity and dedication of the founders, the validity of the principles on which it is based, and the resilience and integrity of the VHWs who benefitted from the process.

CHAPTER 5

Woman and Child Health
You Will Give Birth to a Beautiful Baby

You Will Give Birth to a Beautiful Baby (*Mahine tujhe saran jatil*)

(Chorus)
You will give birth to a beautiful baby
But after delivery, don't cut the cord with a sickle.

In pregnancy don't do heavy work
For some time stop work and rest
Have your urine and blood tested.

Chorus

At the seventh month take a tetanus injection
The child will not get tetanus and mother also will be healthy
Eat vegetables and put dal on your food.

Chorus

After delivery keep surroundings clean
Keep clothes and other things for the baby clean
Avoid uncleanliness near your bed.

Chorus

Within half an hour of delivery breastfeed
your baby. Mother's milk is best for the baby
And helps take care of yourself.

Chorus

After one child don't be in a hurry to have a second one
There should be five years spacing between
two children. This way your life will be happy.

Chorus

The Principle of Equity

The words of the VHW instructional song that begins this chapter serve as a careful guide for the health of women during pregnancy, childbirth, and the postpartum period, and identifies the hope of every pregnant woman—"a beautiful baby." Implicit in these lyrics is the notion of reproductive health as a social phenomenon as well as a biomedical event fundamental to personal integrity and human rights. Reproductive health strategies are tied to economic and social processes and involve the individual autonomy to forestall systems of discrimination against women (Freedman and Isaacs 1993; Cook 1993; Cook and WHO 1994). In addition, gender itself as relations of power "interact with biology to generate differences in needs, capabilities, and treatment requires us to focus systematically on the forms that bias takes and the inequality and injustice that result" (Sen, George, and Östlin 2002, 8).

Equity is the most salient principle of the CRHP primary health care model that relates to reproductive health and addresses the underlying social dynamics of contemporary villages with a focus on defeating gender and caste inequality and highlighting other traditions and practices that affect the health of women. "As the village health workers discussed the social causes of ill health, they saw the need to organize the women in the village if major social changes were to occur. However, they encountered numerous difficulties in doing so. The women, in their isolation, were not open to change and seemed to be trapped in their own fatalism and superstition" (Arole and Arole 1994, 184). Consequently, the VHW educational process taught recognition of local patterns of behavior that prevent women from getting adequate reproductive health care. As practitioners VHWs were able to identify various aspects of village life that contributed negatively to women's health. Thus, central to the role of VHWs is the implementation of appropriate biomedical and social approaches to reproductive health and justice using personal interpretations of the social aspects of gender and caste inequalities to help resist and transform the status quo of village health care.

Everyday Life Experiences and Social Action

By sharing life experiences and a common idea of themselves as social actors, VHWs problematize the hierarchy of Indian life and its social and political consequences as underlying causes of poor reproductive health.

For example, Manjula Gite, a second-generation VHW, explains how negative views of female children directly affected her in childhood and led to an early arranged marriage:

> I was the third girl. I was born in my mother's [natal] village. When my father found out that I was a girl, he disowned me. He said, "take that child and throw her in the river." So, I was left in that place in my grandmother's care. My father disowned me, but my grandmother's neighbors helped care for me and gave me clothes. When it was time for me to go to school my father would not sign. My father wanted to get me married as soon as possible. When I was eleven, he found a husband for me. The man was disabled from polio. He did not have use of one of his legs. I did not like him, and I didn't want to marry. My father told me that he would kill me if I did not agree. We got married and my husband's father supported us. But my father-in-law got TB and died. We had no one to support us. It was left to me. (personal interview, 2012)

Preeti Sadaphule, another second-generation VHW, remembers:

> I was one of four daughters. My father drank alcohol. He beat my mother and blamed her for having four daughters. My mother had to work to feed us. In those days she found no cash jobs, so she bartered her work for food. My father did not contribute to the family. The village community helped to get two of my sisters married. I was fond of school and I went to the third grade, but my mother would not let me continue. My mother could not afford to send me to school. My father decided to marry another woman because he wanted sons. Then my mother got me married. My mother was left alone because all her daughters got married. (personal interview, 2012)

Pushpabai Sanap explains:

> I was the fifth daughter. When I was born my aunt put me under a big pot. She was going to leave me there. But my grandmother rescued me. She told my mother that if she took care of me, she would have a son. So, my mother kept me. Then my brother was born. When we were little, we were always together very nicely. When it came time to go to school only my brother was allowed to go. One day my uncle took me to school. I liked writing with the little chalk slate, so I wanted to stay but my parents said no. Only my brother should go to school. (personal interview, 2009)

Ushabai Bangar, one of the first-generation VHWs, offers her comments on the importance of promoting a girl's self-esteem:

> Educate her and also her brother, do not change that. If a girl is educated, then later on her family will be educated. Any young adolescent girl is very aware about her looks, stands in front of a mirror and looks at herself. What was happening in the past is that her own family members would talk about it in a negative way: "She shouldn't be doing this or that," these are negative comments. And the negative comments are actually an injustice to her. Teach the parents not to get her married until she is eighteen years old. Ask her who she wants to marry, do not go out looking for a husband for her without asking her. You know that when you do that, it creates a big mess. It is very important that the girl and the guy really like each other and know each other. But it is important that she does this for her own self-awareness. (personal interview, 2009)

As Ushabai Bangar asserts, these interpretations of women's lives are necessary to help recognize and defeat gender prejudice in village life in all its many forms. In a rural society that relies on oral traditions, these life stories help make the connections among the numerous ways gender bias affects women's lives from childhood to marriage. These new understandings are integrated into daily practices to negotiate incremental changes in villages. Ultimately, the comprehensiveness of the CRHP model becomes a necessary tool to promote women's health and well-being through introspection, personal consciousness, and the deconstruction of the position of women.

Childbirth: The Value of a Song

Just as personal stories are valuable as frameworks of knowing, the lyrics of "Mahine tujhe saran jatil" ("You Will Give Birth to a Beautiful Baby"), like so many other instructional songs, occupy an essential place in village life. A classroom mnemonic device that is internalized by VHWs, these songs when taught to village women became a guide to good health practices, contrasting new biomedical knowledge with the injurious traditional patterns of the past generations. For village women who have many voiced and unvoiced concerns about labor and childbirth, the practice of teaching songs reassures women of a successful birth experience and becomes a means for VHWs to communicate caring and confidence.

"Don't cut the cord with a sickle"—the words of the song's refrain crystalize a proscription to avoid a practice that leads to postpartum infection and, too often, maternal death. Before safe delivery practices and the CRHP delivery kit (discussed later in this chapter) became standard for VHWs, the sickle (*koyata* or *khurpay*) was used by *dias* and family members to cut the umbilical cord. There are few accessible sharp blades in village households; the *villi* or *soori*, a stationary blade on a wooden base, is the primary cutting utensil used in kitchens. The small four-inch sickle is commonly used by women for most agricultural work activities in the fields. If used in a home delivery it can be the source of bacteria commonly present in soil, dust, and manure that causes a tetanus infection which affects the central nervous system and is one of the major causes of infant and maternal mortality.

A serious cause of fetal loss in the third trimester, especially in the Global South, is excessive physical work, such as lifting and carrying heavy objects like over-sized water containers, bundles of firewood, and sacks of grain that are typically transported on women's heads. The song lyrics are addressed to mothers-in-law to caution them against requiring young wives to continue doing strenuous domestic and farm work late in the pregnancy. Understanding the potential for this serious complication of pregnancy, VHWs spend time during prenatal visits to help mothers-in-law realize the importance of reduced workload and adequate rest in the last trimester of pregnancy. Mediating the complex family relationship between mother-in-law and daughter-in-law is one of the delicate social challenges handled by VHWs.

Nutritional deficiencies during pregnancy are common in India; for example, anemia is a major cause of maternal mortality due to nutritional iron deficiency, which may act as an underlying factor for hemorrhaging, eclampsia, abortion, obstructed labor, and sepsis. In Jamkhed the nutritional taboo of avoiding yellow foods during pregnancy leads to an extreme vitamin A deficiency called night blindness. In village homes *dal* is prepared using pulses (legumes) such as varieties of lentils and chickpeas (*chana*), and sometimes black gram, which are all rich in protein. The danger of avoiding pulses and beans is that these legumes are frequently the only source of protein in the local diet. For example, *dal* is eaten as a type of chutney with other greens, corn, and other seasonal produce when available, with *bhakri* (sorghum flat bread) made daily in households. In encouraging the community to "put dal on your food," the lyrics of "Mahine tujhe saran jatil" support the healthy practice of eating locally available protein-rich foods.

The traditional pattern of breastfeeding, especially in the early days of CRHP, was to wait three days before putting the infant to the breast. Colostrum, the first clear breastmilk produced after childbirth, was considered to be unacceptable for newborns. A usual practice was to use a cotton ball saturated with goat milk to feed the infant; women expressed the colostrum until breastmilk appeared. The song lyrics underscore two health advantages to the practice of breastfeeding: First, the infant benefits from colostrum that contains valuable maternal antibodies that boost the infant's immune system. Second, the woman's postpartum process is enhanced because the act of breastfeeding causes the uterus to contract helping postpartum involution (a physiological process transforming the uterus to its nonpregnant state). In some cases, setting a newborn to breastfeed immediately after birth can help with delivery of the placenta. VHWs understand this as a critical part of postpartum care as the song instructs "helps take care of yourself."

Finally, the song introduces concerns about planning a family and subsequent pregnancies with emphasis on a woman's health and her role in rural villages. VHWs recommend birth spacing of five years as best for the woman who now has the double duty of raising a child and keeping a household running. Once learned, taught, and retaught, these lyrics create a chain of knowledge passed from VHWs to generations of village women to confirm "this way your life will be happy." As will be illustrated later in this chapter through ethnographic interviews and histories of the practice and expertise of first- and second-generation VHWs, major changes in health statistics promoting reproductive health are directly related to the practices, advocacy, and teaching of VHWs.

Gaining Acceptance as a Practitioner

Most VHWs report attending to safe birth experiences and delivering babies as their favorite aspect of village service. Similarly, for many, managing a successful birth experience was the event that signaled their acceptance as a health practitioner. Traditionally, childbirth in Jamkhed villages was attended by women family members and *dias* (local birth guides). Thus, the first generation of VHWs, many of whom were of different castes or religions, had many barriers to breach before they gained approval by their communities. Of course, women who became VHWs were regarded with suspicion even though many became village residents as young brides and had been living in the community for more than ten years. Many VHWs report that the key to a villager's acceptance as a birth attendant was often based on the correct assessment or diagnosis of a problem and a subsequent positive result. As vividly recounted to me in most of the personal interviews I conducted, each VHW distinctly remembers the particular social or health event that helped her make progress toward being recognized as a practitioner and the success of her relentless efforts to win the trust of her village.

For example, Latabai Kadam lived in Pimpalgaon-Alwa. She was called to the house of the *sarpanch*, a wealthy Maratha (dominant caste). This same *sarpanch* had selected Latabai Kadam, a poor, uneducated, twice-widowed Dalit, to be trained at CRHP because he assumed she would be performing menial tasks at the medical center. However, the *sarpanch* had to reassess his opinion of Latabai Kadam when his daughter returned to her natal home village for the birth of her first child. The local *dia* and a women relative were attending the young woman in the delivery of her first child; however, there appeared to be complications. The *sarpanch* heard from other villagers that Latabai Kadam had learned new skills at CRHP and had a growing reputation for safe deliveries. As a last resort he called Latabai Kadam to help his young daughter, who had been in labor for many hours without progressing.

Latabai Kadam explains:

> As I walked into the house, I had to hold my sari close to me so that my garments would not touch the furniture. I did not know how I would help the problem if they did not let me touch the woman in labor. When I reached the room, I was allowed to examine the woman, who was being urged to push. I determined that labor was progressing normally, but she was becoming exhausted. I recommended that she be given something to drink and allowed to rest. After awaking she had the strength to continue and the baby was born and fine. (personal interview, 2009)

This remarkable event ending in the successful safe delivery of a healthy neonate had profound implications on many levels. First, Latabai Kadam was able to demonstrate the knowledge she had gained from CRHP to accurately diagnose a problem and apply the correct remedy. Second, the value of the CRHP primary health care approach over traditional methods was shown. Third, caste prejudice was contested when as a Dalit she was allowed into the house of a Maratha, although she was admonished to hold her sari to allay fears of ritual contamination believed to be linked to low-caste individuals. Finally, Latabai Kadam gained the recognition and acceptance of the Maratha community. Her actions as a health practitioner made inroads to bridge caste prohibitions and changed her position, especially among the upper-caste villagers, who now accepted her as someone with knowledge, skills, and personal confidence.

While first-generation VHWs like Latabai Kadam paved the way, for the second generation acceptance in villages as new practitioners was still based on their personal abilities and proven successes. As the second-generation VHW in Matewali village, Ashti block, Preeti Sadaphule was mentored by the village's first VHW, yet she still needed to gain acceptance as an independent practitioner by demonstrating her own ability and competence. Preeti Sadaphule states:

> One of the occasions that helped me to be accepted by the people in my village occurred when the daughter of a high-caste family was in labor at home and there was a problem. I knew that this family had discriminated against low-caste women. Before I entered the house, I asked if there would be a problem to touch the daughter or have my sari in contact with other family members or objects. The family said there would be no problem. When I arrived, the baby was delivered, but the contractions had stopped leaving the placenta in the uterus. There was a lot of bleeding. After assessing the situation, I recommended that the young woman put the newborn to her breast and start feeding. This was not a typical practice. After a while the placenta was delivered, and the bleeding stopped. (personal interview, 2010)

Based on her classwork and mentoring, Preeti Sadaphule was aware of the relationship between suckling and postpartum uterine contractions as a means of expelling the placenta. She accurately assessed the problem and provided a simple and effective solution to manage the delivery of the placenta. Preeti Sadaphule's application of essential primary health care resulted in an accurate diagnosis and resolution of a potential life-threatening problem. In addition, it allowed her to demonstrate the importance of the continuing educational practices of the CRHP model and reinforce the need to continually challenge traditional unhealthy patterns of maternal and infant health care, especially for breastfeeding.

Prenatal Care

Prenatal, or antenatal, care is considered an indispensable component of reproductive health necessary to prevent potential problems during pregnancy and childbirth and to provide women with access to information about care and decision-making during a pregnancy. When the Aroles arrived in Jamkhed, the number of villages receiving antenatal care was less than 5 percent. Today 95 percent of women have access through the village VHW and government nurses. Following CRHP principles, primary health care practices of essential medicines and appropriate technology are implemented for antenatal care, including medications, tetanus toxoid injections, and folic acid tablets. In the United States the standard of care recommends at least twelve prenatal visits. Due to the structure of primary health care and the implementation of the Jamkhed Model, with one VHW in each village there is a potential to see the VHW every day, especially useful during the last trimester of pregnancy.

VHWs implement comprehensive care using essential medical procedures that meet the basic needs of the community and follow the CRHP primary health care approach to screen pregnant women. VHWs check for gestational diabetes and preeclampsia using portable urine tests. Each VHW can demonstrate the procedure for testing urine using Benedict's solution. This complex procedure requires a glass test tube, test tube holder, and sustained flame made by burning rubbing alcohol on cotton balls. Benedict's solution has been in use since the 1920s and has been replaced by simple urine and blood tests in modern clinical facilities; however, due to lack of finances, this procedure, dated but still accurate, continues to be used by VHWs in Jamkhed. Each VHW has her own test tubes, holders, and reagents to perform the prenatal testing. Another old but effective type of prenatal screening to test for signs of preeclampsia is Heller's test, which identifies albumin in the urine. Preeclampsia (formerly called toxemia) is characterized by an elevation in blood pressure during pregnancy known as gestational hypertension (or pregnancy-induced hypertension), which if it becomes acute may lead to serious complications for both the pregnant woman and the fetus. Each VHW has her own blood pressure equipment, which is usually used in a villager's home during one of the routine prenatal visits. Unfortunately, many of these instruments are outdated; for example, some VHWs use a sphygmomanometer housed in a long metal case (approximately two by twelve inches) consisting of a tube filled with mercury and inflatable cuff to pressure the upper arm and a stethoscope to identify the sounds as a measurement. While still accurate, these cumbersome instruments were replaced in most modern clinics and hospitals more than thirty years ago.

GEETA'S ANTENATAL VISIT

Winters are the dry season in Jamkhed; nights are cool, and days are always sunny with few clouds in the sky. It never rains. On this day we accompanied Pushpabai Sanap on her daily village rounds in Sharadwadi village. As we arrived at Geeta's house, she greeted us at the door. Her house is a typical structure with a large central room with tile flooring and entrance alcove. The dwelling is better appointed than others in the village, typical of a Vanjari-caste home with a TV and a single electric light bulb dangling on a wire, but no source of water. There are a tall, metal, two-door storage cabinet and wall shelves with stainless steel plates and containers for food storage. Bedding is hung on a cord in the near corner where two small suitcases are piled on each other. On a tiny stool there is a stainless plate scattered with onions and potatoes near a two-burner kerosene stove that sits on the floor.

Pushpabai boasted that Geeta was one of the first babies she delivered in this village. She asked me if I remember Geeta reminding me that she was a member of the Adolescent Girls Program at CRHP before she married. We were asked if we would like *caha*. Pushpa, smiling, motioned for Geeta to lie down on the bed that occupies one end of the room under the only window. Pushpabai sat on the bed as Geeta automatically loosened the waist of the underskirt of her sari. As Pushpabai began her examination, she told us that Geeta was twenty-two years old and in the seventh month of her second pregnancy. She married at eighteen when she finished the twelfth standard (equivalent of junior college). She married a man from her mother's village and continues to live in the same village where she was raised, but it's unclear if it was a "love marriage."

The physical examination started with Pushpabai gently moving her hand around Geeta's abdomen to feel the fetus, which is not difficult on a small woman with little body fat. Pushpabai said we check to see if the fetus is positioned like a watermelon seed (head down) or a custard apple seed (transverse). She listened to fetal heart sounds with a stethoscope and smiled at Geeta, saying "good sounds." Blood pressure was taken with a portable cuff wrapped around the upper arm, using a stethoscope. Pushpabai asked if Geeta had noticed any swelling in her feet as she checked for edema by pressing her finger on the top of Geeta's feet and then lower legs. Although she found no swelling, she reassured Geeta that some swelling is normal at this stage of pregnancy. Continuing the examination, Pushpabai assessed Geeta's eyes and tongue for signs of anemia; she turned to us and said she was concerned about anemia because Geeta's last hemoglobin was low, 8.5 g/dL (the US normal range is 10 to 14 g/dL). Although as part of the Adolescent Girls Program, Geeta would have learned about nutrition and health care during pregnancy, Pushpabai still questioned Geeta about eating practices, especially protein intake. As Pushpabai completed her examination, Geeta's father arrived carrying a two-year-old boy who looked at us suspiciously and started to cry. Smiling, Geeta fixed her sari and took the boy. We thanked her for letting us observe the visit.

The competent and thorough prenatal examination conducted by Pushpabai is replicated daily in CRHP project villages. The CRHP continuing-education approach and weekly trainings provide frequent updates about prevention and screening methods to help VHWs detect potential complications of pregnancy, with an emphasis on the most common problems in local populations. For example, anemia during pregnancy, often related to a deficient diet, is one of the major reasons for maternal mortality in this area; consequently, Pushpabai is concerned about Geeta's hemoglobin count and diet as an indicator of anemia. As the reproductive health instructional song lyrics stress, VHWs are always vigilant to promote a well-balanced diet of local food and to avoid food taboos that promote deficiencies during pregnancy.

THE PREGNANCY DELIVERY KIT

A creative innovation of the CRHP methods for childbirth includes the delivery kit, shown in Figure 2, pictured here on a flashcard page showing items necessary for a safe delivery in village households. This kit itself was created in the early days of CRHP to provide a clean environment for all village deliveries in homes where childbirth was carried out on string cots or dung floors. The flashcard page is used to teach VHWs procedures that will take place in the home and to explain to village women what to expect during childbirth. As a symbol of a competent, educated practitioner, the kit inspires confidence, brings new ideas, and carries the promise of a clean and safe outcome. Preparation for a safe delivery begins as soon as a pregnancy is confirmed by the VHW, who helps assemble the contents,

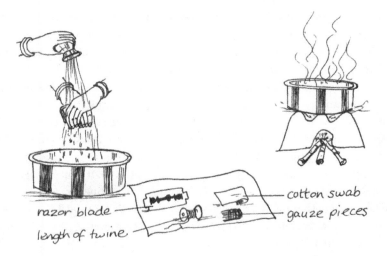

razor blade

length of twine

cotton swab

gauze pieces

The delivery kit

FIGURE 2: The delivery kit originally drawn for *Jamkhed: A Comprehensive Rural Health Project* (Arole and Arole 1994). Courtesy of Ravi Arole, Director, CRHP

which are wrapped in a length of old, clean sari fabric assembled to make a pouch. Later, the sari piece will be used to create a clean, dry surface for the delivery. The kit includes a clean length of twine to tie the umbilical cord and a new double-edged razor to cut the umbilical cord after it is tied. To provide support to the perineum, the area between the anus and the vulva, during delivery there is a sterile gauze pad, provided for the delivery kit by the medical center, to be held firmly on the perineum to prevent vaginal or anal tearing. Each woman is instructed to carefully store the kit in a clean dry place so that it can be easily accessible at the time of labor.

Other appropriate technology is used by some VHWs to follow the growth and development of the fetus. For example, a fetoscope, called a Pinard horn, is made of metal or hollowed wood, and about eight inches long. It amplifies sound when the wide end of the horn is placed against the abdomen; the ear is placed at the other end to listen to the fetal heartbeat. Most women in this part of India have slight builds and are on average 4 feet 11 inches (1.5 meters) tall, and young women are generally slender, which makes it relatively easy to measure the abdomen and to approximate fetal size.

Shilabai Amte explains how she diagnoses and manages a pregnancy currently:

When a woman thinks she is pregnant because she is not having her menstrual cycle for one month, first you must find out why the period has stopped. It may be because a woman might have anemia or a serious disease. If a woman is forty or forty-five years old, she may be at a different stage in her life. When we think she is pregnant, at three months we examine her. We feel her stomach and examine her breasts. Then we can say with certainty, yes, she is pregnant. Then we register her in our notebook to make sure to keep track. We begin to visit with her each month. We examine her at three months and the fetus is only 50 grams [1.7 lb.]. After six months it is 0.5 kg [1.1 lb.]. At seven and eight months the fetus grows about to 1 kg [2.2 lb.]. It is necessary to put always your hand on the stomach of the woman. From that you will know and make sure whether the fetus is growing or not. At six months it is at the level of the navel. At each month the fetus grows two centimeters. So, in the ninth month it is up to the chest [rib cage]. At the ninth month we go to the woman and examine her and we should feel the head of the baby near the pubic bone. From time to time during the pregnancy we give her lessons about nutrition. She should have carbohydrates, protein, and green vegetables. We make sure that she takes a tetanus injection from the government nurse. These injections should be taken at the fifth and sixth months. (fieldnotes, 2010)

GIVING BIRTH

Originally, the first-generation VHWs learned the mechanics of delivery and typical problems of presentation of the fetus by observing Drs. Mabelle and Raj Arole conduct deliveries in the CRHP clinic hospital. First-generation VHWs spent a significant portion of their training observing both simple and complicated deliveries to learn the basics of a safe delivery and what to do in an emergency. However, the methods and patterns of childbirth in the hospital are very different from conducting a delivery in a typical village home. Like the pregnancy kit, procedures were adapted for childbirth in the homes of villagers, especially in the early days of CRHP, when dwellings had thatched roofs, there were few household goods or furniture, and most people slept on floor mats. Childbirth was managed on the cow-dung floors of dwellings using the sari piece from the pregnancy kit to provide a clean surface. Second-generation VHWs had the added advantage of a mentoring relationship with older VHWs, who had the experience of many safe home deliveries.

Gangabai Kulkarni describes a characteristic pattern of attending births in the early days of CRHP, when not all women received prenatal care, especially women returning to their mother's home to give birth.

When we go for a delivery, we ask the woman whether it is the first delivery or second delivery. If it is the first delivery, we take the history. We ask her to lie down for examination. We see how long the head has come down and we hear the heartbeat of the baby. Then we ask her how quickly she is having pain. If she is a primigravida we do not worry because we know it will take fifteen to eighteen hours. If she is having severe pain every five minutes, then we think that this is the time. When it is time, we wash our hands. Then with a cloth [sterile gauze] we support the vagina [perineum] as the head comes down and that is why she does not tear. Then we ask a village women's group member who we also trained to help. We ask for the string and to make the razor red hot to cut the cord. But before that we listen to how the baby is crying. We take out anything from the mouth. And we look at the baby to see if it has any deformities. We check ears, fingers, if it has an extra finger. Whether it has a urinating place and an extra place [anus]. By that time there may be a little fresh blood coming and the umbilical cord becomes long. If the placenta is not expelled immediately, we breastfeed the baby and then it expels. So, the breastfeeding helps. Also, if she breastfeeds the baby, there will be less bleeding. This is important for the health of the baby and the mother also. Then the uterus will contract. We also massage so that the uterus will get back into place. We examine her. If it [cervix] feels like a nose it should be okay. If it feels soft there may be a problem. If she is having bleeding, we put her feet up and her head down, so it will stop. Otherwise we take her to the hospital. (personal interview, 2009)

RETURNING TO YOUR NATAL HOME TO GIVE BIRTH

A pregnant woman in the Jamkhed and surrounding *talukas* returns to her childhood home to give birth, particularly for the first birth, and there is often a stay of some months afterwards. Generally, a woman travels to their mother's village and natal home during the seventh or ninth month but not the eighth month. Since everyone knew about the practice but no one could give me the reason or justification, I presumed it was based on superstition, and a few people tacitly agreed. Most marriages have patrilocal residence, which usually requires a move to the husband's family home immediately after marriage (this was the case even in the days of child betrothal and marriage); going home for the purpose of childbirth was considered a happy time. However, this traditional pattern posed a number of concerns for performing safe home deliveries. For example, if a pregnant woman is living in a CRHP project village, she receives prenatal care from the VHW; while this insures good care and screening, if she returns to her mother's village for the birth or shortly before, the delivery may be conducted by a family member or a local *dia*. Complications of labor and delivery that might be diagnosed during childbirth by the VHW might go unnoticed, leading to more serious outcomes. Alternatively, if a woman returns to her natal home in a CRHP project village to give birth, she may not have had adequate prenatal care, including essential medications or screenings, during her pregnancy while living in her husband's village. If the woman returns in the seventh month the VHW will check the blood pressure and obtain blood and urine tests and sonography, if necessary. However, if the young woman arrives in a CRHP project village in the ninth month, the lack of prenatal care and screening might unnecessarily lead to a complicated childbirth.

Shilabai Amte reports how she managed a case of a woman who is living in a nonproject village:

> When there is a pregnant woman in my village, I see her every month or more. But if it is someone from another village it is difficult. If the woman lives in a nonproject village, that woman may not have gotten adequate prenatal care. Sometimes I am not called for the birth. There was one woman whose mother delivered the baby. I went to visit her mother's house after three days and the young woman was having fever. I asked to see the cloth she was wearing to collect vaginal bleeding. I saw that the cloth had a bad odor. I gave the woman a sponge bath for the fever and Septra [sulfamethoxazole and trimethoprim] and paracetamol [acetaminophen]. I asked how the cloth was washed. I explained the importance of clean cloths and about washing cloths and drying them in the sun. A few days later the woman was fine. (fieldnotes, 2010)

RANI'S TEARS

Rani, an eighteen-year-old girl who is in her ninth month of pregnancy, has returned to her mother's village of Sangavhi-Ashti to give birth even though her mother died when she was a child. This day, Kalawatibai Sawant, the VHW, has called all the pregnant women to her home near the village center because the CRHP mobile health team (MHT) is testing hemoglobin. I had traveled with the MHT to Sangavhi-Ashti. Kalawatibai Sawant used the occasion to check blood pressure and urine and to talk about prenatal care. When Rani's hemoglobin was tested it was found to be low; she reported having prenatal care in her husband's village, but she never had a blood test.

Rani was standing by the door of the house where examinations were taking place. Kalawatibai Sawant said to Rani, "Why are you crying?" and motioned her to come into the room and sit on the mat next to her. Kalawatibai Sawant petted Rani's head and tried to comfort her by putting her arm around her. Then, Kalawatibai Sawant examined Rani by looking at her tongue and the skin beneath her eyes and her fingernail beds. Kalawatibai Sawant said, "Your hemoglobin is a little low. You should be eating four times a day." She started to give other advice regarding foods rich in iron when Rani started crying again. Kalawatibai Sawant silently wiped the tears from her eyes with the *pallu* of her sari and said to Rani, "Why are you crying? We are here with your aunt Phulabai Khedkar who is also a VHW." Kalawatibai Sawant smiled and hugged Rani, joking, "You are not the first woman in the world to get pregnant." She laughed out loud and looked at Rani, who gave a reluctant little smile and wiped her eyes. Kalawatibai Sawant spoke directly to Rani.

> If the slightest thing happens to you, we will take care of you. You should not worry. You have nothing to fear. What are you getting so worried about? Phulabai Khedkar is here. We will make sure. We'll take you and we will show you our love. I've done so many deliveries in my life and even the complicated ones. There are so many people around you. We all love you. So you have nothing to worry about. Even though your mother is not here we have known you since you were a child. I am going to perform the delivery. You have nothing to worry about. I have a phone that CRHP has given me. If we need to go to that hospital, we will tell them that this patient belongs to Kalawatibai Sawant. We all will take good care of you. Why are you crying? (fieldnotes, 2010)

SAFE BIRTHS AND COMPLICATIONS

The CRHP model of one VHW in each village has produced many significant changes in the health profile of villages, yet the greatest benefit is the established pattern of safe deliveries begun by the first generation of VHWs. The record of safe deliveries, whether home births, natural births at the medical center, or caesarian deliveries performed in the medical center operating theater, speaks for itself.

Following a pattern established forty years ago, the VHW is called as soon as labor begins and assists through the entire labor process at the pregnant woman's own home. More importantly, as soon as a potential problem appears, the VHW can identify symptoms of complications that might be high risk. Accordingly, the VHW makes a determination to continue the labor process in the village or to move to the medical center to deal with more serious issues. As part of the CRHP team, the judgement of the VHW in identifying potential problems is helpful in facilitating a transfer of a woman to the operating room for a Caesarean section surgery when necessary.

MANAGING COMPLICATIONS OF PREGNANCY: A SECOND-GENERATION VHW'S EXPERIENCE

I interviewed Preeti Sadaphule, a second-generation VHW, in her village of Matwali in Ashti *taluka*, about how she managed complications of pregnancy. Of the 180 births Preeti Sadaphule attended, only six women had some type of major problem with the pregnancy or delivery. However, Preeti Sadaphule stated that she felt confident about dealing with even the most complicated situations: "We learned from the older women who delivered many babies. They were our mentors and helped us learn the signs. We were fortunate to learn from them" (fieldnotes, 2012).

On one occasion, Preeti Sadaphule recalls that she conducted a manual examination during a prenatal visit on a woman in her third pregnancy and found that the fetus was small for its gestational age. She was concerned and felt that the woman required a sonogram to accurately assess the problem. In India there are stringent restrictions on the use of sonograms to prevent sex determination and the subsequent abortions of female fetuses. In 2002, the Pre-Natal Diagnostic Techniques (Regulation and Prevention of Misuse) Act (PNDT) was amended to restrict access to those with training and licensure. However, there is a sonogram at the CRHP health center that is in a locked room that only Dr. Shobha Arole, the medical director, is certified to operate. Preeti Sadaphule accompanied the woman to the health center; when the sonogram was performed there was a concern that the fetus might have some problem, so the woman was admitted to the CRHP hospital for further observation.

Preeti Sadaphule remembered another incident:

> One night, it was late. I was called to the house of a woman whose daughter
> returned home from her husband's village. She came home to have the baby.
> The mother and aunt were there. They knew there was something wrong. The
> girl was very young and tiny. When I examined her the baby was in the wrong
> position, sideways. I went with them to Jamkhed hospital and the next day she
> had a caesarian operation. (fieldnotes, 2012)

In another case, Preeti Sadaphule reports that she made the diagnosis of
placenta previa, a potentially life threating condition. Unfortunately, when
she tried to explain the situation to the mother-in-law she was met with
opposition:

> There was a woman in my village in her sixth month of pregnancy who was
> bleeding. I had a suspicion that it was placenta previa because there was no
> pain just bleeding. I knew this was a dangerous sign of a serious condition. I
> wanted the woman to take her daughter-in-law to the CRHP hospital, but she
> refused. I got the use of a Jeep and took the woman myself. She got a sonogram,
> which clearly show the placenta in a dangerous place. She remained at CRHP
> and we were better able to watch the pregnancy. Then she had a C-section. She
> and the baby were fine. (fieldnotes, 2012)

For two other women, Preeti Sadaphule used her skill and experience to
identify potential complications of childbirth. On one occasion she was
called to the home of a woman in labor who had a normal presentation
(the fetus was in the correct position for a vaginal delivery) but when her
water broke labor did not progress. After twenty minutes without any sign
of contractions Preeti Sadaphule was concerned about possible complications and accompanied the woman to the CRHP health center. In another
situation, when Preeti Sadaphule examined a woman who was in the very
early stage of labor she discovered that there was an uncharacteristically
small amount of amniotic fluid, which may indicate a fetal abnormality.
Realizing there was no time to get to the CRHP hospital from Ashti, Preeti
Sadaphule was able to conduct a safe delivery at the woman's home and
take care of the newborn.

These personal examples of accurate diagnosis and successful management of health issues are typical of the VHWs' experience. Some VHWs, like

Preeti Sadaphule, are gifted in their ability to combine education and practical experience to diagnose and treat conditions like placenta previa, which is difficult to identify without medical technology even for a skilled clinician.

PERINEAL TEARING

Perineal tearing is a common problem of childbirth, especially in the Global South. During delivery a tear might occur to the perineum, the soft tissue between the vagina and the anus, ranging from small nicks and abrasions to deep lacerations. Small perineal tears may heal automatically; larger rips can damage the anal sphincter causing incontinence, which can become a serious lifelong disability. Tearing is more common among first births, especially with high-birth-weight babies and long deliveries. Episiotomies, a surgical procedure performed by making an incision in the wall of the vagina to prevent uncontrolled tearing during delivery, are obstetrical practice in clinics and hospital settings worldwide. Although common practice over the last several decades, there has been a growing body of evidence critical of episiotomies that questions the benefits of it as a routine procedure and suggests it may contribute to more severe perineal lacerations and future pelvic floor dysfunction.

VHWs use a particular procedure to prevent tearing by applying gentle support to the perineum as the fetal head is delivered. The sterile gauze included in the CRHP pregnancy kit is expressly used for this procedure. Shilabai Amte explains how she routinely uses perineal support to assist the birth process: "After waiting and reassuring her, when it is time for that baby, I unwrap the sterile gauze pad. Depending on the position of the woman at the time of delivery, put gentle support to prevent tearing" (fieldnotes, 2010).

Preeti Sadaphule reports that she has never seen a case of severe tearing, but she is careful to attempt to prevent the problem. She explains, "As soon as I see the top of the head, I begin to put gentle support to the perineum with a sterile gauze pad. Even when I delivered a woman in my village who was pregnant for the first time with a 3.5 kg [7.7 lb.] baby, there was no difficulty or tearing" (fieldnotes, 2010).

Practical Applications: A Discussion about Infant and Child Care

In 2015, I asked women to volunteer to be part of a discussion to demonstrate how VHWs explain their history and present-day activities as practitioners.

I explained that the choice of topics and the conversation would be self-guided; the women could introduce themes and concepts of their own choosing and lead the flow of the discussion. This meeting was not a focus group, because the direction came from the group participants. I recorded the session and asked questions for clarification. The following are excerpts from the transcript of this free-flowing conversation with quotes to clearly emphasize certain points made during the meeting. Some of the responses reinforce other statements made during this chapter regarding maternal and child health and are included here to show the level of knowledge, collaboration, and caring so clearly demonstrated in most interactions I've observed among VHWs in the course of their interactions with villagers.

Six women who agreed to participate were available at the time of the meeting and signed informed consent forms. Sundarbai Paudmal, a second-generation VHW, is a member of the Mang Dalit group from a village, which flies the blue flag to signify a Buddhist community. She was mentored by and succeeded first-generation VHW Sunita Sadaphule, who is the author of the song "Dear Venubai." Gangabai Kulkarni, a Brahmin, is a first-generation VHW from a large, prosperous village. Shilabai Amte is a Maratha who lives in a village that now has a population of almost four thousand partly due to the recent construction of a sugar factory. Hirabai Salve, who straddles the first and second generations of VHWs, wears a wristwatch, an indicator of financial success. Rukhsanabee Shaikh, a Muslim and first-generation VHW, is from a village that is less than 15 percent Muslim; Latabai Kadam, a Dalit, lives in the neighboring community—both are first-generation VHWs and fondly recall their first days at CRHP walking three hours, balancing the metal VHW medical supply case on their heads to attend weekly meetings.

Our session, including a tea interval, lasted for almost three hours, which is typical of CRHP meetings and class periods. The women independently raised issues including low birth weight, infant mortality, immunizations, weighing and feeding babies, pneumonia, diarrhea, and jaundice.

Sundarbai Paudmal started the conversation. "In my village no baby has died in the last six years." The women smiled and nodded. Gangabai Kulkarni stated that in the early years of CRHP, children died from eye infections, ear infections, skin infections, tetanus, diarrhea diseases, pneumonia, fevers, and malnutrition. She reported, "in the last ten years no babies have died in my village, but one ten-year-old boy died of a scorpion bite." Today, she went on, the primary causes of child mortality are from drowning by falling into a well, snakebites, and motorcycle accidents.

LOW BIRTH WEIGHT

Hirabai Salve introduced the topic of low birth-weight babies, which she saw as a continuing concern in her village. She described procedures for infant care:

> The low birth weight baby is vulnerable. First thing is to maintain body temperature. The baby must be kept warm. Someone should always be holding or carrying the baby—mother, grandmother. You must keep the baby close to the body for warmth. When the baby doesn't have ability to suck, the mother must express milk and feed it to the baby. At the same time the baby should be kept near the breast so that suckling can be tried. Be very careful about bathing these children. Once the baby is 3 kg [6.5 lb.] you can bathe the baby if the house is warm.

When Hirabai Salve paused in her comments, all of the women began talking at once about bathing the low-weight baby. Bathing babies is itself a very elaborate process requiring at least two women: one to wash and massage the infant and the other to supply water, soap, oils, towels, and dry clothing. Rukhsanabee Shaikh and Sudarbai Paudmal decided to play-act a demonstration on how to bathe a baby using a rolled-up cloth as an infant substitute. With comic ceremony, Rukhsanabee Shaikh massaged the cloth infant, pouring water on the baby from an imaginary pot and covering the baby with her sari *pallu* as a pretend towel. Another called out, "The bath is taking too long. We don't want the baby to get a chill." Another replied "it's just a play"—immediate laughter broke out in the group. This good-natured banter serves as comic relief, but like similar performances in standard CRHP classes, it also reinforces the purpose and method of the CRHP process while highlighting important aspects of infant care.

Gangabai Kulkarni reiterated the very real danger of too much exposure. She suggested that there are two important points to consider for infant care: maintaining temperature and proper feeding for the child. Rukhsanabee Shaikh agreed that the inability of some newborns to suck at the breast is a serious concern and she reinforced the importance of spoon-feeding breastmilk. She added a general point about infant feeding that after six months solids can be introduced.

Shilabai Amte suggested that she has seen a shift in low-birthweight infants and suggested that it is the result of good nutrition and prenatal care. Noting that the weight at birth has changed over time, she said, "When

I first started delivering babies, they were less than 2 or 2½ kg [4.4 or 5.5 lb.]. Sometimes they didn't have enough strength to pull the milk from the mother. So, I was squeezing the breast and giving the mother's milk to the baby with a spoon. Now babies are born 3 kg [6.6 lb.]. We give the breast within one-half hour at each delivery."

PRIMARY CARE: PREVENTION AND DIAGNOSIS

When the issue of serious health problems causing mortality was raised, VHWs of the first generation spoke about how they each personally witnessed the reversal of mortality and the survival of infants in villages. Latabai remembered that when CRHP began, an average of eighteen babies out of one hundred live births died during their first year of life. After starting work on the solving of basic problems, villagers began to recognize that catastrophic deaths, especially of infants and women, could be reduced: "We could see with our own eyes only two babies might die, not ten or twenty." The women agreed that most people were aware of and appreciated the changes CRHP brought to village life. Shilabai Amte asserted that there was also a record of the VHWs activity, pointing to the notebook she brought with her and reminding everyone of the care that VHWs took to get help to keep the records for CRHP.

Shilabai added that babies stopped dying from diarrhea and that there was a way to treat fevers. Introducing these new techniques through their work and teaching the women's club members was a big part of the solution. All of the VHWs unanimously concurred that these dramatic changes were a combination of many factors; the CRHP health center and hospital, mobile health team, and their own training as practitioners and social actors all contributed to improved health in village life.

Sundarbai Paudmal reported on one of the most important and effective treatments used by VHWs:

The major health problems facing children today are pneumonia and diarrhea. If we see that a child is having diarrhea, we first make *limbu pane,* a sugar and salt solution. We have taught women how to make this in women's clubs. You take a fist full of sugar, pinch of salt, and the juice of half a lemon in clean boiled water. Rice water is much better, but this takes time. To make rice water cook one cup of rice with water. When the rice is cooked, crush it and add a liter of boiled water. This milky rice water is more effective than *limbu pane.*

But, rice may not be available in the house or there might not be enough water or good cooking pot. So first give the *limbu pane*.

Understanding the value of prevention as the first line of defense, Gangabai Kulkarni suggested that,

before we talk about treating colds there must be prevention. The baby must be kept dry. Dress the baby to keep it warm. Use a sweater and a hat in the winter. If the baby has a cold and is not able to breathe properly, we boil water in a kettle take it away from the fire and make a tent with a towel so that the vapor comes. This helps make the respiratory channel clear.

Shilabai Amte added the importance of accurate diagnosis:

Rapid breathing, which is more than fifty respirations per minute, is one symptom of pneumonia. Another symptom is the diaphragm going up and down rapidly. This means there is an air hunger. Amoxicillin is one treatment and Septra is another treatment that is needed. If the baby has pneumonia, it gets amoxicillin. If the baby is too sick, the baby will not suck at the breast. If the baby is very sick, the lips will turn blue; that may mean it is too late. Then the child needs to be transported to the health center for immediate care.

IMMUNIZATIONS: "WHY ARE YOU GIVING A FEVER TO MY BABY?"

Latabai Kadam raised the issue of the difficulties of introducing childhood immunizations in the early days of CRHP. She remembered very few children were immunized, and the deaths and disabilities from childhood diseases were apparent in most villages. At first getting families to agree to immunizations was difficult because they were resistant to new ideas and change. As Shilabai Amte interjected, it was a slow process getting to immunizations because she was prevented from meeting directly with young mothers. The biggest obstacle was the mother-in-law, who actively opposed these new ideas. According to Shilabai Amte, "When I first started it was very difficult to get the women to listen. I started a women's group, but only older women came. They would not let their daughters-in-law attend. We met for almost a year, talking about health education, chit funds, and raising goats. After that the mothers-in-law agreed, and then many babies were immunized."

Latabai Kadam clearly recalled that some women refused immunizations because of the common problem of babies or children developing slight fevers associated with some vaccines. Latabai Kadam explained her approach to convincing mothers of the importance of vaccinations as a means of prevention:

> When we first started working some people in our villages were refusing immunizations. We were giving immunizations, DPT [diphtheria, pertussis, tetanus] and polio, two doses. They were not ready to accept it. They said "If we give immunizations, the child will have a fever. Why are you giving a fever to my baby?" Yes, it is true that one or two babies had a fever after getting immunizations, but I gave cold sponge baths to those babies and the fever is gone. But while I was cold sponging the mother would say, "Don't do that. The child is getting cold. Don't do that." And I would reply, Why don't you trust me, I am from your village and I work for the good health of your baby. I am not going to harm your baby. Whatever calamity happens to your child I am responsible for that. Then I stayed with the baby taking care until the fever came down.
>
> After that they started trusting me. They would say yes, she is very interested in us.
>
> Then, I told them if you don't give immunizations these diseases are life-threatening and you will lose your child. If you do not give polio [immunizations], your child will be disabled. I have a remedy for the fever but not for the disability that comes with polio. The women understood this. Then after two or three years there was real improvement in our village. Before, babies in the village were dying of tetanus or diphtheria. Then after my first three years no babies died. Nobody has become disabled. This the women learned and then I had no trouble giving immunizations.

Sudarbai Paudmal's comments show the changing role of VHWs; while the government provides services, the CRHP takes on the role of advocate for good health, so teaching replaces direct service:

> Convincing mothers to get immunizations changed and was very different for the second-generation VHW. We learned from the older generation. But today most village women get immunizations from government nurses. Children are getting polio boosters every year. They should get the measles vaccine at nine months and a vitamin A shot every six months. Every child is immunized and given a booster, but if the baby is sick there is no vaccine. What we do is help

young women understand what the government nurses are doing. We explain what vaccines are important for a child's health.

Sundarbai Paudmal continued, saying women needed to be reminded of immunization boosters, so it falls on VHWs to help the family to understand these differences. She pointed out that sometimes the battery of immunizations can become complicated; for example, DPT (diphtheria, pertussis, tetanus) is given at one month. There should be a gap of six weeks before the second immunizations.

MOTHERS-IN-LAW (*SASUBAI*)

Shilabai Amte returned to the issue of mothers-in-law, laughing, saying, "Those we make skits and plays about," and "Now we are mothers-in law too." Rukhsanabee Shaikh replied, "Yes, now the women have a different view. . . . Now that I own property, I am leaving it to my daughter-in-law because I know that she will take care of my grandchildren." Shilabai Amte agreed, but explained that she must still remind some women that they must be kind to daughters-in-law when they are pregnant and, of course, the importance of avoiding heavy work late in the pregnancy, telling them, "If you want good crops you prepare the field well. You water the garden, you provide fertilizer, and then you get good results. The pregnant mother should be fed well, and this will help the baby grow. Fertilizer gives good crops. She must be nourished and will give you grandchildren."

Sudarbai Paudmal laughed and said it's always a battle, and in the end the mother-in-law really only cares for her son and the grandchild if it is a boy:

> Mothers-in-law can be a problem. When I was married my mother-in-law noticed that I got my first menstruation. Then when I didn't get my period for four months, she knew that I was pregnant. Then my husband left me. I was pregnant, so she said I could stay but then she threw me out. She was only concerned for her son, never for me.

Suddenly, everyone in the groups started talking at once about the mothers-in-law (*sasubai*). As noted earlier, the *sasubai* is the focus and villain of many of the classroom skits performed by VHWs. The category in village society takes on iconic dimensions because of the amount of control they have over young women marrying into the household. In households, the mother-in-law has complete control over cooking, cleaning, food storage, livestock, and allocating the duties of young wives when they become family members. The group agreed that a primary focus of health education is introducing the mothers-in-law to innovations and convincing them of the need for proper nutrition and sufficient rest, especially for young pregnant women. Rukhsanabee Shaikh reiterated, "We must keep reminding—your daughter-in-law is carrying your grandchild."

BREASTFEEDING

Rukhsanabee Shaikh began a discussion of the importance of breastfeeding. She noted that all babies should be breastfed exclusively for at least the first six months. Rukhsanabee Shaikh described the traditional pattern in the Jamkhed area for breastfeeding. "When we had our own children, we didn't know, and we waited before we gave the breast. It was the way. Before we got education, we did not breastfeed the baby for three days. Instead we dipped cotton in goat milk and gave it to the baby just to suck. That's how it was for our own children." Rukhsanabee Shaikh asserted that this practice has many negative side effects, since babies could easily choke on the cotton and not get the appropriate nutrition. In contrast, she noted that breastfeeding has important health benefits; the colostrum can be described as babies' first immunization, because the infant receives the mother's antibodies from the breast milk. Shilabai Amte added that breastfeeding within one half hour of the birth helps the woman, because it begins the reduction of the uterus to nonpregnant size.

Latabai Kadam strengthened Rukhsanabee Shaikh's comments with her own recollections about teaching breastfeeding:

Today, we tell the women the value of breast milk. So, we tell them it is important to breastfeed right after birth and the first three days. If you give the breast milk to your baby it prevents diseases. It is like a tonic for the baby. If you give the breast milk the child's brain will develop and the baby will go to school and become a [government] officer. [She laughs]. The boy or girl will be physically strong if he drinks milk. That is what we tell them. If you see the cow in your courtyard, when the calf is born the cow gives the milk immediately and the calf jumps. The cow cannot talk. The cow does not have many brains. Still she knows to breastfeed the calf right away in one day. How come you are not doing that? So, I am teaching women to follow my advice. I am telling you I am responsible. So, when the woman delivers her baby, I clean the breast and immediately give that baby to feed. If you follow my teaching and breastfeed immediately after birth—good will happen. You can take me to the police if something happens to your baby. [She laughs again].

Latabai Kadam's joking about the police makes all of us laugh.

On-demand infant feeding is aided by the typical practice of constantly holding the infant except at night. Most infants sleep in a hammock made of old sari cloth that is usually tied under the mother's bed, approximately twelve to sixteen inches off the floor. For women who work in the fields, infant care becomes a problem if the baby must be taken to the worksite because the child is carried by the mother but never swaddled or strapped to her body. Sudarbai Paudmal summed up her perspective on breastfeeding, "All babies should be on continuous on-demand breastfeeding and should be with the mother at all times. An advantage of on-demand is that if the child cries the mother can comfort the baby."

WEIGHING BABIES

Weighing babies is an essential aspect of VHW infant and childcare. One of the women brought the standardized yellow form used by VHWs to chart each child's weight and development. It is similar to the standardized form used by American physicians. "We measure the weight of the infant. Even babies born at 3 kg [6.6 lb.] can lose weight. One infant had a fever and some respiratory infection and lost weight. So we take the weight and keep track to make sure the baby stayed within the normal range."

To make sure babies and small children were weighed at home, scoop scales like the type found in grocery stores were adapted to be portable. The child is placed in a cloth seat attached to the bottom of the scale, which is easily hung from a rafter or doorframe. In the early days there was some opposition to this practice. Rukhsanabee Shaikh pointed out, "It was not possible to get the parents to weigh the child. People believed that if the child is weighed the evil eye will attack the child and make the child sick. Many infants were not weighed in the first month because the grandmother would not allow it."

FEEDING BABIES

Shilabai Amte reintroduced the topic of feeding babies.

Women were not feeding the baby [solid food] until the age of one, when the child had teeth. I told them after six months that baby increases its appetite and should be given supplementary food. They would say yes, yes, but they would not give food to the baby. So CRHP would give sorghum flour to their house. I would tell them to take some oil and fry the sorghum flour, add water, and make a porridge that is semi-thick. I would take the baby on my lap and feed the baby with a spoon. Then the baby will want more and more. The woman will be surprised. Then she understood that the baby is hungry.

Latabai Kadam explained one of the stories she uses and the joking relations she creates with women to enlist their cooperation.

If there is a small rat in your house how much grain does it eat? Now, this is a baby of 6 kg [13.2 lb.], how much food will that child need? So give that baby the food. Then, I would buy a banana and take my own banana and give it to the baby. And the mother said, "Don't give the baby a banana." Then I started giving banana. The mother would say, "This will give my baby pneumonia. If my child had pneumonia you have to come and cure my baby." Then for eight days I will go continuously after giving the banana. Each day I would ask, "Did the baby get pneumonia?" I showed that it is not true that bananas give pneumonia. So that is the way I made them feed that baby everything. The baby should be in the habit of eating everything. Then I tell them not to go to the market just to feed the baby. They should give the baby what is available. When banana is available, give banana. In papaya season, give papaya. In mango season, give mango. In mango season make a juice for the baby but do not put the hair [pulp] from the seed in the juice this will make the baby vomit. So I tell her to strain the juice and then give it to the baby. Then she asks, "Why are you giving mango juice and papaya juice to the baby?" I tell her it will make the eyes of the baby very nice. The baby will not have night blindness. You have seen that so many children are not having night blindness since I am giving them a papaya and mango juice. So, this is how I convince people.

JAUNDICE

Regarding jaundice in newborns, Sundarbai Paudmal asserted, you must check the eyes of newborns for yellowing, which might be a sign of jaundice, which she described as a problem of the babies' blood. The CRHP clinic does not have the special equipment that emits light in the blue-green spectrum to treat the high bilirubin that causes jaundice. However, because most babies are born at home, Sundarbai Paudmal recommended a simple treatment. "If in the first few days, the baby's eyes have a yellow color. This may not be serious. You can solve the problem if in the early morning you expose your child to sun rays for a short time. Hold the baby in your arms, remove some blankets, but cover the eyes. Make sure the baby stays dry."

SKIN INFECTIONS

Hirabai Salve remembered a serious endemic problem that was solved by cooperation between the VHW and villagers and was one of the successes of the early days of CRHP. When she began working in villages, a common problem was scabies, tiny mites that irritate the skin. For some children, itching and scratching led to breaks in the skin that had the potential to result in systemic infections like staphylococcus. These infections may be life-threatening for small children and require medical treatment. To solve this situation, several remedies were used instead of immediately resorting to a biomedicine. According to Sunita Sadaphule, first, it was found that the source of scabies was the bedding used by the family that is stored during the day and spread out on the floor of the dwellings for sleeping, so the bedding and garments were washed and dried in the sun. Then to sooth the skin and eliminate itching, a salve made from leaves of the neem tree was applied to the skin. The salve is prepared only from neem leaves just off the tree; the uncooked leaves are ground with a mortar commonly used for cooking. This produced a green ointment that was applied directly to irritated skin as necessary. Within a short period of time the problem was solved using these home remedies. In India, neem trees are considered important to Ayurvedic and homeopathic medicine for gum disease, stomach problems, and heart disease.

Hirabai Salve remembered the formula, "Take leaves from the neem tree; grind the leaves. Just grinding. Make a paste. It looks green. Apply to the skin and infection goes away. Remember to also treat the bedding. Make sure that the clothes are boiled. It's been more than twenty years since we have seen a child with a skin infection from scabies."

The range and depth of this free-flowing conversation about VHW practices demonstrates the effectiveness of VHWs as practitioners and validates the educational methods of the Jamkhed model. Of course, the women who participated reported that they enjoyed the conversation and were happy to spend the afternoon with friends talking about their life and work.

Neonatal Death: Changing Medical Technology in Jamkhed

Rukhsanabee Shaikh, the VHW of Pimpalgaon-Unda, with a population of one thousand, accompanied us to the multifamily dwelling of her lifelong friend Sunita. It is notable that Rukhsanabee Shaikh is a Muslim and Sunita is Hindu. Their stark differences, marked by social standing—Sunita's family are a landowning wealthy farming family—and religion, have not prevented a lasting relationship. Sunita is the mother and head of a household of three children; one daughter lives in Pune, a large city four hours away by car from Jamkhed, and the two sons live on the compound, each with a separate dwelling surrounding a central open courtyard.

One warm morning in July we met Rukhsanabee Shaikh at her home and walked through the village to the entrance to Sunita's household. I sat in the courtyard on a metal bed without a mattress with Ratna Kamble, who has known the family for many years. Sunita's daughter-in-law Padma was playing with her toddler, who was encouraged to sit on the bed with us, but she clung to her mother. Sunita crouched near an open oven making *bhakri* for the family's lunch as we talked.

With a knowing grin, Rukhsanabee Shaikh introduced me to Padma and asked me if I know her mother. I was surprised by such a question. All the women were smiling at me and chuckling. Rukhsanabee Shaikh revealed that Padma is the daughter of Ratna Sutar, the VHW from Padali. Of course I knew Ratna, but now I was even more confused because she is from a Sutar caste and not one that would likely marry into this wealthy family. In fact, Rukhsanabee and Ratna developed a longstanding friendship at CRHP and they were instrumental in arranging the marriage of the family's eldest son, Mandan, to Ratna Sutar's daughter Padma. This marriage arrangement, itself, was even more unusual because it crossed caste and religious boundaries— two VHWs, one low caste and one Muslim, were instrumental in matching a man from a wealthy Maratha family with carpenter caste woman. Of course, the strong relationship that Rukhsanabee developed with the family during her years providing health care and social progress to her village and her personal friendship with Sunita was part the motivation for the marriage. However, the arrangement started a controversy. Ratna Sutar's husband opposed the marriage and did not attend the wedding because the father of the bridegroom had once been treated for leprosy.

After twelve years of marriage, Padma finally became pregnant and was receiving prenatal care from Rukhsanabee Shaikh. During a regular pre-natal check Rukhsanabee noticed that Padma's blood pressure was high. Concerned because at age thirty this was her first pregnancy, unusual in the area, Rukhsanabee Shaikh recommended that she visit the CRHP health center for further testing. Rukhsanabee's assessment of the potential danger for the pregnancy was confirmed; Padma remained at the CRHP hospital for the duration of the pregnancy. Due to complications, the baby, a girl, was delivered by caesarean section. The family was very happy that there was finally a grandchild. During our conversation, the little girl, almost two years old, grew comfortable with the group of us in the courtyard and began interacting and playing with us. Her mother and grandmother doted on her every smile, giggle, and word.

As we are all engaged in watching the adorable granddaughter, Sunita asked Rukhsanabee to tell me the story of Venita, Sunita's daughter that had taken place the year before. Rukhsanabee reluctantly begins:

Venita lives in Pune with her husband. She returned to her mother's village for the birth of her first child at age nineteen. All the blood work was done in Pune. It was okay. All of her lab results looked good. The doctor from Pune warned her that there might be bleeding and told her to be careful and not pick up heavy things. She came here at the ninth month. I examined her. The baby was very small.

At the birth there was a lot of bleeding. I advised her to put the head down and the legs up and the bleeding stopped. She was in labor for three hours. The baby was less than 2 kg [4.4 lb.]. After the birth the child was okay. And on the third day I went to Jamkhed for class. Later I learned that the mother had a fever. Husband's family preferred to call private doctor who gave Sunita's daughter an injection. She already had tetanus toxoid, but he gave her tetanus again. When I got back the baby was five days old and he was having trouble breathing. I thought maybe the child had pneumonia. The family all got into the Jeep and went to Jamkhed. They took the baby to the private clinic in

Jamkhed to a doctor who says he is a children's specialist. They kept the baby for one day and he died. Why didn't they go to CRHP hospital? I don't know. [Rukhsanabee Shaikh and Sunita begin to cry.]

Rukhsanabee Shaikh continued to cry, wiping her tears with the *pallu* of her sari, and said:

It was August, maybe there was too much cold air. Why didn't they go to the CRHP hospital? In the morning when they went to Jamkhed town I was praying. They said he was okay. The family told me the baby was doing better. But then I heard the child died the next day. That was one of worst experiences of my life after thirty years. The first time a baby died after being born alive.

Sunita began to comfort Rukhsanabee Shaikh. Mandan, the eldest son, tried to console Rukhsanabee Shaikh by praising her for the care and support she gave his own wife and his sister during the delivery. Mandan voiced his anger at the physician and the staff at the children's clinic in Jamkhed, who he described as incompetent for substituting medical technology instead of understanding the real problem. He explained that although the family spent the entire time at the hospital, they were not adequately informed of the baby's condition and were only allowed to visit the baby for short periods of time. In addition, he was concerned that his sister was not permitted to breastfeed. The family of Venita's husband chose the Jamkhed Pediatric Hospital over the CRHP medical center because they believed this, a new pediatric facility, would have the most up-to-date technology. As the county seat and market center, the town of Jamkhed has grown, and there has been a steady increase in the number and type of new medical facilities there, including the small pediatric hospital chosen by Venita's husband. However, Mandan lamented that the decision was made against his advice and that there was no advantage to having more money to access private health care services if there is such disrespect for the families and medical incompetence.

The morning at Sunita's household revealed a situation of a death of an infant that was largely out of the control of the VHW due a decision to pursue new technology. However, the family clearly respected the relationship established over many years between a Rukhsanabee and family. The son expressed his respect for the Rukhsanabee even in the face of this tragic events. There is no way of knowing the cause of this neonatal death, which could have been related to any number of problems including a genetic or congenital condition. Just as VHWs are eager to report their successes as health practitioners, they are reluctant but honest in remembering and reporting the circumstances surrounding difficulties and negative outcomes.

Conclusion: Global Reproductive Health and the Jamkhed Model

Based on a controlled study of CRHP project villages, McCord et al. (2001) found that between January 1996 and July 1999, 85 percent of 2,861 pregnancies beyond twenty-four weeks resulted in home deliveries. The research was conducted to understand obstetric outcomes, patterns, and costs of obstetrical care in rural India. In addition, the study suggested that a referral service that identified local patients in need of care for complicated deliveries was appropriate for medical management. For example, the results showed that a total of 14.4 percent of deliveries after twenty-four weeks had identified complications, but the caesarean section rate for all deliveries was 2 percent. The research concluded that maternal and perinatal deaths would be prevented by early and appropriate referral to hospitals as demonstrated by the Jamkhed Model. Consequently, the practice of careful and systematic hospital referrals as instituted by CRHP contributed to the successful outcomes. The hospital's case-fatality rates, overall fatality, and perinatal mortality are better than those reported in similar rural environments for all of India (McCord et al. 2001). This study concluded that the CRHP referral system for reproductive health care implemented by the mobile health team and VHWs has the potential for changing the health profile of rural villagers.

The goal of the Jamkhed Model to reduce maternal and infant mortality resulted in a dramatic decline in the first five years of CRHP. Notably, as practitioners living in villages, VHWs became central to the health of women and children and a pivotal link between the medical center and mobile health team. Eliminating detrimental traditional practices while introducing comprehensive health care emphasizing prenatal care, safe delivery, postpartum care, infant care including immunizations, and birth spacing successfully changed women and children's health status.

Over the many years of my fieldwork and continuing visits to CRHP, I observed the VHWs in the classroom and the hospital, at festival events, weddings, and funerals, and most importantly, as health practitioners and social activists. Through these encounters I was able to learn and understand the magnitude of the agency, resilience, and intellect of the VHWs who persist in their dedication to improve everyday village life. CRHP demonstrated the possibilities for change by following principles of comprehensive primary health care, especially local community participation and capacity building and using essential biomedicine as appropriate. That resulted in a sustainable design for planning and implementing rural health programs. Clearly, from a variety of perspectives and analysis, the health statistics of the CRHP Jamkhed Model are consistently better than the Indian national averages. This is not merely an artifact of a small sample comparing regional to national statistics, but is due to CRHP's recognition that in communities with scarce resources, attention must be paid to all residents, especially those in the most precarious situations who suffer the greatest consequences. Simple and appropriate tools, even songs, promote health and wellness and show that a community-based primary health care model using these local solutions, especially for the health of women and children, are able to resolve even the most intractable global problems.

CHAPTER 6

Money in Her Hand

Mahila Vikas Mandal

Husband Don't Be in My Way (*Dhani adwu naka mala naduwu naka*)

(Chorus)
O husband don't be in my way. Let me go
to the project. And learn about health.

There are many responsibilities at home.
However, I have prepared to get an education in health
And thereby serve our community
Please allow me to serve

Chorus

Behind everything is money. The girl is burnt for dowry
Don't take dowry. Don't give dowry.
Let me lead a happy life.
Please allow me to lead a happy life

Chorus

Many people opposed me. And I was disappointed
There will be many calamities
Yet I will live to serve the community
Let me take the weight of that child

Chorus

Self-Help Groups

In August 2010, Sunita Gite, the VHW of Sangavi in Ashti *taluka*, walked through her village telling women she will hold a meeting in her home. She was organizing a new self-help group (SHG) as part of her work to improve health and economic development in her home village, whose population is two thousand. Women assembled in the eight-by-ten-foot front room of Sunita Gite's house, which contained a solitary string cot, a foot-peddle sewing machine, and a stainless-steel water jug with a spout. We sat on a cloth mat, moving closer and closer together as women fill the room. Sunita Gite and Mrs. Ratna Kamble, the social worker, began the conversation with eight women; the exchange became lively, with much joking and laughter. During the forty-minute meeting, more than thirty women entered and left the room, replacing each other on the cloth mat. More women appeared at the door and some husbands asked if their wives can enter but they were told that the group was closed at twenty. If there are enough prospective members, another group would be formed. Sunita Gite took out a hardcover notebook and gave it to Mrs. Kamble who began to enter the names of the women joining the SHG. The names of the twenty members were written into a notebook and read aloud. By voice nomination and votes, the new members elected a president and secretary, both with women's club experience, who would open a bank account when sufficient funds are collected.

The women decided that they will contribute ₹100 (about $2 US in 2012). Next on the agenda was a discussion about the name of the group. One of the members, Vanita, suggested the name Savitribai Phule, a nineteenth-century woman educator who started schools for girls. This choice reflected an appreciation of the local history and a commitment to the education of young girls. Finally, the women started putting rupees in the center of the woven floor mat next to the list of names. After the money was collected and counted, the women signed the agreement by writing or thumbprint. The meeting ended midmorning with some women rushing off to work in the fields.

Health and Development: Two Sides of the Same Coin

Development requires the removal of major sources of unfreedom: poverty as well as tyranny, poor economic opportunity as well as systematic social deprivation, neglect of public facilities as well as intolerance or overactivity of repressive states. (Sen 1999, 3)

Throughout the 1970s, women's groups proliferated across India, usually "led by middle-class women to access government welfare programs or initiate income-generating activities" (Purushothaman 1998, 82). Micro-finance is defined as the provision of financial services to low-income clients or solidarity lending groups who traditionally lack access to banking and related services. This concept gained enormous attention due to the activities of the Grameen Bank of Bangladesh and its founder, Nobel Prize–winner Muhammad Yunus, who created a system of microcredit loans for women with the promise of alleviating poverty through the empowerment of women. Consequently, in the 1980s international financial institutions like the World Bank, and private funders such as the Ford Foundation, the Rockefeller Brothers Fund, and IBM supported programs that sponsored neoliberal mechanisms sometimes called "trickle-up" (Farnesworth 1988). These financial institutions and others made the assumption that merely providing monetary resources would lead to automatic financial empowerment for women without accounting for social class. Yet, for women without alternative financial support or readily available capital, the promise of microfinance as a means for change and transition out of poverty is elusive, even for those motivated to join self-help groups.

Dr. Raj Arole was fond of saying "health and development are two sides of the same coin." Integration of services is one of the basic principles of CRHP; consequently, an objective of village improvement is initiating and adapting economic projects for use by local women through community participation (Arole and Arole 1994, 251). Innovating social and economic programs required a complicated and multifaceted effort of the clinic staff, mobile health team, and VHWs. In Jamkhed, there was a general lack of financial acuity, and few women had personal experience either working for a salary or participating in activities that would potentially generate income. For example, a common practice affecting some women who were day laborers was to pay wages directly to their husbands. As the lyrics from the song that opens this chapter express, "behind everything is money," but for women with limited or no access to cash even for their own work, the process of learning and gaining practical experience handling money required a loosening of the constraints of traditional caste values, family, and above all, gender inequality.

Creating a Social Space for Economic Change

Like the morning meeting in Sangavi, organizing to create self-help groups in Jamkhed villages was relatively common during my fieldwork years. The effortless assembly of women and the desire to participate and contribute is evidence of the success of the Jamkhed Model, which incorporates health, social awareness, and income generation as part of a comprehensive approach for community well-being to benefit the everyday lives of women.

Weekly meetings initiated by VHWs became a social space to introduce health information, begin a conversation about financial matters, and, most importantly, to encourage women to speak about their own problems. In the early years of CRHP, village women had neither the freedom nor the experience of assembling together for discussions or to develop new friendships. Most women, but especially newly married young women, were discouraged from making associations outside of the immediate family. Social interactions were discouraged even though women participated in parallel activities like going to the well or taking children to *anganwadi* (nursery school).

The first generation of VHWs learned to advocate for themselves and actively introduced new ideas:

> As the village health workers discussed the social causes of ill health, they saw the need to organize the women in the villages if major social changes were to occur. . . . Opposition came mainly from older women. They did not like the idea of their "daughter-in-law wasting their time," listening to new ideas about bringing up children or getting prenatal care instead of working either in the house or on the farm. (Arole and Arole 1994, 184)

VHWs persisted even though they encountered many levels of resistance, which demonstrated their own conviction of the value of community participation and gender equity. Wary of potential reprisals or actual punishment from husbands or family, first-generation VHWs conducted organizing activities in secret, gathering women when men were working in the fields, meeting at the well or at night. As Hirabai Salve says, "Is it possible for a single bullock to plough a field? It takes six or more to do a good job" (qtd. in Arole and Arole 1994, 186). Shilabai Amte, remembered that her initial attempts to bring women together were discouraging because when village meetings were called only a few mothers-in-law from the dominant caste attended (personal interview, 2010). Encouraged by the support they received at weekly classes at the CRHP center, VHWs persevered, as Hirabai Salve told the Aroles:

> I was able to convince only seven women to come together in the beginning. We gathered together to socialize in one of the women's houses, to sing songs and listen to each other. In between, I taught them childcare. One day I was about to talk about childcare, when one woman's husband came with a stick, ready to beat his wife. I pleaded with him, why do you object to your wife learning how to take care of your own son? I am just teaching her about his life [child

growth and development]. He thought we were gossiping. I invited him to sit outside and listen to our talk. He left without a word. (Arole and Arole 1994, 18)

Whether forty years ago or today, VHWs credit their resistance to societal constraints as the core of their ability to promote change.

Weekly meetings with village women developed into an informal women's club that provided a regular space and time for VHWs to continue discussions about health and gently and deliberately introduce new concepts and ideas while reinforcing home remedies for health promotion and disease prevention. For example, almost all village women learned the process of how to make the oral rehydration solution *limbu pane* as a quick fix to prevent dehydration of infants with diarrhea. Built into every meeting was time to listen to women about personal and household problems. This type of listening and caring is modeled from the same treatment that VHWs experienced with Dr. Mabelle Arole, which they found so compelling and reaffirming in their own educational process and training. In addition, at their own CRHP weekly continuing education classes, VHWs reported on their own observations and experiences managing weekly meetings, in order to learn successful techniques and methods from each other. Accordingly, Arole and Arole (1994) note that VHWs want to communicate the same of type of liberation to village women that they experienced in learning new ideas.

Women's Seminars

As progress continued in the early days of CRHP and informal village gatherings grew in size and frequency, VHWs asked if village women might accompany them to the weekly classes in Jamkhed to experience how VHWs were taught about health and wellness and to help continue building solidarity. Aware of the success of the farmers' clubs seminars organized by CRHP to introduce new business and farming techniques and alter caste social relations, the VHWs were eager to introduce a series of workshops to focus on women's issues and concerns. In the late 1970s, a Women's Seminar was set up as a three-day event for local village women to stay at the CRHP training center. At first fifty women attended.

The gathering was a great occasion for them [women] to meet together and exchange ideas. They ate together and slept together under a huge canopy. They composed songs on social evils like alcoholism and exploitation and discussed issues such as the status of women, poverty, dowry, atrocities inflicted on Dalits and corruption rampant in society. Through these songs they exhorted women to unite to end untouchability. (Arole and Arole 1994, 188)

Subsequently, another series of women's seminars was set up over a three-month period that resulted in hundreds of women attending to hear health professionals and government and business leaders from the Jamkhed area. Topics such as starting kitchen gardens, raising goats and chickens, and negotiating bank loans, along with discussions about agricultural innovations and money management, drew popular attendance. Away from the observation of husbands and families, free from household chores and farm work, women were able to learn new ideas, consider the complexity of women's issues, and begin to communicate with each other with in an unbiased environment free from traditional constraints. Arole and Arole (1994) noted the value of raising persistent but hidden social issues that cause emotional or physical pain, and promoted themes like the burden of dowry, physical abuse due to husband's alcoholism, corruption in local government, and the exploitation of women's work. Equally important, these rare occasions when local women left their home villages helped establish a sense of community among women. Because VHWs played a prominent role in facilitating the seminars, the professional connection between CRHP and VHWs was confirmed, adding to the growing acceptance of VHWs as agents of change.

These patterns of seminars and educational workshops continues at CRHP to help introduce current ideas about women's standing in village life and new social and economic possibilities. Introducing these opportunities are a continuing part of the Jamkhed Model. For example, in 2007, I participated in a conference on microfinance loans for women organized by CRHP and sponsored by professional, business, and government officials from Ahmednagar district. The program was presided over by Dr. Raj Arole and led by CRHP staff, with presentations from local dignitaries, business leaders, and bank managers; four hundred women attended the one-day event. Gangabai Kulkarni explains her impression of the value of seminars:

Formerly the life of women was terrible. There was no freedom to leave the house. Everything was controlled by men. How did these things change? CRHP. There were seminars here with legal officers, social workers. They explained to women about their legal rights. Social workers told us how we can improve things. The bankers talked to us about money and government loan schemes. Legal experts told us our rights. The main thing was that women were able to leave their place and come here. (personal interview, 2012)

Gender Equity and Finances

Women's seminars established an atmosphere for learning, collaboration, and trust that continued during informal group meetings in villages and was essential to the process of integrating services. These sessions enhanced relationships among women that supported introducing complicated and challenging new ideas, particularly against money lenders, faith healers, and other charlatans who preyed on poor villagers. According to Arole and Arole (1994), as village women's club meetings grew in size a platform was established by VHWs to encourage women to express their own views on topics formerly avoided, like alcoholism, wife beating, treatment of unwed mothers, corruption in local governments, and exploitation of women's work. VHWs reported that discussions about the treatment of women and girls—specifically, the differential treatment of boys and girls, the lack of good and sufficient food for girls, and prohibiting girls from schooling—became topics of conversations that were raised often and explored from many different perspectives. As Kaushalya Gaikwad remembers, "Before there was really no communication. There was no unity. Women got along but they really weren't talking to each other. Now there are a lot of small issues women are getting together to talk about, [including] personal things" (field notes, 2010).

Ratna Kamble, a social worker, commented on the early work of organizing. "It is individual flowers strung one by one that makes the beautiful flower garland. We had to get the women one by one. The village health worker would convince just seven or eight women . . . we would sit together and share each other's problems" (qtd. in Arole and Arole 1994, 185). In some ways these exchanges created a form of consciousness-raising, incrementally focusing on understanding gender equity and the everyday activities of village women.

Mahila Vikas Mandals (Women's Development Associations)

Mahila vikas mandals (MVMs) were the next step in organizing women. They adhered to the repeating theme that health and development move together as two aspects of a comprehensive approach to wellness and community economic advancement. While many women worked on family farms without a salary, the wages of a married woman working as an agricultural day laborer were often collected by her husband. Still, in the early days of CRHP few women, except for some mothers-in-law, had access to or control of money.

Drs. Mabelle and Rajanikant Arole used a variety of methods to promote development and increase income to ultimately put money in women's hands. For example, one very successful approach was adopting the local practice of *bhishi*, an informal self-financing credit plan of pooling funds contributed by individual women. This cooperative credit plan is similar to other indigenous collectives, traditional savings plans, and credit funds called *chits* elsewhere in India, *susus* in Ghana, *tandas* in Mexico, *arisan* in Indonesia, and *tontines* in West Africa.

This *bhishi* model helped women financially and built a sense of trust:

> We need money for different kinds of things for our families. Each time we need a loan, for somebody who is sick, or money for seeds, we must go to a moneylender or someone who will charge us high interest. So, we thought why not collect our own money and this is the way friends came together with the help of the Village Health Worker. There are eleven members, each one paid ₹30 and from that each one gets a loan. The *Bhishi* stays together until each woman gets a share. (Arole and Arole 1994)

Based on this adaptation of the *bhishi* system, women contribute money, in this case monthly, with the objective of giving a particular sum to one of the members for her own use. Hirabai Salve explained, "In our village we put the names in a pot and let one of the children select a name. That woman got the money. And then the next and the next until everyone had a turn" (personal interview, 2010). The relationships established by these practices lead to a growing sense of solidarity for financial reassurances. For example, Kaushalya Gaikwad points out:

> Six months ago, there was a girl who wanted to go to the 11 and 12 standard (grade). For this there are many expenses like clothes and books and other things. So all of the women from the group contributed ₹100 each so that the girl would go to school. But this is not a loan. It is not expected to be paid back. This is one of the things that women do for each other. (fieldnotes, 2012)

Clearly, these monetary alliances had a variety of values for the women. Manjula Gite, a second-generation VHW, emphasized that income-generating schemes contributed to a sustainable change for herself and her family. "No one knew my value. How did I do it? I improved my family, my neighbors, and my village. My husband was disabled. We were very poor. Because I learned about income generation, we came up from poverty. Now that I am earning, my family respects me" (personal interview, 2012). Within a relatively short time the process of creating *bhishi* showed success: by 1978 there were thirty-one villages with *mahila vikas mandals* (Arole and Arole 1994).

CRHP Self-Help Groups

The CRHP *mahila vikas mandals* established self-help groups at the same time that the Indian government joined the international trend to support women's financial endeavors. Consequently, village women in the Jamkhed area qualify for government-guided microfinance loans from local banks. Women without property, particularly those who are widowed or living alone, remain in very precarious financial and social situations in local villages. As Shantabai Sathe explained to me:

> A big thing is the self-help groups. There are four or five self-help groups in my village. What's happening now is they get to use their own money. Women really did not get out of the house. Now, a lot of women start small income projects, small convenience type stores or sell bangles. Some women borrow money to go to the weekly markets to buy dry fish and bring it back to the village to sell and then they pay the money back and have some. (personal interview, 2012)

Mahila vikas mandals established in project villages had an even larger advantage for local women who qualified for government-sponsored programs for women living below the poverty level (BPL), which includes the majority of families in the Jamkhed area. CRHP staff were instrumental in assisting VHWs with acquiring and managing bank loans and providing information, education, and support to make projects fit local women's needs. Becoming part of a VHW-sponsored self-help group adds immeasurably to women's stability both for social support and to learn money management. At regular group meetings women learned how to count money, keep ledgers, collect and store cash, and equitably distribute funds—all necessary skills for maintaining successful personal and group income-generating projects. For example, in 2012 I attended a group meeting in Jawalke village and asked the president of one of the SHGs, a woman named Preti, why her group was so successful. She responded by praising the two VHWs who worked in her village.

> Hirabai Salve and Shantabai Sathe gave us the idea to form our new self-help group that is the *bhishi*. They are trusted and have influence in the village. The VHWs encouraged us to be part of the self-help groups. They help us and show us new ways. When we start a group, we must make sure that everyone gives money. And we must help each other. (fieldnotes, 2012).

The pattern of starting an SHG is relatively the same in every village as described at the outset of this chapter for Sangavi-Ashti. Typically, a president and secretary are elected who are responsible for money storage and record keeping, and when sufficient funds are collected, they open an account at the local bank as signatories for the group. The newly constituted group agrees on the frequency of meetings and the number of rupees each woman will contribute. Another favorite part of the process is selecting a group name. Some choose names of goddesses or gods, like Parvati or Ganesh; some groups select names of flowers; but other SHGs prefer names of political and social leaders like Dr. Babsaheb Ambedkar, Indira Gandhi, or Dr. Mabelle Arole. Others used the name Gayatri, after the famous princess, or the song (*raga*) "Saraswati Gat." At the meeting described at the beginning of this chapter, the group selected the name of Savitribai Phule, a woman famous in Maharashtra who was an educator, poet, and champion of the social-reform movement. Recordkeeping is a necessary part of organizing, beginning with the initial meeting when new members sign the hard-covered ledger or place their thumbprints on the page. At each subsequent meeting the amount of each member's contribution to the fund is recorded.

A Small Sample

In 2012, I collected information on SHGs in seventeen project villages with the help of CRHP staff using VHW records that are transferred weekly to notebooks. Information given included the name of the organization, number of members, number of years in existence, amount of each contribution, and the bank in which the money is deposited. Each of the SHGs followed the pattern of elected officials and record keeping, and most had accounts in local branches of large banks, such as the State Bank of India, with branches in Halgoan or Ashti, while others used the Cooperative Bank in Jamkhed, Patoda, or Nanaj. Two groups used the CRHP Cooperative Bank, which was originally set up for CRHP workers.

In CRHP project villages there are usually several independent SHGs running simultaneously, some of the groups having worked together consistently for twelve years, while others are newly formed, running for only two months. The number of members in each ranged from twenty to ten women; twelve was the average number. Not all the women in a given village are members of a group. Joining a group requires having sufficient funds to be able to make the payments at meetings whether weekly or monthly. Commitment to the groups or to a specific group project is a primary concern because the success of the SHG relies on all members attending all meetings and providing the agreed upon remuneration. Shantabai Sathe, a VHW who has initiated and been a member of several groups, points out that in some large families only one woman will become an official member, but the others will benefit.

The groups even in this small sample are representative of the potential longevity of each established group. Some groups started as a *bhishi* and took advantage of government loans. Other SHGs represent only a small segment of the village and members may be of the same caste or religion. None of these factors predict whether the group will be successful, particularly whether it was initiated as a group project or supporting individual and personal needs. In some cases, the longevity of some *bhishi*-type groups is variable; some groups disband when all the members receive a loan or agreed-upon amount of money. The contribution of the groups in this small sample of SHGs was typically ₹100 (about $2 in 2012) per month. The purposes of groups differ considerably; some are formed as a single-purpose group to complete a particular project, while others support individual women's personal use of money.

Income-Generating Activities: Success and Failures

As various recent studies have shown, microfinance SHGs that typically qualify for microcredit loans often fail because of lack of additional financial resources, insufficient information about the particulars of the project, or a basic lack of general information about financial matters, especially among women who have never handled money (Purushothaman 1998; Karim 2011; Eisenstein 2009). For example, Arole and Arole (1994) note that some women

eager to begin a project were convinced by government development officers to purchase Jersey cows as an income-generating project. However, the
women were unaware of the care and feeding requirements for these animals as well as the inability of this breed of cow to withstand the hot season
in Jamkhed, when temperatures can rise to 43°C (>110°F). The project failed
and the group was forced to repay the loan, causing family hardship; however, they were undeterred and again pooled resources after learning about
livestock that were appropriate to the area—they purchased and successfully raised local goats.

Most women report that the first use of the small amount of money
generated from income projects is primarily used to "support the family"
with extra food, paying for medical care, and buying uniforms and books
for school children. Larger sums are necessary for weddings but presum-
ably not for dowry. While the original intent of these endeavors was to put
money in women's hands, larger sums were used to support family farms.
Funds were given directly to husbands to buy seeds or livestock, and more
recently for the purchase or rental of tractors for ploughing. Frequently,
women's money is given to men specifically for their own discretion, often
to buy motorcycles which, in the Jamkhed area, are driven exclusively by
men. Gangabai Kulkarni suggests that the different uses of money by the
women and men is striking. However, she feels that when women gained
access to money, relations between men and women changed, which she
hopes would lead to an improved value of women in the family and an
understanding of women's rights:

> Income-generating activities were very important. We had cash money in our
> hands. When women started getting money, people from the CRHP explained
> to the men that they should treat us like human beings and that will help us
> contribute to the family. Now, when women get money they registered the
> property in the wife's name. Formerly, the man went to the market and spent
> all his money. When a man has money, he spends large amounts of money for
> himself. He buys a watch, a motorcycle or parties with his friends. Women are
> better at dealing with the money for the family and maintaining the house-
> hold. (personal interview, 2012)

In rural Jamkhed villages one can hear the ubiquitous bleating of
skinny black goats, some with blue painted horns, walking in small groups
guided by women, often members of SHGs. This is a common type of

income-generating project that began at CRHP in the early days when live-stock was given to VHWs to help improve their family's income. Women learned about the care of goats from each other through informal women's clubs led by VHWs and from women who attended CRHP seminars on animal husbandry.

Another type of inventive activity begun by some women was selling bundles of small dried fish purchased at the weekly Saturday market in Jamkhed town. These odoriferous bundles of dried fish are purchased and transported back to the village to be sold to other women. Essentially, women acted as a broker, transporting the product. Then, local women were able to purchase dried fish by taking a short walk in the village, saving time and money on bus fare. It takes all day to travel by bus from some villages to the market in Jamkhed town.

In Matkuli village a few resourceful women pooled SHG money to buy large cooking pots and audio equipment that they rented for weddings and festivals in nearby villages. These large metal pans are used to cook food over fireplaces for weddings that may have more than one hundred partici-pants. The sound systems were super-sized box speakers used to play music for large crowds and to broadcast the wedding ceremony.

In many Jamkhed villages women used SHG funds to purchase sewing machines, powered by foot pedals or in homes where electricity is readily available some women use motorized foot pedal machines. Saris are the typical attire for married women in Jamkhed, and since most women are married by age eighteen and saris are never sold with ready-made blouse pieces, stitching blouses for saris is a reliable source of income for many village women. In the homes of women tailors, blouse pieces of many colors and patterns are usually hung above a sewing machine as a display and advertisement of the quality of work. During some ritual holidays, like Sankranti, a day of women's worship and celebration, the need for tailor-ing increases greatly because every woman buys a new sari for the festival activities of sharing sweets with women friends and relatives and visiting the many Hindu temples in Jamkhed town. While there are tailor shops in Jamkhed town, with mostly male stitchers, local women often prefer female sari blouse makers.

In Kusadgaon village one SHG initiated a vermiculture business as a large cooperative project. Vermiculture is one of the appropriate organic agriculture technology ventures of the CRHP model farm. The nutrient-rich fertilizer produced from vermiculture is a compost comprised of vermicast (worm manure) from the breakdown of organic matter. This fertilizer is used on the CRHP farm and sold to other local farmers. The SHG members attended teaching sessions at the model farm to learn from the female farm managers the appropriate care and treatment of the worms and the methods of harvesting fertilizer. The income-generating project was planned to produce fertilizer to avoid the enormous cost and other negative effects of commercial fertilizer. The project failed within the first six months.

As part of my inquiries into SHGs, I travelled to Kusadgaon village to learn about the progress of the vermiculture project that had been in preparation during my visit the year before. I was told that the project had been unsuccessful but I could see the remains of the structure. I was surprised by the size of the cement enclosure (3 feet by 7 feet), which appeared small for its purpose of producing fertilizer, and I was puzzled that there was no easily accessible nearby source of water. In addition, the enclosure was shaded by a plastic corrugated roof that was three feet above the cement trough. The vermicultural structural set-up of a waste-level cement basin and plastic roof appeared inadequate for the time and effort that went into creating the project based on successful examples. The location and structure in the village differed considerably from the original vermiculture containers on the CRHP model-farm, which were close to the ground and protected on all sides from the sun with an adequate source of water. In addition, the farm troughs had ample tree cover for additional protection for the growth and survival of the worm population in the hot summer months.

This Kusadgaon SHG disbanded after working together on the vermiculture project. When I asked former members their opinion of the problem, some blamed other women for not providing sufficient water and nutrients to keep the worms alive. Other women explained that the difficulty of transporting adequate water to keep vermiculture worms alive in temperatures above 38°C (100°F) was the issue. Others characterized the project as an embarrassment and a failure and declined to comment or said, "It was in the past and we have forgotten about it."

JAWALKE WOMEN'S CLUB MEETING

Women from Jawalke assemble near the center of the village in a community hall, fifteen by twenty feet. The green stippled walls of the small room almost look like an intentional design, but the color is due to damage from rainwater, humidity, and age. Upon entering the room, the women find places to sit on a woven floor mat. About fifteen women are present but not all are SHG members. Women enter and leave the room amid crying babies and children who climb on and off women's laps. There are two young women caring for small infants. Jawalke's two VHWs sit in the center of the group that formed a semicircle three women deep facing the visitors, a group of seven men and women from an American Christian philanthropic organization, one of the many small donor organizations for CRHP, who have come to visit the village. The women gathered in the community center are encouraged to speak about their income-generating experiences. One SHG member begins reluctantly, "I took ₹2,000 and I bought fertilizer for the farm and cooking pots. The next time I got ₹5,000 and bought fertilizer plus goats. The third time they provided me with ₹20,000. I paid each back, including the ₹20,000." The group applauds.

The president of the SHG shows the group's bankbooks and record ledgers. One woman reported that her group took two bank loans amounting to ₹25,000 "I keep it [money] in the bank so our savings grew, and we are able to take the loans from our savings." From that original SHG loan one woman took four loans totaling ₹5,000 to buy goats, and another borrowed ₹10,000 for her daughter's marriage expenses. One woman borrowed enough money to, with help from her husband's family, open a convenience stand in the village, which she runs with her husband. Finally, a woman spoke from the back of the room in a loud voice: "I got a loan of ₹5,000 to buy onion seeds and germinated them into small plants and planted them in my fields. At harvest time I sent the entire crop to be sold in Solapur [a nearby city]." She concluded triumphantly: "I made ₹50,000 on my ₹5,000 investment." This caused spontaneous talking and some applause in the room. [As noted earlier, at the 2012 exchange rate ₹100 was equivalent to about $2

WOMEN ENTREPRENEURS: KHOYA PRODUCTION

When I asked women in Jawalke village about successful projects, I was taken to an open-sided shed where *khoya*, a milk product used in making sweets was produced. Two village women, Leelabai, the mother-in-law, and Jija, her young daughter-in-law, were busy inside. On a brick fireplace platform sat an enormous metal cooking pot .75 meters (39 inches) wide and .4 meters (18 inches) deep filled with cow's milk. When I was introduced I started asking questions about the process of making *khoya*. Jija, the younger woman, looked at the ground and avoided eye contact. Her mother-in-law, a member of the women's club in Jawalke village, answered my questions and affirmed that her daughter-in-law was shy. Leelaabai explained that they use milk from her own two cows, but she also buys milk from other women in the village. Leelaabai describes the process:

> She [the daughter-in-law] boils the milk to make it into *khoya*. Every day she takes 20 liters of milk and makes 5 kg of *khoya*. At seven o'clock in the morning she starts by heating milk and stirring and stirring it until it becomes like a solid. It is done at eleven o'clock. She packs it up in a large bundle wrapped with cloth and string. She sends it to a village that is forty kilometers from here. We put it [the bundle] on the bus by itself. It goes from one bus to the other bus. The bus conductor takes that responsibility and we pay for that for the transportation. For one kilogram of khoya she earns ₹100. She sends 20 kg each day she works and makes ₹2,000 per day. (fieldnotes, 2012)

The final product of the morning's activities was a package of *khoya* solid approximately four inches by four inches by fifteen inches. The women's entire project depended on the help of a trusted government bus conductor who would transport the product from the village to the sweets maker. I learned sometime later that production had stopped at the *khoya* shed. After years of making money for her family and other women in the village who contributed additional milk, the project was left without a way to get the milk product to market. The bus conductor who had been paid a small fee to help transport the *khoya* bundle retired. When a new bus conductor began service on the village route, he refused to transport the package and, with few other means of transportation at that time for the forty-kilometer trip to the sweets maker, the project failed.

THE FISH SELLER'S HUSBAND

Gosala's husband, a cobbler, sat on the ground in front of his house near the center of his village wearing Western clothes. He held between his legs a cast-iron shoe anvil attached to a wooden platform atop a steel tripod about twelve inches high. He was adding rubber heels to leather *chappals* (sandals) using what appeared to be a cobbler's hammer without a handle. Many villagers dropped by. The VHW asked for his wife. He explained that

she had gone to her family home to celebrate a festival. While he continued to repair a sandal, Gosala's husband answered questions about loan
his wife received from the bank.

> We go from village to village on market day. My wife sells dried fish and I sell
> and fix shoes. Each village has a market on a different day, and we would go
> to several villages. The original loan was ₹3000. My wife is a member of the
> women's club. We got the information that we could get a loan from a private
> bank. We repaid the loan and then took another loan from the CRHP women's
> bank. The loans were to increase business. With the loans the land was bought,
> and the house was built. My sons went to school one to tenth standard and the
> other is sixth standard and both of them work in Pune. Because I am alone to-
> day, I am not making new shoes. Today, old shoes are repaired. (fieldnotes, 2010)

The shoemaker was asked to show us the room where dried fish (Bombay
Duck) is stored. He declined, saying that there was too much moisture in
the air which is not good for the dried fish.

Government Schemes

In India, since the second five-year plan in 1956, various programs have developed measures for poverty alleviation. Government programs introduced in
Maharashtra in the 1970s and 1980s include Development for Women and
Children in Rural Areas (DWCRA), the Desert Development Programme
(DDP), the Drought Prone Areas Programme (DPAP), and the Intensive
Agricultural District Programme (IADP) (Purushothaman 1998). In 1974 a
statewide program under the auspices of the Planning Department was
started in Maharashtra to guarantee work for the poor, and by 1979 it had
evolved into an act paying minimum wage to unskilled workers for manual
labor. During the previous Congress party administration, the National
Rural Employment Guarantee Act of 2005 (renamed for Mahatma Gandhi
in 2009) guarantees a hundred days per financial year of wage employment
for unskilled manual work for adult members of rural households.

Indian government initiatives to extend financial services for those traditionally without formal access began in 1992 with five hundred women's
self-help groups gaining access to bank loans. Since 2004 these microcredit
programs are initiated primarily by the National Bank for Agriculture and

Rural Development (NABARD) (NABARD 2013, 1). Further, the 2006 National Rural Employment Guarantee Act (NREGA) creates wage work. For example, the NABARD report (2013) noted that by March 2002 there were five hundred thousand SHGs, and in March 2012 there were eight million (3). Further, the report claimed that informal self-help groups had blossomed into a "monolith" microfinance initiative, and that these decentralized Indian financial initiatives are "cost-effective and [the] fastest-growing microfinance initiatives in the world, enabling over 103 million poor households access to a variety of sustainable financial services from the banking system" (1).

LOCAL GOVERNMENT CORRUPTION

Arole and Arole (1994) reported that when CRHP began VHWs overwhelmingly feared local government officials, which made them reluctant to deal with police, local politicians, and bank officials, presenting an impediment to accessing local loan programs. The first women's seminars tried to dispel this dread of even entering a court or police station and helped women stand up for their own legal rights. One of the sources of their reluctance was that most women or family members had personal experience with corrupt officials. They had witnessed first-hand how local government officials intervened in relief programs, favoring one caste affiliation over the other, usually based on bribery. This local interference could impact people's ability to access ration stores, purchase land, settle disputes, deal with criminal arrests, and even obtain a driving license.

Clearly, the direct support of CRHP in teaching VHWs and providing seminars for local women broke social barriers, especially the fear and lack of information that prevented women from even attempting to be part of the economic life of villages. In Halgaon village, on the occasion of the opening of a new bank, *panchayat* politicians, bank officials, and government block development officers (BDO) attended the ceremony, as did Shilabai Amte, the village VHW, and her women's SHG. Shilabai Amte used this occasion to speak to the crowd about eliminating harassment of women. She was concerned about what she saw as the "corruption and inefficiency of the village level bureaucracy" (Arole and Arole 1994). Shilabai Amte is one of the first-generation VHWs; she lives in a geodesic dome house with a diameter of eight meters (twenty-six feet) that was built by CRHP after the Latur, Maharashtra, earthquake in 1993 that resulted in the deaths of more than nine thousand people. Shilabai Amte was one of the VHWs of CRHP who volunteered to help the injured and traveled 163 kilometers (one hundred miles) to the disaster area.

On a visit to Halgaon village in 2015, I spoke with Shilabai Amte about the early days of organizing and resistance in her village. She recalled that speaking out at the bank opening was an example of what she learned at CRHP, to stand up and be heard. She talked about her views on women and income generation and how conditions for women using banks had changed over the years. After talking in her home, Shilabai Amte suggested we take a walk through the village to meet the head of Bhairavnath Vidhyalaya bank. In the one room bank there are paintings of four famous men and a respected local deity as well as three portraits of famous women of Maharashtra, including Savitribai Phule. We had tea at the home of the bank manager, just next to the bank building, and met his wife and daughter, who was looking forward to attending college.

Learning about women's rights within the legal system helped VHWs overcome their fears of government officials and enabled them to navigate the loan systems of local banks. With this new knowledge and experience, VHWs and women's club members were able to access government schemes that provided economic assistance. However, women were mindful of the obstacles hidden within these new benefits, especially the complicated interstitial village politics and corrupt government officials. According to VHWs, the source of many of these difficulties were generated by the actions of the *talathi*, an appointed government official. A *talathi* is assigned to five or six villages to collect land revenue; maintain accounts, records, agricultural statistics, and government forms; and inspect crops and boundary markers ("Maharashtra Zilla Parishad" 2010). Yet, as financial opportunities became available for VHWs, they were also aware that with changing patterns hegemonic powers tend to reemerge that reinforce traditional gender and caste relations.

In order to become successful borrowers, CRHP social workers recommended that, because the government bank scheme allowed SHGs to repay only half of the principle, when the loan was granted half of the principle should immediately be placed in the SGH's bank account. In 2012, the interest on the regular savings accounts SGHs used was 6 percent. Hirabai Salve, a VHW of Jawalke village, was very astute in learning the criteria for government monetary schemes and bank loans. In her village most households are below the designated national poverty line (BPL). With her SHG, she applied for a government-sponsored loan from the bank in her village, but she was initially refused because she owned no property and had no collateral security. With the help of a CRHP male social worker, the group reapplied and demanded a loan or the reason in writing for the refusal, citing recent regulations for government-designated loans for women. Finally, the first loan was received; Hirabi helped the SHGs in her village navigate complicated loan repayments. When the SHG completed the terms of the first loan and applied for a subsequent loan to continue their income-generating projects, the second attempt was refused. According to the bank, the application was rejected because four of the eleven women in her group no longer have the proper BPL documents.

> In our self-help group those women who are below poverty have special benefits from the government. But the government has done a resurvey of the poor people in the village and their names are not there. When we looked at the list, we saw that the names of rich people were there. Not ours. So, what should we do about that? We are below the poverty line and someone has cut us from the list. Now the whole group is not eligible because those four members are not at the poverty line. (Hirabai Salve, personal interview, 2012)

According to Hirabai Salve, the *talathi*, who evaluates families' financial status and designates those who are BPL, had done something wrong because nothing substantial had changed in the economic status of the women who lost their BPL status. Hirabai Salve suspected that this was another example of local corruption and assumed that the *talathi* was paid a bribe by wealthy villagers to approve their BPL status in order to gain access to low-cost government loans.

Due to her keen sense of how to manage money and her ability to understand banking systems and sponsored loans, Hirabai Salve has become one of the wealthiest VHWs. When asked about her success, she proudly lists the property she has acquired, including land, cows, a wristwatch, several sewing machines, and a Jeep, although she is unable to drive. Her married son is the primary user of the Jeep and keeps it at his home. Even with her accumulated wealth, Hirabai is still a member of SHGs, sells bangles, and participates in other income-generating activities. While she owns these items, her worth straddles BPL status.

Conclusion

Aside from the direct effects of market employment in adding to the economic independence of women, outside work is also causally important in making women have a better "deal" in intra household distribution. Needless to say, women's work at home can be
backbreaking, but it is rarely honored or even recognized (and certainly not remunerated),
and the denial of the right to work outside the home is a rather momentous violation of
women's liberty. (Sen 1999, 115)

Clearly, Indian women who start their days before dawn have arduous
lives, yet, the current presumption that merely placing money in women's
hands will change village and local economies is without evidence. This
raises again the importance of understanding the dynamics of a woman's
quality of life and of asking questions like, Can economic status be understood without attention to caste and gender inequality? Will these income-
generating projects in fact alleviate poverty as the Grameen Bank example
presumes? Will improving family income through the government intervention of loan programs solve the unyielding problem of poverty, or is
more government intervention necessary? Are there real on-the-ground
advantages to microloans for women and their income-generation projects?

The obvious signs of economic change in villages show up in families.
As households gain more money, changes usually progress in a particular
pattern: Dung floors are covered with ceramic tiles; an armoire with cab-
inets and drawers is added to rooms formerly without furniture; the last
large item added is a TV. Motorcycles, driven only by men, become common,
and in some villages with large multifamily farms, tractors are purchased.
In prosperous villages, wealthy farmers install irrigation systems and build
large houses on farm property. In India the BPL is an official designation
measured by a complicated formula about land and local goods, and as of
this writing, the current Bharatiya Janata Party (BJP) government headed by
Narendra Modi has not officially designated a level for the Indian population and is still using 2012 figures of less than $1.25/day. The World Bank
Group defines extreme poverty as an income of less than $1.90 per day per
head of purchasing power parity (World Bank 2016). In Jamkhed, day wages
in 2017 for a woman working on an agricultural farm ranged from ₹90 to
₹120 ($1.40 to $2.10 in 2017 dollars); however, the work is sporadic and primarily seasonal.

Gangabai Kulkarni, a Brahmin woman and one of the first-generation
VHWs, is certain that income-generating projects created real change when
it put "money in our hands." She emphasized that it is not just about the

money, but also the support, education, and training that VHWs and other villagers received from CRHP. Gangabai Kulkarni said that even though women understand their rights, the underlying issue of gender inequality is always a consideration: "When a man has money, he spends large amounts of money for himself. When a woman starts getting money, she spends it on her family" (fieldnotes, 2012).

CHAPTER 7

Standing on My Own

Women and Equity

Parliament's Leaders Live in Bungalows (*MP nete bangola rahatata*)

(Chorus)
If parliament's leaders live in bungalows
Then how will they see poor people's sorrow

They get new cars without effort
They sit on thick matts covered with velvet
All the time they are busy eating luscious food

Chorus

Just like a king they are surrounded by servants
They follow capitalism
And agree to do black marketing

Chorus

Every village is having *panchayat*
These are the keys to unlock civility
We see how fighting is growing wildly

Chorus

The *panchayat* mayor and parliament's leaders work together
How they work is seen from their potbellies
We need not say it—they are dishonest

Chorus

Women, Power, and Processes of Empowerment (*Sakshamikaran*)

The concept of empowerment for women is ubiquitous in the development and public health literature and so universal that it has become formulaic as a panacea for women, especially those who are economically disadvantaged. In the early days of CRHP, before the construct became commonplace, a concept of empowerment was incorporated as one of the three underlying principles of the CRHP model. Empowerment is defined as a necessary aspect of the learning process for VHWs: first, to develop self-awareness and self-confidence; second, to achieve personal growth through education; third, to become part of a health care team to treat and educate others; and fourth, to understand societal constructs that cause inequality.

> Human beings, regardless of their station in life have innate unlimited potential within themselves. People have been empowered through a process of discovery, experimentation, trial and error, rerouting when necessary and by being nondogmatic in sharing values and skills. Only people empowered and empowering others for the common good can find and keep the respect, cooperation and peace so much needed in this world. (Arole and Arole 1994, 252)

The Aroles' definition of empowerment became a cornerstone of their project and centers the value of the individuals in a society to develop community participation and consensus. Thus, enabling empowerment is a process that must be anchored to social relations as part of a continuum, founded upon "the realization that knowledge not only gives power, but that sharing knowledge also increases self-esteem [which] is important in the development of team spirit" (Arole and Arole 1994, 248). Like other promising approaches in the 1970s that coupled adult education with philosophical and political ideas, such as Paulo Freire's programs in Brazil and liberation theology in Latin America, the CRHP approach instilled biomedical learning with awareness of the underlying issues of cultural hegemony and the maintenance of the status quo in rural society through caste and gender inequality. Built on adult education that identifies external political and economic factors, CRHP challenges local patterns of inequality, common in village life, as impediments to learning. The song "Parliament's Leaders Live in Bungalows" poses the question, How will members of the Lok Sabha in Delhi, so removed from rural society, understand the everyday life of villagers? It indicts the *panchayat* (local elected officials) as adopting the same hierarchical attitude. What level of understanding is necessary to enable VHWs to write a song that connects national legislation to district and local power to memorialize the consequences of an unequal society? Clearly, a benefit of the Jamkhed Model is that it enables women to recognize and understand the underlying issues of cultural hegemony as they learn about the complexity of their position in rural patriarchal society.

Social Empowerment and Community Participation: For the Public Good

The development of self-worth that began with the simple exercise by the first-generation VHWs of viewing themselves in a mirror to acknowledge their individual identity apart from familial norms led to a type of professional empowerment that "gives them [VHWs] self-confidence to share boldly their experiences with formally educated professionals" (Arole and Arole 1994, 209). Themselves enabled, the cadres of VHWs are able to advance newly learned and heartfelt ideas and serve as intermediaries between their villages and CRHP. This attention to women's capabilities instilled self-worth and confidence and led to a sense of consciousness that combined an understanding of women's rights and legal entitlements. Thus this participatory approach based on personal empowerment built a dynamic team that values an individual's experience and knowledge of her community and relies on creating conditions for social empowerment in individuals who in turn become advocates. Community participation and consensus building contributed to the ultimate goal of this process to communicate health and medical information to all community members for the benefit of all. Contradicting standards of medical hegemony, the Aroles believe that knowledge about improving health should not be in the hands of a few professionals, because "as communities become more empowered, more and more of the responsibilities of primary health care [are] taken over by the village people" (Arole and Arole 1994, 237). Clearly, the Aroles' depth of conviction and their faith and confidence in individual capabilities frame the underlying philosophies of the CRHP model.

In 2012, I attended a VHW class on reproductive health and during a tea interval I casually asked the woman sitting next to me, a first-generation VHW then in her early sixties, why she had been a VHW for so many years. She responded:

Why do we come to CRHP? Why do we come for years and years? We come to see each other. We come to see you. [She laughs]. We come to gain knowledge. In the villages now, health knowledge is shared. If the VHW is not there, who in the village can help? What we learn we share. We unite the women. We organize them and give them skills and help them to stand on their own feet and give them social consciousness. (fieldnotes, 2012)

This sense of connection between self-actualization and building group consciousness persists. For example, Sunita Sadaphule responded to a similar question posed almost thirty years before and noted in the 1994 publication: "We don't come [to CRHP] just for training. We come mainly to experience closeness with other workers. We are live coals; together the fire keeps us burning. Alone we shall be extinguished" (Arole and Arole 1994, 153). Consequently, creating the conditions for empowerment as the Aroles define it while organizing and uniting other women and men is a clear example of the dynamic process of community building that sustains the Jamkhed Model.

Germinal work in anthropology and the social sciences on women and empowerment emphasizes the centrality of social relationships in the context of power to understand empowerment as "a process aimed at consolidating, maintaining, or changing the nature of the distribution of power on a particular cultural context" (Bookman and Morgen 1988, 4). Kabeer (1999) explains empowerment as a process by which those denied decision-making acquire the ability to make strategic life choices. Others argue empowerment is a process of analysis of power from women's experience through collective action that produces an outcome for both men and women that considers global and national forces (Parpart, Rai, and Staudt 2003).

Resistance, Struggle, and Social Change

Is adopting the CRHP model and teaching it to other women a form of resistance and agency? What motivated the first generation of VHWs to so completely absorb the values of CRHP that more than forty years later they are still promoting those values and the ideals of community participation and primary health care? Are the CRHP rights-based perspective and kinetic teaching methods motivating factors? Resistance and struggle against common everyday inequality is lived, discussed, and deconstructed by women village health workers as an integral part of the CRHP learning process to become a health-care practitioner and village advocate.

As Latabai Kadam's quote at the outset of this book explains, her life was unalterably changed when she was selected to be one of the first village health workers. Through the CRHP educational process, women began to interrogate the reality of their situation. As VHWs learned to introduce a support system for social change and development, teaching and organizing in villages became the earliest examples of resistance to traditional health and social norms. For the first time in their lives, women VHWs, together, recognized the possibility of a different position in society that previously relegated them to roles only as daughters, wives, or mothers, with no standing or privileges either within families or as villagers. More importantly, by learning about and actively working against their own oppression and toward improving the position of women in village society, VHWs validate the underlying principle of equity that is central to the Jamkhed Model. In addition, they appreciate the value of collaborating with each other, something previously prohibited in daily village life. Even given all of this, the question remains: How were women with no position or status in their patrilocal villages able to become independent health practitioners and community organizers in one generation?

Some researchers propose that values and patterns of relationships derived from social conditions generated the patriarchal and caste orders that embody values and beliefs; consequently, to treat beliefs "purely as ideologies which can be transformed with a change in consciousness is to ignore their social roots" (M. Mohanty 2004, 20). Further, M. Mohanty (2004) suggests that the way colonial and post-colonial capitalism developed foreshadows sources of power and control over the means of production such as land and industry. Ironically, one of the explanations for the ability of the women of Jamkhed to make the enormous step to leadership, autonomy, and self-determination may be rooted in the systems of inequality themselves: "Due to manual labor in agriculture and forest economy, *shudras* and so-called outcastes [Dalits] and tribals already had a relatively high degree of equality between men and women" (M. Mohanty 2004, 20). For those living in precarious circumstances, the need for manual labor by both men and women to contribute to the below-the-poverty-line family economy might undermine the traditional patriarchal caste- and gender-based division of labor.

From the early days of CRHP the concept of caste was presented as a contested category rather than accepted tradition. As a way of introducing challenges to structural inequalities, every activity initiated by the Aroles incorporated a method or action to oppose conventional relationships that sustained caste inequality. With every new project or program, whether providing breakfast for children, hiring workers, supporting new housing, introducing agricultural innovations, convening seminars and training programs, instituting adolescent girls clubs (and later adding adolescent boys clubs), or directly promoting income-generating programs for women, practices were introduced to disrupt typical patterns of caste segregation. Gangabai Kulkarni, discussing the 1970s, stated:

> twenty years ago, it was unheard of for a Brahmin woman like me to sit with men or socialize with Dalit women. As a woman I was confined to my home and sometimes I worked on our ancestral farm. Now I am free and serving the entire village as a health volunteer. In the beginning it was difficult for me to visit Dalit women and particularly to deliver their babies. I have never been to school. I look after the health of the mothers and children. I have been a village health worker for the past seventeen years. I have conducted over 550 deliveries and have not lost a single mother during this time. This village has about 250 couples and 150 practice family planning. . . . I visit all the families in my village and follow up the children. Ghodegaon was a different village before I became a village health worker. (qtd. in Arole and Arole 1994, 12)

The village of Ghodegaon is constructed within ancient walls built by the stonecutter caste. Today the stone walls are in partial disrepair, but the boundaries are evident. Each year CRHP draws a village plan as a record of each household, road, water well, and temple, as well as the houses of dignitaries. The plan marks households by indicating Dalits in brown, Buddhists in blue, and Muslims in green. In Arole and Arole (1994), there are two monochrome hand drawings of Ghodegaon village, one from 1971 with the Dalit households huddled together on the outside of the village wall. In contrast, the 1992 plan of the village shows a major difference: the Dalit households are scattered throughout the village. These drawings are evidence of a particular type of success of the mission of the CRHP because they demonstrate much more than the integration of households into the physical structure of communities. Of course, merely moving to a house built within the confines of a village does not ensure acceptance unless it is accompanied by constant and gentle pressure from the farmers' clubs and women's clubs and the VHWs' daily modeling of acceptance of equality among villages, all exerting pressure for community change.

For forty years, Gangabai Kulkarni has been an active VHW who participated in the implementation of CRHP programs and continues to make a difference in her community. Her understanding of village politics is informed
by an assessment of how health care policy has influenced local problems.
Much like the sentiment of the song that begins this chapter, she sees a
disjunction between what is needed for the health of villagers and policy
decisions. In fact, she negatively refers to parliamentary leaders as "men
in air-conditioned rooms," indicating just how geographically and socially
distant they are from rural villagers. Her hands-on training and experiences
as an effective health practitioner equip Gangabai Kulkarni with the tools
to assess the underlying causes of local problems. Her critical analysis of
both health professionals and parliamentarians was articulated based on
her ability to evaluate rather than absorb the status quo, and to use this
perspective to teach other village women ways to understand and deconstruct village life, especially caste and gender relations.

The first generation of VHWs learned to not privilege caste in personal
interactions and everyday experiences at CRHP symbolically and practi-
cally by "sleeping under one blanket." VHWs were in the forefront of making changes in love relationships and intercaste marriages. During a focus
group on caste with five VHWs, I asked a complicated question about intercaste marriage and asked Mrs. Kamble to translate it. She replied that there
was no need to pose such a question because marriage arrangements were
fixed by caste groups. I reframed the question in a simpler form basing it
on the example of couples VHWs knew personally who had intercaste marriages. Mrs. Kamble was shocked by the responses. Not only was there evidence in all five of the villages they represented, but the VHWs themselves
had been instrumental in arranging one marriage between a Hindu girl of
the Sutar caste and a Muslim boy.

Agency, History, and Hegemony

How are the everyday lives of women constrained or enabled by power and
privilege? Does the VHWs' historical perspective enable them to assess
larger social, political, and economic processes? VHWs at CRHP, even those
with little formal education, know important historical facts about Maharashtra and talk about currents news events in India and the US, especially
during presidential elections. In conversations they regularly refer to significant political and religious figures such as Bhimrao Ambedkar, Annabhau

Sathe, Lahuji Raghoji Salve, and Jyotirao Phule, and know about Savitribai Phule, who founded the first women's school in 1848. Women talk about movie and TV stars and some village homes have a satellite television dish. Marathi-language TV began in 1984. Full-length silent films started in 1912 with Marathi intertitles, and the first talking films in Marathi were in 1932.

In Maharashtra state in the early twentieth century under the British Raj, education was conducted largely in English. Performances in that period in the local Marathi vernacular reached a broader audience, including women, especially those without a formal education. For example, Anagol (2007) describes *Purushance band* (Men's rebellion), a play written in 1912 by a woman that was performed for public audiences throughout the state of Maharashtra in the Marathi language. In the play a ruler decides that women and men should form single gender societies as parallel kingdoms. Left to their own devices, the men's society soon descends into an unruly dysfunction; in contrast, in the women's kingdom there is collaboration and cooperation, and in no time, banking and manufacturing are established, and women's society is prospering on all levels. Performances in the Marathi language were accessible to urban dwellers and rural villagers alike without formal education, and plays like *Purushance band* communicated ideas and raised questions about historical events and contemporary issues of gender, politics, and differences in Indian life.

Anagol (2007) used her own class background to depict growing up in a Jain household. There she heard stories of Marathi- and Kannada-speaking women who had made major impacts on the society, religion, and politics of the region. She also vividly remembers hearing sagas of other women living in extreme hardship, deprived of family support and even shelter. Anagol suggests the use of the vernacular, in this case Marathi, rather than English, allowed uneducated rural villagers to incorporate these ideas into oral histories and local tales as amusements to be told and retold to understand current and changing societal experiences.

These abstract notions of essential differences between men's worlds and women's worlds are writ large in the everyday lives of people in villages where all aspects of their lives are marked by physical gender separation. For example, every morning men are seen in the village center talking in groups, drinking at tea stalls, or preparing to journey to town on motorcycles. In contrast, women are unseen, at home making breakfast, washing clothes, or doing other domestic duties. At village meetings and assemblies, men sit together in the front of the group while women are relegated to the back or periphery. These traditional patterns are the manifestation of the underlying patriarchy in rural villages. Such patterns are expressed in myriad ways in family relationships despite laws and even amendments in the Indian constitution to protect the rights of women. For example, the Prohibition of Child Marriage Act of 2006 followed the Sharda Act (or Child Marriage Restraint Act) of 1929 and legislated the age of marriage at eighteen for females and twenty-one for males. In 1961, the Dowry Prohibition Act was passed. While the Indian Penal Code was amended in 1983 (498-A) to make domestic violence a criminal offense, more recently the Justice Verma Committee issued a report on the need to further protect women from domestic violence including acid attacks, sexual harassment, voyeurism, stalking, and sexual trafficking. This report led to changes in the criminal code. VHWs were aware of the changes in these protections as well as other laws affecting economics and microloans and used that awareness to address practices they saw as restraining women's position in everyday life. The 73rd and 74th constitutional amendments direct the decentralization of political, administrative, and fiscal systems, creating reservations or statutory quotas for specific groups in legislatures, local governments, and public service, and introducing allocations for women for equity in governance. Learning about these legal and historical processes enabled a growing understanding of how far the margins of change could be nudged by each VHW in her own village, and how collectively these incremental changes lead to altering the capabilities of village women.

As a white American researcher, the interpretation of Western notions of freedom, equity, and difference were uppermost in my mind during interactions with the women and men of Jamkhed, especially when my questions were misunderstood or led to a quizzical look. I was careful to frame queries, particularly regarding advocacy and activism, using local perspectives. Agency, neutrally defined as the capacity for individual choice and action, has to be examined as subverting norms of gender performativity to reverse power (Butler 2007). In another sense, agency connotes the realization of "one's own interests against the weight of custom, tradition, transcendental will, or other obstacles (whether individual or collective)" (Mahmood 2011, 206). Others identify the value of understanding rights-based justice in the face of neoliberal practices (Hodgson 2016). Observing women's agency at a particular place and at a particular time gives us an ethnographic snapshot of everyday patterns of behavior that can be diagnostic of resistance to the norms of power. With the ability to untangle hegemonic structures that are influenced by the historical moment, VHWs are able to understand the pressure on everyday activities that may present a pragmatic limitation of agency, which Lopez (2008) describes as limited choices. Yet without the advantage of deconstructing the historical depth of political and economic changes that generate social trends and modifications on women's life experience, these relentless and nuanced alterations of circumstances would be opaque.

Shakila Shaikh explains her experience in the face of family and community constraints trying to manage her life with her growing understanding of women's individual rights:

I am a Muslim. In my society young married women do not go out except in purdah. The mothers-in-law force it. When I was young, I was married as a second wife to a man who was older. He was a drunkard. My family lived in poverty. I was twelve years old when I was married, and my husband used to beat me every day. My in-laws knew that I was from a poor family and they would treat me very badly. I wasn't given enough food to eat. If I was given food, it was leftovers. Once I went to my parents to tell them what was happening to me. They said, "You are dead to us and it is your fate and you must face whatever you face alone." And you must not come back here anymore. When my first child was six months old I got pregnant with my second child. While I was pregnant my husband took a knife and cut me. I needed eight stitches in my arm. So, I was fourteen when this happened. I went back to my mother again and told her he beat me and cut me. She said you must go back to your husband. But I did not want to go back.

There was an older woman in the village, her name was Radabai, she was the VHW. She talked to me and took me to CRHP. So, after that the village women's group invited me to be a part of them. They were not Muslim. Most Muslim girls were not allowed to go to school, so I couldn't read or write but I enjoyed being with these women, and they supported me. Then once when Dr. Mabelle Arole came to the village with the mobile health team they saw me in the women's group. They asked Radabai, do you think she will be able to learn and become a VHW? I said I have no education, I don't know anything. I cannot read or write. But I was selected.

My brother would take me to CRHP for the training there. We would lie to the family and say that we were going to a relative's house. But actually, I was going for training. So, when I would get the honorarium my brother would say give me the money. I moved to my brother's house to get a better life. Then I said it is my money I need it for my family. Then I knew what I was doing. So I would not just hand it to my brother. Then he said don't go there, you are learning too much and getting too smart. So he threw me out and I had no place to stay.

But then I learned how to spend money. I learned how to make decisions. So in my village there is a high Muslim population and they are strong. A woman who was from a fisherman group helped me. So, I got three hundred rupees and started selling bananas in a bus stand. The people said you are young and a Muslim, how dare you sell fruit in the bus stand. But I said to them, "If you don't want me to sell bananas then each family must give me money, so I can survive." Where I would sit near the bus stand it was local government land. I learned my rights at CRHP and if this land belongs to the government then I have a right to be in this area. I said, "You do not have a legal right to kick me out. I have a right to sell." I learned to stand on my own feet. I got confidence. I learned to sign my name. Then, I was able to buy my own house. I was able to do many things with what I learned at CRHP.

I wanted my daughter to get education. She studied until twelfth standard. My daughter walked twenty minutes to travel for twelfth grade. I inspired the others to send their daughters. People started to ask for my daughter to get married. My dream was that my daughter should be a doctor or a nurse or a teacher. My father and the rest of the people in my society were determined that she should get married. I was against it. Because I was a widow my family said it would be bad for the family if she did not get married. But I said, "Whoever comes to marry my daughter they must have an HIV test first." My father said if you do that then no one will come for your daughter and she will never get married. I said, "Getting a test is the correct thing." Now, my daughter is married, she has children, I have my grandson.

But I have achieved a lot in my life. I stand on my own two feet. My daughter and son were educated and slowly my family started respecting me. Now they say she has really done something with her life. Now I am esteemed in my village. If there is a dispute, they come to me. If there is a fight, they come to me. We have a prayer every evening, they all come and pray. Doesn't matter if you are Muslim or anything else, people believe in prayer. Muslims are known not to teach their girls but after what I did, they send their girls to school. Muslims are not known to use family planning, but people will ask for tubectomy after two children.

My son is married, and he has children. My daughter's husband is being good. I told my son-in-law that if he does not behave, I will make a court case after him. But I learn how to love. At CRHP, I learned how to love my enemies. Before he died, my husband who beat me up and abused me got cancer of the throat. He got very sick, but I went back and took care of him because I learned from others, I learned to love my enemies.

Social Empowerment of Women

Nobody valued me. Not only did I not know my value, my family did not know my value. I did not know what I expect from society. Initially there was a big change in my family. Initially I improved my family and then my neighbors and then I went to the village. My husband is a disabled person, so I can't tell you how poor we were and how much poverty we had. Because I got the knowledge here [CRHP] about income generation and farming, I started income-generation activities. I have three buffalos, I have milk. I sell the milk. My husband sells the milk to the dairy and I make and sell yogurt. Now instead of getting one sack of grain I get ten sacks of grain from my land. This is how I came up from poverty. When I was earning, the family started respecting. Once your family respects you, your community will also. (Manjula Gite, personal interview, 2009)

Wallerstein (2006) suggests, "health professionals, non-governmental agencies, multi-lateral and bilateral aid agencies, foundations, and governmental agencies have increasingly turned to empowerment and community participation as major strategies for alleviating poverty and social exclusion and reducing health disparities" (7). To assess empowerment in the VHWs in Jamkhed, Kaysin (2010) adopted a 1990s model developed by Carl Taylor for women in Afghanistan. As part of an MPH project for Johns Hopkins Bloomberg School of Public Health, Kaysin incorporated a public health model and undergraduate anthropological experience to use an ethnographic perspective. Kaysin found that no matter which age or generation of training, VHWs' scores were consistently remarkable on measures of agency, self-confidence, and efficacy. In fact, the Aroles predicted their model would create the conditions to reduce gender inequality; they envisaged that "as women become more empowered attitudes [e.g., acceptance of female children] will change" (Arole and Arole 1994, 221). Kaysin concluded that Taylor's adapted model was a valid instrument to assess women community health workers' agency and empowerment. Further, he asserted that Jamkhed VHWs were decidedly outside the normal range of measurements and beyond expectations for empowerment using these indices.

In addition to structured studies, even casual observation of everyday village life gives indications of the role of VHWs in Jamkhed communities, especially when villagers meet to discuss introducing new projects and programs generated by local officials or CRHP. On one occasion in 2010, I attended a meeting in Sharadwadi village for a CRHP project on adding latrines to existing houses. A meeting was called by the mobile health team with some volunteers from the farmers' clubs from other villages to report on progress of implementation in their own villages. Pushpabai Sanap helped the mobile health team set up a place near the village temple by laying out large woven mats to demarcate a sitting area. Then with other MHT members she began gathering villagers and alerting them that the meeting was about to begin. At first a few men dressed in the typical white kurta and pants with *topi* caps arrived and sat at the front of the sitting area facing the elected officials and MHT members who sat with informational charts and notebooks. As more people arrived a few women joined but sat together at the back of the space. After a while thirty villagers had assembled and the MHT began presenting the project. Several of the men asked questions and joined in the conversation. However, the women, with Pushpabai, sat in the back with heads covered with the sari *pallu* as they silently observed the proceedings. As the meeting progressed Pushpabai moved herself forward, still in a sitting position. She carved a path for herself, moving forward until she was at the front of the group with her *pallu* still over her head, adjusting it as she moved forward. As she approached the front of the crowd, she started asking questions. Finally, Pushpabai became a commentator and interpreter for those who had not fully participated, especially the women. In this way she began to quietly and forcefully intervene to redirect the emphasis to include everyone in attendance.

The purpose of the meeting was to get villagers to sign an agreement partially funded by CRHP to begin work on installing latrines. While most of the signatories were men, Pushpabai encouraged women who were living alone to agree because CRHP would provide assistance. Pushpabai's subtle but decisive actions during the meeting clearly demonstrated her confidence interacting with men and her efficiency in dealing with various groups in the community. This pattern of gentle assertiveness was learned through trial and error alongside other VHWs who understand the most effective methods of creating space as women and advocating for those who need help declaring their position.

Economic Empowerment

The United Nations Women's Economic Empowerment website features a photo of a woman using a power tool and states, "investing in women's economic empowerment sets a direct path towards gender equality, poverty eradication and inclusive economic growth. Women make enormous contributions to economies, whether in businesses, on farms, as entrepreneurs or employees, or by doing unpaid care work at home" (UN, n.d.). The assumption of poverty alleviation through women's economic empowerment is largely based on claims of the success of women's financial empowerment programs, especially banking through microloans. This neoliberal presumption of how markets or financialization affect everyday life reduces broader societal factors to a simple zero-sum equivalent. However, these successes are frequently measured by an analysis that examines an incomplete set of results, like debt repayment alone, without evaluating whether there is real change in household income or if woman's quality of life is improved (see Chapter 6). In the Jamkhed case, when some women become transporters of goods from the market to the village, they take the lead in providing services to other village households. This affords a small remuneration for the women transporters who take the initiative to use public transportation to a weekly town market to acquire goods, but can this activity be considered entrepreneurial? In fact, the practice of goods transporter was effectively eliminated in a relatively short period of time as more families acquired motorcycles and easier access to town markets. In addition, these interim enterprises do not generate sufficient funds to expand or even continue, especially when the woman who took the initiative has no other means of support, financial or otherwise. In rare cases, these market activities led some women to open convenience shops that supply a small sample of household and personal necessities, but how many such shops can one village support? Often, those who identify these surface changes as signs of financial success fail to take into account how the wider historical, social, and political contexts affect a woman's well-being and whether these changes are real and sustainable. As Purushothaman (1998) asserts, women's empowerment in India is largely a class-based endeavor, with those having access to financial support being better able to sustain projects that have the largest gains. In Jamkhed, evidence of women's empowerment for some has taken a lifetime, even with consistent support from CRHP in initiating the conditions for personal, social, and economic change.

Shilabai Amte describes how she incrementally changed her own situation:

> I am from a caste where women are not allowed to leave the house. We have to wear our *pallu* like this [she pulls the veil part of her sari over her face]. In

the beginning the mobile health team was coming to my village. They helped organized the women's groups and I was starting the main one. At that time my husband was a gambler. I had to do farm labor on other people's farms to earn money. Those days I had only one sari. To have one complete nine-yard sari I would stitch old saris together. To wash the sari sometimes I would go to the river and wash one part of the sari and dip into the river so that no one would see. When that part of the sari was dry, I would put it on and wash the other part. That is the way we would survive.

At CRHP, I got a ₹500 loan from the project. With that money I bought dry fish and vegetables at the market [Jamkhed central] to sell in my village. Every time I came here [to CRHP for weekly training], I was buying vegetables and dry fish and I was having my medicine kit. Selling things and giving health education and giving medicine also earned. I gave *bhakri* [bread] to my son to sell before school. He would sell the *bhakri* and then go to school.

After that I managed to get one goat and that goat produced one more and then I got a herd of ten to fifteen goats. We had farmland, but the well was dry. Then one day Dr. Mabelle asked me, How much yield do you get from your farm, and I said one sack of *jowar* (sorghum). Then I learned about how to get bank loans. I got an ₹11,000 loan. Then, I took two more loans. I deepened the well and then I built a pipeline for irrigation. Now I have a variety of crops from my field. I get twenty-five sacks of *jowar*.

The early days were hard. I had three sons and I had only my farm to get money. When my oldest son was seven years, I took him with me to harvest. He would help me. This is how we would survive. So, when I came to CRHP, Dr. Raj said why don't you send your children to school? Then I had a little money and I did, one went to fifth standard, one went to sixth, the last one graduated. But my father did not speak to me for two years because I became a health worker. He would not give me food or clothes. He said, "you are working with this Christian community." It was hard for us, but we got courage.

Nobody gave us the key to our brains. Now we have new ideas and we have prospered. We have courage. Who would have ever thought that a woman would be standing on her own feet? I never thought that a woman would go to a bank, but I have gone for loans three times. Now, bank people respect me because CRHP people showed us the way.

At present I sell bangles from my house. In the past if my rich relatives were having a marriage ceremony, they would put a curtain between us, so they did not see my poverty. Now, those people who put a curtain between them and me respect me. Now their girls are my daughters-in-law. (fieldnotes, 2010)

Shilabai Amte lives in the home that she built in the early days of working at CRHP, and she still tends her kitchen garden. Her description of these aspects of her life show marked changes in her understanding of her position in Halgaon village and Jamkhed society. Her life course continues to advance, as does her sense of herself and the remaking of her identity as a woman with independent and transferable rights. She believes she contributes to her community through administering health care and providing practical information to her village. She does not own a vehicle or have furniture in her home, and she sleeps on a floor mat, but she does own land in her own name and has written a will to leave the land to her daughter-in-law. Shilabai Amte, like Rukhsanabee Shaikh and other first-generation VHWs, understands the value of supporting her family both now and in the future by writing a will to bequeath property to her daughter-in-law, who she believes will stabilize the household. These actions identify changes in understanding, self-awareness, and self-determination that demonstrate the connection between the economic power of women and the ability to challenge the structure of religious and societal codes of belief.

Social Stigma and Social Change

In a society structured on supposedly immutable stratification, stigma expressed as the exclusion or discrediting of individuals is accepted and reproduced. In Jamkhed villages, individuals with leprosy, a disfiguring disease, were shunned and segregated from villages no matter their caste or status. Whether due to fear of the unknown or fear of contamination, lepers were relegated to a lonely existence apart from village life. Often people with leprosy were ostracized and left to fend for themselves, living in the forest or the outskirts of villages with no means of livelihood except for begging or living on gathered or discarded food. Marriages were affected because daughters of those with leprosy were not considered marriageable; in a society in which all women are married, this compounded the pattern of social exclusion.

In the 1970s, while multidrug regimens were being tested, there was one effective medication available to treat leprosy. The Aroles believed that integrating treatment of leprosy into the process of primary health care would eliminate stigma. Badambai Dalvi, a first-generation VHW from an upper caste, was affected by this type of stigmatization because her father had leprosy. He was rejected by her family, and as a young girl Badambai learned to participate in his rejection:

I did not know the meaning of humanity. My father had leprosy. My grandparents (his parents) and my mother left him. No one wanted to stay with him. We did not treat him with sympathy.

When the mobile health team came to my village, first Dr. Arole and the staff would go to the Dalit area. They would go to the Dalit houses but as the VHW I had to go with them. But as an upper caste person I thought, my village is such a big village, why are they only going to these places? When I began training, I would stay outside the house and look at what they are doing. I saw the doctors touch the hand of the leprosy patient. The sisters (nurses) or doctor would clean the wounds and give service to patients who are not related to them. So I thought that these doctors were taking medicine to protect themselves from leprosy.

Though I came to CRHP for two years of education I still did not change my ideas. I thought leprosy is infectious and if I go to my father, I will also get it. But then as I learned, I thought my own father has leprosy, why don't I take care of him? But I did not have the courage to ask the question of Dr. Mabelle Arole. Then I did ask Dr. Mabellebai, if I go to my father's house will I get leprosy? Then I learned and understood more about leprosy and I changed. And then I understood, yes, I can go and take medicine to give to my father.

As a child I remembered that sometimes my father would come to our house to give us fish that he caught, but our mother will not let us eat it. When I told my mother my plan to help my father my mother said don't go. She said, "I have spent my energy to bring you up and if you go you will get leprosy and who will take care of you then." But I had the knowledge and I took time to trust that leprosy is not easy to get, and I was able to help my father. (personal interview, 2009)

The lessons learned in overcoming the stigma of leprosy were already part of the CRHP model when HIV/AIDS began to appear in local villages. In the transcript below Rukhsanabee Shaikh explains how she was able to use her understanding of the health and social factors about HIV/AIDS as a teaching moment that benefited those in her village who were becoming concerned about the epidemic and were predictably succumbing to misinformation. This situation is an example of the relationship between the individual social empowerment of the VHW and her ability to communicate this learning for the good of the local community. Rukhsanabee Shaikh explains:

Two young men from my village went on a truck for work to Gujarat state which is next to us. When the majority people from my village migrate, they go husband and wife together, this is what we recommend. But these two men went alone. So one of the men who went to Gujarat came back to the village. He complained about having trouble with his leg.

His family told him to stay in the village and get married. His family told him that his aunt had a lot of property. If he would stay and get married, his aunt's family would give some property to him. So then he got married. I spoke with the girl [about his condition]. I told the girl not to try to get pregnant for six months.

When he got married, he slowly became thinner and thinner and lost weight. When he became more seriously ill the family said it was because of his leg. So, he was taken to the hospital in Ahmednagar, which is seventy-five miles away, for an examination, but they did not disclose whether he had HIV. Then they went to another hospital but never was it openly disclosed that he had HIV.

Only his mother and wife would go near to him, no one else in the family were taking care of him. I knew that he was sick, I knew that he was having fever and I thought I know why. But his father said you should not make noise that he is having fever and that you should keep quiet. So, after the last time I never spoke anything. When I entered the house, they said don't go near to him. I said, no I will go. At that time, he was having a high fever. He was urinating on himself and nobody was taking care of him. Then the mobile health team came to the village. I sent them to visit him. When the team went to the house the father came into the room, he took his scarf and covered his face and mouth. The team told the father this disease doesn't go to you through your mouth or in the air. Don't worry. Whatever he has treat him well and feed him well, but one day he is going to die. Then his grandmother and I took care of him. We cleaned him. He could barely drink, we tried to give him milk. But soon after that he died.

Then his friend also got HIV and people thought it was because they were living together and eating and sleeping together. But I told them that you can only get it through sexual contact. Someone else said maybe it was like malaria through a mosquito bite. I said no it will not happen through mosquito bites. The only way that you can get this is through sexual contact. But they treated this person with fear and panic. They did not treat him like a friend, like a person who was sick.

To show the importance of understanding health education I organized a meeting of the men's and women's groups. And I explained that HIV is contracted through sexual contact. It used to be thought if someone had an accident and they gave them blood they could get it through the blood. But nowadays they check the blood. It is also possible through injection also. When women go to some government nurses for immunizations, I tell them to buy a new needle. I explained that the wife of the man who died was living in another village and she was HIV positive from her husband. After they listened to me and there was an improvement for the way people treated the second man. There was not so much stigma attached. Villagers would give him food and visit him. Everybody was different and started to change because I gave education, they changed their ideas about HIV. (fieldnotes, 2012)

When Rukhsanabee Shaikh talked about sexual contact she did not say whether she thought the two men were with sex workers in Gujarat or having sex with each other. Although villagers know of several men who have sex with men, it is not a topic that is openly or easily discussed. Arranged marriages are common and most villagers are married in their teenage years, even with recent laws mandating age eighteen as the legal age of marriage. If the marriage lasts only for a few weeks, women still wear the *mangalsutra*, the neckless with a gold pendant and black and gold beads that indicates married status. Consequently, individual sexuality is often masked by traditional early marital patterns. Nevertheless, Rukhsanabee Shaikh demonstrated her understanding of HIV/AIDS and tried to both take care of medical needs and change the stigmatized understanding of the disease. If empowerment is measured, as the Aroles suggest, as people inspiring others for the common good, Rukhsanabee Shaikh earned respect. Through years of service to her village she provided health education and generated cooperation among villagers who, in this instance, were able to overcome what she describes as a type of panic about someone with HIV living in the village. With this action Rukhsanabee Shaikh demonstrates her self-recognition, self-determination, and ability to challenge medical misinformation, stigma, and potential for social reprisals.

Divorce and Violence

At the end of each life history personal interview, which often occupied an entire afternoon with breaks, tea intervals, and interruptions, I asked women if they had any questions for me. Most questions were about my marriage, family, and children and the differences between everyday life in Jamkhed and America. When Shilabai Amte asked if I was currently married, I got the sense that she was prompted to interrogate me by other women who had learned I was divorced but wanted to know more. Shilabai Amte pressed for more information, and when I replied that I asked for the divorce she seemed taken aback, but her only response was: "He didn't leave you?" When I reviewed the videotape, I was unnerved at the length of time it took me to answer this personal question, especially since I had just spent most of an afternoon probing her own life. I finally replied that I asked for the divorce because even though my husband was a very nice man and very supportive of my own education, I was unhappy in the marriage. Shilabai Amte, not someone who smiles easily, grinned and said, "Here we can never do that, we must just stay and be unhappy." In Jamkhed many husbands leave their wives and live with other women without formal divorce. Often an unwanted wife is coerced to leave her husband's home. While many of the VHWs live without their husbands in the home, the official divorce rate in India is 13 percent. I was aware of only one official divorce by a VHW. Suvarna Gite was forced to migrate to work in the sugar cane fields by her husband. At the time, she was unaware that she had leprosy. The difficult and demanding work in the cane fields caused damage to her hands that eventually resulted in severe deformity. Before her hands healed from the injuries incurred harvesting sugar cane, her husband intimidated her into leaving her marital home. Suvarna was able to move back to her mother's house. After several years of pursuing legal actions and encouraged by CRHP, she was successful in being awarded a divorce based on being abandoned by her husband. Sharmila Rege (2013), an Indian sociologist, points out that the Hindu Code Bill proposed by Ambedkar was rejected in the 1950s because of the threat of women gaining access to property, the removal of caste restrictions in marriage, and "the dawn of the right to divorce" (200).

Most Hindu VHWs daily wear the *mangalsutra* necklace symbolizing the sacred cord of marriage even though their husbands are no longer living with them. Some were married as briefly as one month before being forsaken whereas others were rejected because there were no male children. Some men leave because they had been forced into an arranged marriage though they had a previously established love relationship with another woman. Many of these departures are related to requests for additional dowry, especially cash. Nonetheless women wear the *mangalsutra* and red *bindi* every day until the death of their husband, no matter who he is living with or where he lives.

Violence against women is an everyday occurrence in India, with reports of rape, beatings, burnings, and dowry murder in newspapers and on TV. As one VHW told me, "Every time I suspect, I ask a woman if her husband troubles her, I get a story of a recent physical or verbal abuse. It is happening all the time but not in the open" (Shakuntala Moholkar, personal interview, 2010). These disclosures are made to VHWs who are trusted members of village communities and understand the sensitivity of the issue. However, a study about women living in urban Delhi shows women are reluctant to answer structured questions about domestic violence and unlikely to give detailed reports (Snell-Rood 2015). A recent systematic review of a decade of quantitative studies of domestic violence against women reports that a median 41 percent of women reported experiencing domestic violence during their lifetime and 30 percent in the past year of the survey (Kalokhe et al. 2017). Another review of worldwide sexual violence (Abrahams et al. 2014) notes there are problems identifying risk factors and definitions of rape, sexual violence, and sexual abuse, which vary considerably based on locality, especially for intimate partner abuse. For example, intimate partner violence is consistently underreported in India. One study based on recorded cases showed that intimate partner abuse results in a deceptively low prevalence of 8.5 percent but noted that only 1 percent of affected women reported sexual violence to the police (Raj and McDougal 2014). An earlier report (Visaria 2008) using survey-based studies (the National Family Health Survey 2) notes that 35 to 75 percent of women in India face verbal, physical, or sexual violence. Yet a news source reported that even after India's National Family Health Survey 3 introduced questions on intimate partner abuse or violence, 80 percent of women who have experienced sexual violence never tell anyone about it (Pathak and Frayer 2019). In addition, Indian legislation passed in 2013 by the Lok Sabha and Rajya Sabha to amend the penal code for sexual offenses after a highly publicized gang rape of a student in Delhi prompted one writer to question whether these laws rushed through parliament can change society's attitudes toward women (Sankaran 2013).

In Jamkhed, one form of domestic violence by husbands against women is the use of kerosene to immolate women. Burns are survivable if the injuries do not cover a large percentage of the women's body, but based on severity, some burn victims might stay for months in the CRHP hospital being treated and recovering. These injuries are often compounded because women in the Jamkhed area wear saris exclusively. Most six-yard saris are carefully draped to create the pleated bodice; unfortunately, the majority of saris are made of synthetic materials that are highly flammable.

For women who have spent time in the CRHP hospital recovering from injuries or having scar tissue removed, the description of the burn incident usually follows a typical pattern. At first the woman claims the fire and subsequent burns were an accident, often blaming themselves for being careless while cooking. However, as the woman becomes more comfortable with the hospital staff and are not under the watchful eye of their husband and his family, she may confess that the fire was not an accident but an intentional attack. Consequently, actual reports of domestic violence to authorities are rare, skewing the real reports for violence against women and further normalizing these incidents. Estimations based on reported cases of violence even in the extreme case of near fatal bodily harm are often underreported or not reported at all, resulting in current statistics being suspect.

Understanding and in some cases experiencing domestic abuse, VHWs with the cooperation of village women have tried to change patterns of violence, especially the most common complaint: being beaten by a drunken husband. Shakuntala Moholkar described one incident in 2010:

> There is a woman in my village who works all day at the farm and takes care of her children. She'd come home her husband would beat her up. He was drunk every day. The women's club members tried to talk to him. But it didn't work. They told the woman to lock herself inside her home and not let her husband in. We said no matter what he does do not open the door. She followed our idea but when she opened the door the next morning he came in and beat her up. The women's club went there again and told him that if he didn't stop, they would bring police action. He did not believe any of that and continued beating her. So, one day the women's club convinced her to pack up everything and go to her mother's village. He started begging the women's club members to bring her home. After eight or ten days she returned. She has been back and there have been no incidences. If he does anything, now he knows we will go to the police. (fieldnotes, 2012)

VHWs are aware of the changes in the penal code making domestic violence a criminal offense; consequently, threats to abusive husbands are not seen as idle but rather have the weight of women's groups and support of local law authorities.

Bold Women *Sakshamikaran*

In 2005, the village of Jawalke held an election for the *panchayat*. It conformed to the spirit of the 73rd and 74th amendments to the Indian constitution

passed in 1992, which mandated that one-third of the seats be designated
for women and one-third of the seats reserved for Scheduled Castes and
Scheduled Tribes. At this time, Shantabai Sathe, a Mang Dalit, was elected
to the *panchayat* and then elected by the *panchayat* to be village *sarpanch*
for a five-year term. In her words:

I was elected to the *panchayat* and named *sarpanch*. I was bold and worried.
First, I had some fear. I was not literate. I was hesitating because I did not have
faith on my own. The village was having faith in me. Of 1,882 households, four
hundred voted for me; the largest group was Maratha with three hundred but
also Mang, Mahar, Chambhar, Dhangar, and Muslim. My brother had a lot of
experience about the *panchayat*. I used to ask my brother to read everything.
Before the meeting there was an agenda. But my brother was not permitted to
come into the room. They closed the door. Even though my brother was not
with me I used to conduct the meeting alone. Slowly, slowly I learned what to do.

There were some problems in the government program of distributing money.
The Maratha people (the dominant caste) on the *panchayat* wanted to get more
houses. But I said that the other poor people should also get housing. I said it
should be fair.

I sanction twenty houses of government. Only six for Maratha, the other went
to Mang, Koli, Chambhar, and Muslim. For the Indira Awaas Yojana Housing
Program each person got ₹28,000 [about $600 in 2010] but they must be below
₹15,000 [annual income]. Some said that the Maratha family were not below
₹15,000. Marathas' previous houses were built on sites of their old houses. Sometime Harijan [Dalit] don't have enough land. But landless people can get land
from the government. The houses usually have one room and one for kitchen
and an outside latrine also very small. They are all the same plan. Dirt floor. If
they want to add other improvement, they use their own money for the flooring
or if they want something fancy.

In Dalit *vasti* [area] they did not have electricity or water or a good road. I
gave money to build a road for the public bus. There was a common well twenty
years old but there's no water. I sanctioned money for a new well and new pipeline for seventy households.

I had one bad experience when I was just new after two months. I was going
through so many chits for so many things. There was rice for the primary school,
housing for the poor people, road work, water problems, so many subjects. I was
at home making *bhakri* and the schoolteacher of the Jawalke primary school
came to my home and wanted money to purchase the rice for school lunches.

He wanted me to sign a chit. I said no I am not going to sign that chit. He said you know me very well. I am not going to deceive you. I did not want to sign because there was no one to help me read the chit. But I could read the figures and I noticed there were no numbers on the chit. So, I asked him how much money and he said, "Just ₹800." I trusted him, and I signed. Then, I told my brother that he did not write the amount on the chit, but I signed it.

My brother was very angry. He said we will go to the bank now. At the bank the manager showed us the chit and it said ₹8,800 (about $190 in 2010). We went to his house, but his wife said he has gone to Jamkhed to the government block office. I went with my brother. We caught him. When we asked why he did it that way, he lied that it was ₹800. I told him we have gone to the bank and seen the chit. I said I will talk the *taluka* officer. He showed the receipts that it was rice, dal, and oil and whatever else he bought. I said I wanted the remaining money. He gave the ₹4,000 remaining. He said sorry. I said this is the first time but the next time your job will go. Then within six months he was no longer at the position as head teacher.

For five years I was the mayor and did so many things people gave me respect and love for taking care. I am like chief minister of the *panchayat*. The *gram sevak* [an appointed government official] tried to dominate me. But, I made my own decisions. I held a meeting every month and all the members met every three months. I took care of my caste of people who had been neglected. At end the of my five years I gave each family four saplings from the government nursery to plant for their house or farm, custard apple, *amba* (mango), *badam* (almond), and bamboo. God has given a gift to me. The village had faith in me. I knew what to do. I use my brain in a very good way. I am proud of my knowledge. (fieldnotes, 2010)

For my formal life history interview with Vatsala Chande, a first-generation VHW, she arrived with a folder containing an award certificate, some frayed newspaper clippings, and photos. I began the interview with a reading of the informed consent and then Vatsala Chande signed her name. She replied to the basic questions with meticulous detail. However, when I asked her an opinion question about how the water supply affects health, she began telling a story that happened in the late 1980s:

My village is five hundred people of the nomadic Dhangars. The only available well was almost four kilometers away. It was a dangerous walk downhill and people were getting hurt. I helped organize the women of the village then everybody joined together, and we dug a well and built a pipeline to the village on the top of the hill. Then we asked the chief governmental official to come to our village to see what we had done. He was so impressed with our settlement that he agreed to make it a separate village, so we would govern ourselves. We wanted to build a hall and the government official agreed to give us ₹35,000 The official told the story to the prime minister Rajiv Gandhi and he invited me to New Delhi.

I travelled to New Delhi, it took one day on the train. I was invited to talk about health to the prime minister, but the conversation lasted for two and one-half hours. I told him about my village and the work of the community. I told him about my work as a VHW. I told him that women should be equal in governing the village and that 50 percent of those elected to the *panchayat* and *lok saba* should be equal (not just dominant groups) and that 30 percent reservations should be for women.

Vatsala Chande stops to show me her documents, the official letter of invitation, the award certificate, the newspaper article, and her photo with the Prime Minister. According to Sindhuja and Murugan (2018), Prime Minister Rajiv Gandhi made several attempts to introduce a constitutional provision in the late 1980s to ensure regular and fair elections; however, the 73rd constitutional amendment was not passed until 1993. Whether Vatsala Chande's meeting with the prime minister influenced his position is not known, but the dynamic way she presents herself and her ideas are more than impressive, even among a group of women confident of their ability to teach and advocate.

Conclusion: Standing on My Feet

Some researchers raise concerns about whether the concept of empowerment should be perceived as an "unquestioned good" when embraced by entities like the World Bank, Oxfam, local nongovernmental organizations (NGOs), and women's collectives (Parpart, Rai, and Staudt 2002). Rege (2003b) agrees that the concerns of the 1980s and 1990s about the visibility of women in India as conduits of the economic renewal are based on inordinate emphasis on concepts of empowerment fostered by international financial and development agencies. For example, Sharma (2008) asserts that the use of empowerment as state-driven development policy in India is pervasive in local economies based on a presumption that there is some movement away from dependency and precarity, especially for subaltern women. The term *empowerment* pervades the public and professional imagination whether in books, magazines, newspapers, television, cinema, or the internet. The overuse, misuse, and, all too often, abuse of the concept is pervasive. Nevertheless, I suggest that the omnipresence of the term *empowerment* makes it useless as an explanatory concept in and of itself to understand the experiences of working and poor women unless it is part of a gendered and class analysis that examines particular communities mediated by historical, social, political, and economic factors and global influences on everyday lives. Trickle up, without financial governmental inducements, is as useless as trickle down.

Local women are disrupting and challenging gender norms that are effectively ascribed to both Hindu and Muslim traditions by using the conditions created by CRHP to become practitioners and advocates in their home villages. Gender inequality and caste discrimination are the underlying aspects that framed Jamkhed society. In a community where class differences are directed by national standards, more than 90 percent of the population in villages are below the poverty line. Incrementally, for some forty years, the CRHP and the VHWs have worked together, supporting each other toward change while pushing the limits of the possible through their own capabilities. The result of this method of advocacy, created through community participation, is to build a buttress against current trends and government processes and schemes and show measurable social change. All of these changes must be regarded as byproducts of the conditions created by the principles of CRHP that guided the education and training of the women selected by village officials and later the VHWs themselves. However, the first group of women selected who largely sustained the project were in effect randomly chosen. Village leaders had little idea what the role of VHWs would entail; in some cases, poor women were chosen; in others, high caste women. Each of those who continued on to become practitioners were guided by their own subjectivities, motivations, and understanding of gender and caste constraints. But using different imagery each woman expressed her own understanding of how the men in bungalows and the men in their families who once controlled them now see women as bold and "standing on their own feet."

The Jamkhed book begins with a description of a May 1988 global health conference in Washington, DC, attended by Drs. Mabelle and Rajanikant Arole. Janabai Pol, a first-generation VHW, was invited as a representative of Jamkhed VHWs. Janabai Pol, dressed in a local-style Maharashtran sari and speaking in a rural dialect of Marathi, stood in front of an audience of nearly five hundred health professionals, academics, ministers of health, and officials from WHO and UNICEF the presentation was translated by Dr. Mabelle Arole. Janabai Pol, with the grace of a seasoned professional, spoke:

> "This beautiful hall and the shining chandeliers are a treat to watch," she says.
> "One has to travel thousands of miles to come to see their beauty. The doctors
> are like these chandeliers, beautiful and exquisite, but expensive and inacces-
> sible." She then pulls out two wick lamps from her purse. She lights one. "This
> lamp is inexpensive and simple, but unlike the chandeliers, it can transfer its
> light to another lamp." She lights the other wick lamp with the first. Holding
> up both lamps in her outstretched hand. "I am like this lamp, lighting the lamp
> of better health. Workers like me can light another and another and thus en-
> circle the whole earth. This is Health for All." The audience rises to its feet in
> a standing ovation. (Arole and Arole 1994, 1)

When I conducted a life history interview with Janabai Pol, I asked her about her trip to the United States and her presentation at the conference. I was especially curious about her symbolic use of an oil lamp. This is her response:

> A researcher came to CRHP to do a study about self-esteem and in part I was
> selected based on that. Then Dr. Mabelle Arole took me on a trip to Mussoorie
> near the Himalayas to give a talk at a school for administrative service. After,
> Dr. Mabelle asked me if the travel was okay and if I wanted to go to the United
> States. I said yes immediately because I was confident at that point. For the
> trip to America I prepared what I was going to say but I did not tell anybody.
> As part of the preparation I took two small brass lamps, wicks, and oil with
> me. I had no idea how many people would be there, but I prayed for strength.
>   I am an illiterate person, but I own my own small convenience shop. I also
> sell bangles. And I am on my own feet and I am willing to make a difference in
> my village. I truly believed in possibility of Health for All for the year 2000.
>   When I spoke, there were pictures and a slide show so the audience realized
> that I wasn't just talking but they could see the things that I was actually doing.
> Through pictures I showed how I cared for pregnant women, TB, leprosy, chil-
> dren under five and also adolescent girls. I spoke a lot but at the end I took a wick
> lamp and pointed to the large electric light above me. I said, "The chandelier is

for the rich but for the poor we have these lamps. With one matchstick you can light millions of these lamps. It is the same with health: you can bring the light of knowledge and health with women like myself.

"If I can make a difference anyone can make a difference."

I felt that just like in Jamkhed. You can make sure that health reaches everyone in all countries throughout the world. The medical practices of the doctors who have made it a business and it is not about health but about business. For no reason they give injections and some of the medicines they prescribe don't make people better, they have reverse effects. But instead what we have learned is that many illnesses can be treated at home, especially many waterborne like typhoid, diarrhea, cholera. We take therapies from home remedies. Before, we did not know how to treat children with fevers but now we learned, and we taught our villagers about how to treat fever. With diarrhea we would give them electrolyte solution. If it worked it worked, if not we would take them to the hospital. We worked very hard to learn. Together we kept repeating and repeating. And songs, lots of songs we wrote to remember. We made flash cards [visual aids] with people who looked like us in village life. I still feel the spirit of Dr. Mabelle in everything she did and everything we do. She would be so happy to see the effect of her work [wiping tears from her eyes]. I am very happy to [be of] service. It makes me happy to help and as long as I can move my hands and feet, I am going to serve people. The educated people and the rich should unite and they should unite for the development of the poor. (personal interview, 2010)

In Jamkhed, the process of educating women to be VHWs is based on the principles of CRHP that acknowledge innate unlimited potential and demonstrate the necessity for teaching a broad view of structural power and the value of learning about hegemonic structures that affect women's everyday experience. While the concept of empowerment is defined as measures to increase autonomy or self-determination, it cannot be understood without an analysis of the larger context within the constraints of political and economic parameters within a historical context. As Wolf (2001) suggests, structural power shapes the field of social action, and "the notion of structural power is useful precisely because it allows us to delineate how the forces of the world impinge upon the people we study" (385). Understanding women's empowerment without attention to the relations among agency, resistance, and power does little to explain the shifting patterns of everyday strategies. As Abu-Lughod (1990, 1999) explains, an analysis of women's actions, sometimes marked as resistances, becomes diagnostic practices that help us understand theories of power in assessing the details of quotidian struggles. CRHP created the conditions for VHWs to learn about their own position in village society shaped by women's caste- and class-based inequalities and to realize their own capabilities for dignity, proficiency, and success.

CONCLUSION

Local Solutions to Global Problems

In a noteworthy publication in the *American Journal of Public Health*, Farmer (1999) cites the 1948 Universal Declaration of Human Rights regarding health and well-being, special care for woman and children, and access to scientific advancement. He affirmed that "social inequalities based on race or ethnicity, gender, religious creed, and—above all—social class are the motive force behind most human rights violations" (1488). Based on his work during the AIDS epidemic and especially listening to the voices of subaltern groups, Farmer identifies a definitive position: promoting social and economic rights is the key goal for health and human rights in the twenty-first century. Physicians Mabelle and Raj Arole devoted their life's work to the ideals of human rights by helping people living in rural villages in India and rejecting top-down attempts to change course away from an equity-based model of primary health care. The Jamkhed Model was painstakingly developed and continually refined to represent a template for providing health through equity that is sustainable and reproducible.

The World Health Organization defines health as a "state of complete physical, mental, and social well-being and not merely the absence of disease or infirmity" (WHO 2014, 1). Callahan (1973), a bioethicist, suggests that biomedical professionals are largely critical of this definition because it challenges the tendency toward medicalization of social problems and the cultural context of illness. Instead, he defends the term for its wider ethical, social, and political meaning, and because it implies "an intrinsic relationship between the good of the body and the good of the self" (77). Can health be calculated? Is well-being quantifiable? Wali (2012) questions whether happiness can be measured by a statistical composite like the Gross Domestic Product or Human Development Index (HDI). Instead, she suggests that long-term comparative studies of cultural formations permits anthropologists to "offer measures of happiness found in different places than the statistics that inform the economists' standards: we craft a concrete visualization of the conditions necessary to attain happiness through our analyses of the stories people tell, the webs of relationships people build, their expression of emotions, and the aesthetics of the everyday" (12). Further, Wali proposes fostering dignity as a way of creating value and respect and thus motivating people to be happy, healthy, or content.

In offering local solutions to global problems, the Comprehensive Rural Health Project created the conditions for the promotion of health and well-being by integrating social science, public health, and biomedical perspectives. As physicians, the Aroles' primary health care model centered on promotive and preventive medicine while fostering health and social well-being with a firm understanding of the exclusive and hierarchical nature of biomedicine. For them the ideal of "health for all," the motto of Alma-Ata, meant understanding that the ordered division of rural Indian society based on caste, gender, or class reproduces an unequal system that reinforces the direct opposite of their objective. In the community-based model, equity in health requires attention to the weakening of local prejudice and the promulgation of change. Accordingly, CRHP successfully added the crucial dimension of community participation, from the bottom up, to frame and organize interventions. This provision of medical care focused on essential medicines and treatments that directly satisfied the most urgent public health care needs of the population based on relevance, safety, and efficacy. Following principles of primary health care, CRHP collaborated with the local community in all aspects of health and social planning. Drs. Mabelle and Raj Arole understood that before any project, program, or biomedical measures could be implemented, a realistic assessment of the everyday struggles of rural villagers was essential.

The Aroles recognized that the material necessities of health and well-being were tangled in the local hierarchical ranking of traditions that reinforce social inequalities, and that health policies dictated by both local and national administrations are often at the mercy of changes in political dominance. So they began by targeting local embedded inequalities in village life using the mobile health team and VHWs as agents of change, setting in motion an innovative process to incrementally improve health and social well-being. Thus, over more than forty years, CRHP demonstrated the successes of a participatory community-based primary health care (PHC) model with unprecedented improvement in health and social and economic welfare for more than 130 Jamkhed project villages with a combined population of approximately 1.25 million.

The Aroles' Jamkhed Model as a workable primary health care experiential approach, exclusively selecting village women as community health workers, proved especially effective in applying a local solution to one of the most intractable global health problems: maternal and child health. Inexperienced family members or *dias* (traditional birth attendants taught through apprenticeship) assisting at home births were replaced by well-trained VHWs who introduced new techniques and eliminated unsanitary traditional practices to accomplish safer home deliveries. With at least one VHW in each village trained in the CRHP appropriate and practical methods, villagers had access to a trusted, skilled practitioner who was primarily responsible for introducing innovations such as techniques for safer deliveries, early breastfeeding practices, and treatment for infant diarrhea and fevers that changed village health profiles. Consequently, the focus on these made-to-measure solutions became the foundation for medically appropriate practices by women who were of the village and worked for the village.

Local women, especially first-generation VHWs, changed the trajectory of their lives from child brides and sequestered wives to health practitioners, social advocates, and village leaders. Their dignity is demonstrated daily through their personal strength, persistence, and resilience, strengthening their own agency with new ideas, adopting complicated medical procedures, and teaching health and health care in their own villages. The worldviews of women who became VHWs gave them no reference to imagine the dramatic transformations for their lives, families, and communities that CRHP would introduce. VHWs resisted traditional patriarchal hegemony and consciously reversed the practice of silence by learning about structural economic and political power in the local context (Wolf 1999), and by defeating what Achino-Loeb (2006) called silence as the currency of power, to forge new identities through the process of building social relations.

Village women themselves became part of the process to overcome the double problem of caste and gender inequality by first changing their own understanding of village life and then actively supporting the transfer of these social innovations to others. Additionally, learning about local and national politics that directly affected their lives helped them understand the position of rural women in Indian society. The strenuous work of rural Indian women whose day starts before dawn is well documented, yet adding the supplementary work of a VHW to their daily routines produced satisfaction, self-respect, and pride voiced unassumingly in conversations and interviews: "I'm standing on my own feet," "I delivered four hundred babies in my village," "I own land," "Children in my village are healthy," "People call me doctor," "I got divorced," "I gave medicine to treat the problem," "I tested her urine and found diabetes." "I taught the women about birth spacing," "I started a self-help group," "I built my own house," "My daughter-in-law will inherit my land," "I met with the prime minister," "I travelled to help earthquake victims," "I was elected *sarpanch*," "I understand friendship and *maya* (affection)." The CRHP model, through the integration of professional and local knowledge accompanied by simple tools like songs, eliminated local endemic health problems and reduced infectious diseases common in the Global South, and it maintains sustainable health profiles that resemble countries in the Global North. Inspired by the CRHP principle of equity, VHWs collaborated in promoting their own agency and performing everyday resistances to local power dynamics by confronting entrenched caste- and gender-based inequality in village life for the public good.

Sustainability, Cost Effectiveness, and a "Virtuous Social Cycle"

I do not want a salary from CRHP, I am not working for the money. My whole life changed because of CRHP. I was very poor. I didn't know how to talk to people. I didn't know anything about government schemes, so I learned a lot of things from CRHP. I hold my own money. I am not working just for the money. For my whole life I would like to work with CRHP. I want to be part of CRHP because I want knowledge. (Kaushalya Gaikwad, personal interview, 2010).

Of the thirty-three VHWs who participated in a life-history interview for this research project, most answered a question about salary with a variation on the answer above. The majority of those interviewed considered themselves independent practitioners. They did not see themselves as employees or volunteers; some women, especially those who formerly worked as day laborers, felt that a salary would make them like servants. Almost all VHWs have benefitted financially either by small loans, being part of *bhishi* or self-help groups, or through individual or group loans from banks. All VHWs interviewed for this research reported being part of a financial group and using funds to start small income-generating projects like raising goats, tailoring, selling produce and dried fish, selling bangles, starting vermiculture, or collaborating in an upscale dairy commune.

Why in an area of extreme poverty and inequality did the Aroles elect not to pay VHWs a salary? Other workers, such as sisters (mostly auxiliary nurse midwives), social workers, laboratory technicians, and even drivers received wages. The first consideration was purely financial—the initial operating budget of CRHP based on grants without government support was not sufficient to pay salaries for fifty to sixty VHWs. But this was not the primary reason for the lack of a regular salary. In the Jamkhed area where more than 80 percent of villagers live in poverty, giving a wage as compensation for VHWs would create a separate status that effectively would change their position in village society.

One of the basic principles of CRHP is to select residents of the community to be representative of and accepted by the poor. Would financial benefits set them apart, providing an autonomous status different from quotidian village life? Clearly this raises a thorny ethical concern. Subsequently, the Aroles developed a complex set of arrangements to create financial benefits for workers, especially VHWs, that promoted income-generating projects for women and created structures to effectively access government programs designed for those living BPL, including bank loans, which helped lead toward individual self-sufficiency. Of course, VHWs were given food and lodging when they stayed on the CRHP campus. An honorarium was given for the time spent attending classes equivalent to the high-end typical day's wage. While showing appreciation for local practices, these measures were designed to best fit the residents and support the underlying values of CRHP, especially in times of scarce resources for nonprofit health providers.

Do these practices penalize VHWs financially or prevent them from having professional autonomy? The Aroles' model for monetary remuneration of VHWs was based on their past experience of trying to attract professional staff to work in a rural area situated more than a four-hour drive from a major city. While CRHP has been responsible for introducing agricultural innovations that benefited farmers with both small and large land holdings, those changes affecting caste relations were absorbed, with some regressions, into local social organizations, thus also helping the introduction of health care. The wholesale insertion of a new financial status for village women would have inadvertently restructured local fiscal arrangements in a way that would, in effect, disorder the basis of economic life and disrupt the social contract, negatively affecting the already tenuous organization of health delivery for the majority of impoverished villagers. Instead, over the years of CRHP, VHWs achieved their own financial and social position within the community through their own engagement in village life.

In his discussion of the ways health and human rights can solve public health problems, Farmer (2008) makes a distinction between the community health worker and the volunteer and recognizes the importance of compensating community members who contribute to health work. This analysis is set against the backdrop of assumptions made by NGOs and government that local people do not need be paid; that they work because of some inchoate desire to serve. Some researchers reject the idea of volunteerism that presumed some return for mental satisfaction (Maes, Closser, and Kalofonos 2014). Farmer (2008) makes the basic point that "experts who argue that we should encourage volunteerism, and not pay the poor for their labor, have not imagined themselves in the situation of the vast number of rural or urban poor people who would happily become community health workers" (8). While CRHP may qualify as an NGO based on certain definitions, volunteerism was never a concept accepted by the Aroles. VHWs are respected by villagers as health practitioners, and they see themselves as autonomous actors in an area where men and women without land are forced into difficult and dangerous agricultural and government road-building work and are often exploited by employers and moneylenders. As independent practitioners and remaining part of a traditional society, women gained the unique position of reframing local communities and attaining respect, status, and dignity.

Social Disparities of Health

The success of the Jamkhed Model to identify and actively intervene in local gender and caste inequalities as a function of a comprehensive PHC approach demonstrates the direct relationship between reducing social disparities and achieving health and well-being for all. Anthropologists use intersectional models to investigate underlying disparities in a particular community, such as racial discrimination, class exploitation, and gender subordination in the Harlem neighborhood of New York City (Mullings and Wali 2000). To examine issues of reproductive justice, some analysts reframe hegemonic neoliberal thinking to include structural vulnerability and human rights concerns (Zavella 2016). Baer, Singer, and Susser (2013) emphasize unambiguously the necessity to apply a political economic perspective for medical anthropology with an attention to power and inequality as a central explanatory context. Public health researchers assert that the elimination of bias in the health care system, especially gender inequalities, are necessary to secure human rights (Sen and Östlin 2008).

In the last part of the twentieth century, social factors affecting health were assessed in epidemiologists' studies through the distribution and determinants of diseases in human populations and the implementation of standardized surveillance, intervention, and evaluation (Mausner and Kramer 1985). Some models, like the web of causality, inferred the inter- activeness of the environment, genetic influences, and disease, while lin- ear continuum approaches informed biomedicine by assessing individual behavior, sometimes called lifestyle, to help identify, diagnose, and cure the disease in order to return the individual to his or her "normal" life. Other researchers began to center on social network models to examine effects on health (Berkman and Syme 1979), and some methodologies considered the relationship between social conditions and risk factors as the funda- mental causes of disease (Link and Phelan 1995).

Marmot (2017) defines social determinant of health [SDOH] as "the condi- tions in which people are born, grow, live, work and age; and inequities in power, money and resources that give rise to inequities in the conditions of daily life" (1312). The social determinants of health perspective intro- duced a necessary approach to understand the influences of social and eco- nomic factors on health (Marmot 2005). However, some researchers point out "healthcare systems and services can promote health equity if they are designed to maximize the 'fit' between patients and provider" (Taylor and Marandi 2008, 266). Both medical doctors and individuals seeking health care are embedded in social class and societal relationships; when these are not taken into account, typical medical interactions can be mediated by unconscious bias even when physicians are well intentioned. Recent stud- ies suggest that unconscious bias in health care requires careful identifica- tion and modification, especially regarding doctor-patient interaction and hiring and promotion of practitioners (Marcelin et al 2019).

In *When People Come First*, a medical anthropology anthology, Biehl and Petryna (2013) assert "the global health community has overemphasized individual risk factors that ignore how health risks are shaped by law, politics, and practice ranging from industrial and agricultural policies to discrimina- tion, violence, and lack of access to justice" (3). While identifying gaps in social determinants of health, Marmot (2017) is careful to explain that there is an additional burden for low-income countries when comparisons are made between countries. Yet when assessing social factors and absolute and relative poverty for low income residents of a large US city, Marmot (2017) implies that determinants are reducible to individual risk because, he sug- gests, for some urban residents, ultimately "healthy lifestyle choices are low priority" (1313). Does this statement adequately assess structural constraints? Navarro (2004) cautions that a failure to see issues such as class (as well as gender and race) "rather than people's choice as the roots of the problem puts the blame on the victims themselves" (96). Mullings and Schulz (2006) suggest so-called cultural and lifestyle explanatory constructions "locate the cause of health disparities within individuals or groups rather than in sets of social relations" reproduced within localities (4).

How will the health status quo of localities and nations be altered if these markers are considered discrete characteristics of individuals without an analysis of the intersections and expressions of health disparities at a particular place in real time? Navarro (2007) is concerned that the WHO Commission on Social Determinants of Health is not emphasizing the problems that determine poor health "that are rooted in class as well as in race and gender power relations and in the political instruments through which such power is exercised and reproduce" (61). Krieger (2008, 2011) is critical of approaches of determinants of health that use models or terminology like proximal (or downstream) and distal (upstream) to generate what she describes as a type of causality in public health. As Krieger (2000) points out, "We are a long way from thinking our variables are 'value free' or that the numerical method guarantees objectivity; underlying theoretical frameworks and ideological assumptions are brought out into the open, spurring much-needed debate and reflection" (161). Consequently, she asserts health disparities are created by biological consequences and social dynamics, which lead to inequities that affect living standards, working conditions, and environmental exposure, especially for subordinate groups (2008, 2011). As one study suggests, "achieving greater equity in health is a goal in itself and achieving the various specific global health and development targets without ensuring equitable distribution across and within populations is of limited value" (Blas and Kurup 2010, 8).

Primary Health Care and Global Neoliberalism

Navarro (2016) asserts that neoliberalism is the dominant ideology motivating public policy in both the Global North and South, bolstered by international financial institutions and responsible for the growth of social inequalities. Labonté et al. (2017) are confident that the future of comprehensive primary health care is achievable even if "initiatives are occurring in the context of continuing dominance of neoliberal economics that has escalated wealth inequalities, promoted austerity policies, and challenged the ability of states to build sustainable public health systems" (292).

The Alma-Ata 1978 goal to protect and promote health for all by the year 2000 was never achieved. The current dominant model of evidence-based medicine is employed by most national health care systems and reinforced globally by the World Health Organization and the World Bank Fund policies. Faced with structural adjustment programs in the 1980s and 1990s, countries that were signatories of Alma-Alta were unable to comply with the consensus recommendations for primary health care, instead, adopting vertical health programs that reinforced market-based systems, as noted in Chapter 1 regarding India's devaluing of the rupee and reducing allotments for education and health care. Further, today India is moving toward adopting an insurance plan that is bolstered by neoliberal policies that privileges hospital financing over community based care (Ahlin, Nichter, and Pillai 2016).

On the thirtieth anniversary of the Alma-Ata Declaration, Margaret Chan (2008), then director-general of the World Health Organization, stated that she wanted to revitalize values, principles, and approaches of primary health care, especially mechanisms for reaching vulnerable populations (1118). Proponents of primary health care emphasized growing evidence that biomedical interventions require, and assessment of health is a result of, social, political, and economic environments, not merely of control of diseases and infirmities (Bhatia and Rifkin 2013). Still other researchers consider primary health care the missing link for global health and emphasize that 90 percent of health care demands can be managed by primary health care (Rao and Pilot 2014), and another study shows that community-based primary health care has been growing slowly in importance over the last fifty years for improved maternal, neonatal, and child health (Perry et al. 2017).

Navarro (2004, 2016) points out that categories of per capita income show divisions between dominant economic groups and social classes that impact health and health care. The gross domestic product (GDP) measures the total number of goods and services produced each year; the amount of GDP spent on health broadly indicates the number of people able to access health care, ultimately reflecting morbidity, mortality, and life expectancy as a function of the efficacy of national and local health care systems. While any one of these measures or statistics may not give a complete picture of a population's health, the comparison of health indicators and financial expenditures for medical care can provide a broader explanation of equity within health systems. As noted in Chapter 1, Cuba's primary health care approach has a much better outcome for infant mortality than the US health system. Still, one study demonstrated that Cuba spends only 7 percent of its GDP on health care compared to the US which spends almost twice the GDP at 13 percent (Rao and Pilot 2014), causing some to consider the inability to reduce the infant mortality rate in the US a national embarrassment (Ingraham 2014). Consequently, using the IMR measured against GDP shows that Cuba's thirty-year national primary health care program, which provides universal care, is more effective than the United States' fee-for-service market-based model, which leaves approximately fifty million citizens under the age of sixty-five either uninsured or underinsured (Collins, Bhupal, and Doty 2019). In India, the health expenditure was 4.7 percent of the GDP in 2014, raising the question of whether as the Modi government moves firmly to commercial Western free-market models, can the 2018 insurance plan, Ayushman Bharat, solve India's urgent and growing health problems, or will millions be unable to pay for insurance?

Global health funding since the passage of Alma-Ata has shifted from public to private sources for health programs, ushered in by the adoption of neoliberalism allowing market forces to shape and dictate health care and health systems development and directly affect global interventions (Rylko-Bauer and Farmer 2002; Pfeiffer and Nichter 2008). For example, the United Nations Millennium Development Goals (MDGs) ratified in 2000 identified eight specific health and development targets to be accomplished by the year 2015, which were supported by International Financial Institutions (IFIs) including the World Bank Group, the International Monetary Fund, and G8 foreign ministers. In the past, WHO and UNICEF led research and funding in global health; today, private and bilateral donors and pharmaceutical companies are moving to the forefront of leadership (Cueto 2013), further impeding the progress toward community-based health care. In addition, the "projectification of care" redefines the role of governments and entrepreneurial projects (Biehl and Petryna 2013) sanctioning donor organizations to recruit "clients" for sponsored programs and dedicated medical treatments that effectively isolates the individuals and treats conditions exclusive of a communities health patterns (Whyte et al. 2013). Finally, Farmer et al. (2013) suggest that addressing the social, political, and economic forces that drive ill health must include both clinical medicine and public health "to address the fundamentally biosocial nature of global health problems" (9).

TABLE 1. Health Statistics from CRHP Project Villages (1971–2016)

	1971	1976	1986	1999	2007	2011	2016	India[1]
Infant mortality rate (per 1,000 live births)	176	52	49	26	24	18	18	41
Crude birth rate (per 1,000 population)	40	34	28	20	14.8	23.1	23.1	19
MATERNAL HEALTH SERVICES								
At least 4 ANC visits (%) by skilled provider	0.5	80	82	97	99	99	99	51.2
Skilled birth provider at delivery[2] (%)	<0.5	74	83	98	98	99.4	98	81
CHILD HEALTH SERVICES								
Under-5 received 3rd dose of DPT and polio vaccines[3] (%)	0.5	81	91	99	87[4]	99	99	78/73[5]
Under-5 underweight (%)	40	30	5	5	<5	<5	9	36

SOURCE: Monitoring and evaluation data from a representative sample of project villages in Ahmednagar district; Comprehensive Rural Health Project health information system

1. *National Family Health Survey NFHS-4, 2015-16: India* (IIPS and ICF 2017).
2. CRHP counts village health workers as skilled birth attendants if they meet all training and supervised apprenticeship requirements.
3. CRHP tracks DPT and polio immunizations together.
4. In 2001, CRHP transferred control of the immunization program to the government.
5. For all India, DPT-3 is 78 percent and polio is 73 percent.

Accomplishments Sustained

The Comprehensive Rural Health Project created a positive health profile in villages that demonstrate a sustained change almost forty years later. Drs. Raj and Mabelle Arole, based on principles of equity, integration, and empowerment, conscientiously developed and fostered a design to provide maximum care for many villages with a mobile health team of professionals, and introduced the position of woman VHW at the village level. This assemblage contributed to the lives and well-being of countless Jamkhed villagers propelled by community participation through bottom-up interventions with dramatic improvements to stimulate agricultural advancement, provide clean water, introduce sanitary conditions, sponsor women's economic empowerment, reduce child mortality, attenuate gender inequality, and weaken social discrimination based on caste. Health statistics from CRHP project villages are consistently better than the Indian national average; this is not merely a product of a small sample, because there are valid comparisons of other regional-to-national statistics.

A local solution to the intractable global problem of infant mortality was accomplished in Jamkhed by CRHP within the first five years. In 1960, India's national IMR was 165 per 1,000; today, after the United Nation Millennium Development Goals global health project, the national 2014 IMR in India was 38 (Barros et al. 2012). When the Aroles introduced the CRHP comprehensive PHC model to rural villages, the IMR in Jamkhed was 176 deaths per thousand births. As discussed earlier, within only five years, the IMR showed a precipitous decline, with only 52 infants out of 1,000 dying. Today, more than forty years later, the infant mortality rate at CRHP remains astonishingly low at 24 per 1,000. How was this dramatic transition achieved and maintained? In 1971, the percentage of women receiving antenatal care in Jamkhed villages was .05 percent; since 2005, 97 percent of women in Jamkhed villages received antenatal; today, the overall percentage of women accessing antenatal care in all of India is only 50.7 percent. The precipitous decline in morbidity and mortality demonstrated the maintenance of positive health indicators, marking a dramatic health transition and showing the effectiveness and sustainability of the Comprehensive Rural Health Project primary health-care approach. The Jamkhed Model establishes conclusively that in communities with scarce resources, attention must be paid to all residents and the underlying, sometimes intangible, social, economic, and political factors affecting health, especially those in the most precarious situations who suffer the greatest consequences.

Women, Health, and Equity

CRHP created the conditions for women to change their lives and awakened a consciousness about themselves and their lives in villages and the wider Indian society. The model of one practitioner for each village introducing and managing prenatal care, better nutrition, and safe deliveries proved to be the right solution at the right time. Thus, the Aroles' focus on a gendered approach and an advocacy for women's rights explains the broader changing social relationships that makes possible the active transitions of local women from housebound wives to health workers and village leaders. As Freire (1970), Gramsci (1971), and M. Mohanty (2004) suggest, understanding the relationship between one's position in a local community and the larger political and economic processes produces a transformational experience.

Collective and individual agency expressed as resistance served to deconstruct and challenge the relations of power, both in traditional village life and the wider structures of the neoliberal Indian political economy. Susser (2011) explains that Gramsci understands "organic intellectuals as two-sided as they transmit ideology to subaltern groups from above and also transmit innovative ideological approaches upward" (734). As VHWs reflect on their long-term connections to CRHP, their individual expressions of accomplishments, and the very use of the pronoun *I*, demonstrates their positions against hegemony and patriarchy even within the contradictions and the structural constraints of local and hierarchical power. As Narotzky and Smith (2006) assert, "people pursue the leverage they need to make their own history" (218). The sustainability of CRHP is evident in its forty-year history promoting health in Jamkhed project villages and continues today as a source of dignity for VHWs who still work to maintain health and foster social well-being. In one of my many visits with Sunita Sadaphule, one of the first-generation VHWs, she spoke of the pride of her accomplishments: "Before our eyes we saw that babies survived. In our villages, we could see that they didn't die. We learned to know changes, to keep records, to know the progress." Another first-generation, longtime VHW, Salma Pathan, reflecting on her years of experience, said, "The first thing I learned was how to be with others, then how to talk to others, and how to love, and later how to do good for others."

BIBLIOGRAPHY

Abu-Lughod, Lila. 1990. "The Romance of Resistance: Tracing Transformations of Power through Bedouin Women." *American Ethnologist* 17 (1): 41–55.

_____. 1999. *Veiled Sentiments: Honor and Poetry in a Bedouin Society*. Berkeley: University of California Press.

_____. 2002. "Do Muslim Women Really Need Saving? Anthropological Reflections on Cultural Relativism and Its Others." *American Anthropologist* 104 (3): 783–90.

Abrahams, N., K. Devries, C. Watts, C. Pallitto, M. Petzold, S. Shamu, and C. García-Moreno. 2014. "Worldwide Prevalence of Non-Partner Sexual Violence: A Systematic Review. *Lancet* 383 (9929): 1648–54.

Achino-Loeb, Maria-Luisa. 2006. Introduction. In *Silence: The Currency of Power*, edited by M. L. Achino-Loeb. New York: Berghahn Books.

Agnes, Flavia. 2002. "Transgressing Boundaries of Gender and Identity." *Economic and Political Weekly* 37 (36): 3695–98.

_____. 2012. "From Shah Bano to Kausar Bano: Contextualizing the 'Muslim Women' within a Communalized Polity." In *South Asian Feminisms*, edited by Ania Loomba and Ritty A. Lukose. Durham, NC: Duke University Press.

Ahlin, T., M. Nichter, and G. Pillai. 2016. "Health Insurance in India: What Do We Know and Why Is Ethnographic Research Needed." *Anthropology and Medicine* 23 (1): 102–24.

Anagol, Padma. 2007. "From the Symbolic to the Open: Women's Resistance in Colonial Maharashtra." In *Behind the Veil: Resistance and the Everyday in Colonial South Asia*, edited by Anindita Ghosh. New Delhi, India: Permanent Black (Macmillan).

Antoniello, Patricia, 2015. "Banking the Unbanked: Women and Microfinance in India." *Urbanities: Journal of Urban Ethnography* 15 (1): 63–71.

Arole, Mabelle. 1995. *Voices of South Asian Women*. New York: UNICEF, United Nations.

_____. 1998. *Religion and Rights of Children and Women in South Asia*. New York: UNICEF, United Nations.

Arole, Mabelle, and Rajanikant Arole. 1975. "A Comprehensive Rural Health Project in Jamkhed (India)." In *Health by the People*, edited by Kenneth W. Newell, 70–90. Geneva: World Health Organization.

_____. 1994. *Jamkhed: A Comprehensive Rural Health Project*. London: Macmillan.

_____. 2007. "Village Health Workers—Agents of Transformation." Unpublished internal report. Jamkhed, India: Jamkhed Institute for Community-Based Health and Development.

Baer, Hans A., Merrill Singer, and Ida Susser. 2013. *Medical Anthropology and the World System: Critical Perspectives*. Westport, CT: Praeger.

Bailey, Frederick George. 1957. *Caste and the Economic Frontier: A Village in Highland Orissa*. Manchester, UK: Manchester University Press.

Balagopal, K. 1990. "This Anti-Mandal Mania." *Economic and Political Weekly* 25 (40): 2231–34.

"The Bank and Structural Adjustment." 1996. World Bank in India (website), Indian Economy Overview. www.ieo.org/world-c10-p1.html.

Barros, A. J., C. Ronsmans, H. Axelson, E. Loaiza, A. D. Bertoldi, G. V. França, J. Bryce, J. T. Boerma, and C. G. Victora. 2012. "Equity in Maternal, Newborn, and Child Health Interventions in Countdown to 2015: A Retrospective Review of Survey Data from 54 Countries. *Lancet* 379 (9822): 1225–33.

BBC. 1984. *East of Bombay*. Documentary video. British Broadcasting Company.

Benería, Lourdes, and Gita Sen. 1981. "Accumulation, Reproduction, and 'Women's Role in Economic Development': Boserup Revisited." *Signs* 7 (2): 279–98.

Beteille, Andre. 1996. "Caste in Contemporary India." In *Caste Today*, edited by Christopher John Fuller, 150–179. SOAS Studies on South Asia. New York: Oxford University Press.

_____. 2012. *Caste, Class and Power: Changing Patterns of Stratification in a Tanjore Village*. New York: Oxford University Press.

Berkman, L. F., and S. L. Syme. 1979. "Social Networks, Host Resistance, and Mortality: A Nine-Year Follow-up Study of Alameda County Residents." *American Journal of Epidemiology* 109 (2): 186–204.

Bhatia, Mrigesh, and Susan B. Rifkin. 2013. "Primary Health Care, Now and Forever? A Case Study of a Paradigm Change." *International Journal of Health Services* 43 (3): 459–71.

Biehl, João, and Adriana Petryna. 2013. Introduction. In *When People Come First: Critical Studies in Global Health*, edited by João Biehl and Adriana Petryna, 1–29. Princeton, NJ: Princeton University Press.

Blas, E., and A. S. Kurup, eds. 2010. *Equity, Social Determinants and Public Health Programmes*. Geneva: World Health Organization.

Bookman, Ann, and Sandra Morgen. 1988. *Women and the Politics of Empowerment*. Philadelphia, PA: Temple University Press.

Boserup, Ester. 1970. *Women's Role in Economic Development*. London: Allen and Unwin.

Brown, Theodore M., Marcos Cueto, and Elizabeth Fee. 2006. "The World Health Organization and the Transition from 'International' to 'Global' Public Health." *American Journal of Public Health* 96 (1): 62–72.

Butler, J. 2007. *Gender Trouble: Feminism and the Subversion of Identity*. New York: Routledge.

Callahan, Daniel. 1973. "Science: Limits and Prohibitions." *Hastings Center Report* 3 (5): 5–7.

CDC. 1989. "National Infant Mortality Surveillance (NIMS) 1980." *MMWR Surveillance Summaries* 38 (SS-3, December 1):1–46, 1989. www.cdc.gov/mmwr/preview/mmwrhtml/00001551.htm.

Chambers, B. D., J. T. Erausquin, A. E. Tanner, T. R. Nichols, and S. Brown-Jeffy. 2018. "Testing the Association between Traditional and Novel Indicators of County-Level Structural Racism and Birth Outcomes among Black and White Women." *Journal of Racial and Ethnic Health Disparities* 5 (5): 966–77.

Chambers, Robert. 1994. "The Origins and Practice of Participatory Rural Appraisal." *World Development* 22 (7): 953–69.

Chan, Margaret. 2008. "Return to Alma-Ata." *Lancet (London, England)* 372 (9642): 865–66.

Chandra, Uday. 2015. "Rethinking Subaltern Resistance." *Journal of Contemporary Asia* 45 (4): 563–73.

Channa, Subhadra Mitra. 2013. *Gender in South Asia: Social Imagination and Constructed Realities*. Delhi: Cambridge University Press.

Chatterjee, Partha. 1989. "Colonialism, Nationalism, and Colonialized Women: The Contest in India." *American Ethnologist* 16 (4): 622–33.

Chitnis, Ketan S. 2005. "Communication for Empowerment and Participatory Development: A Social Model of Health in Jamkhed, India." PhD diss., Ohio University.

Collins, S. R., H. K. Bhupal, and M. M. Doty. 2019. "Health Insurance Coverage Eight Years after the ACA: Fewer Uninsured Americans and Shorter Coverage Gaps, but More Underinsured." *Commonwealth Fund*, no. 7: 2–26.

Colvin, Christopher J., and Alison Swartz. 2015. "Extension Agents or Agents of Change? Community Health Workers and the Politics of Care Work in Postapartheid South Africa." *Annals of Anthropological Practice* 39 (1): 29–41.

Cook, Rebecca J. 1993. "International Human Rights and Women's Reproductive Health." *Studies in Family Planning* 24 (2): 73–86. doi.org/10.2307/2939201.

Cook, Rebecca J., and World Health Organization. 1994. *Women's Health and Human Rights: The Promotion and Protection of Women's Health through International Human Rights Law*. Geneva: World Health Organization.

Coreil, Jeannine, and J. Dennis Mull, eds. 1990. *Anthropology and Primary Health Care*. Boulder, CO: Westview Press.

Coriel, Jeannine, 1990. "The Evolution of Anthropology in International Health." In *Anthropology and Primary Health Care*, edited by Jeannine Coreil and J. Dennis Mull. Boulder, CO: Westview Press.

Crenshaw, Kimberle. 1989. "Demarginalizing the Intersection of Race and Sex: A Black Feminist Critique of Antidiscrimination Doctrine, Feminist Theory and Antiracist Politics." *University of Chicago Legal Forum*, no. 1989: article 8. chicagounbound.uchicago.edu/uclf/vol1989/iss1/8.

———. 1990. "Mapping the Margins: Intersectionality, Identity Politics, and Violence against Women of Color." *Stanford Law Review* 43 (6): 1241–99.

CRHP. 2009. *Comprehensive Rural Health Project Annual Report*. Jamkhed, Maharashtra: Comprehensive Rural Health Project.

Cueto, Marcos. 2004. "The Origins of Primary Health Care and Selective Primary Health Care." *American Journal of Public Health* 94 (11): 1864–74.

———. 2013 "A Return to the Magic Bullet? Malaria and Global Health in the Twenty-First Century." In *When People Come First: Critical Studies in Global Health*, edited by João Biehl and Adriana Petryna, 30–54. Princeton, NJ: Princeton University Press.

Davis, Nicola. 2016. "Maternal Deaths Worldwide Drop by Half, Yet Shocking Disparities Remain." *Guardian*, Sept. 15, 2016. www.theguardian.com/science/2016/sep/15/maternal-deaths-worldwide-drop-by-half-yet-shocking-disparities-remain.

Dirks, Nicholas B. 1993. *The Hollow Crown: Ethnohistory of an Indian Kingdom*. Ann Arbor: University of Michigan Press.

———. 1992. "Castes of Mind." *Representations*, no. 37 (Special Issue): 55–78.

Djukanovic, V., E. P. Mach, and WHO. 1975. *Alternative Approaches to Meeting Basic Health Needs in Developing Countries: A Joint UNICEF/WHO Study*. Geneva: World Health Organization.

Dube, Leela. 1997. "Caste and Women." In *Caste: Its Twentieth Century Avatar*, edited by M. N. Srinivas, 1–27. New York: Penguin.

Dumont, L. 1970 *Homo Hierarchicus: The Caste System and Its Implications*. Translated by Mark Sainsbury, Louis Dumont, and Basia Bulati. Chicago: University of Chicago Press.

Eisenstein, Hester. 2009. *Feminism Seduced: How Global Elites Use Women's Labor and Ideas to Exploit Women*. Boulder, CO: Paradigm Publishers.

Espinosa, M. C. S., M. E. Lauzurique, V. R. H. Alcázar, B. L. C. Pacheco, M. D. C. M. Lubián, D. C. Cala, R. T. A. Fumero, and B. M. Teruel. 2018. "Maternal and Child Health Care in Cuba: Achievements and Challenges / Atención a la salud maternoinfantil en Cuba: Logros y desafíos". Special Issue: Health System in Cuba. *Pan American Journal of Public Health*, no. 42 (April 24, 2018). doi.org/10.26633/RPSP.2018.27.

Farmer, Paul. 1999. "Pathologies of Power: Rethinking Health and Human Rights." *American Journal of Public Health* 89 (10): 1486–96.

_____. 2008. "Challenging Orthodoxies: The Road Ahead for Health and Human Rights." *Health and Human Rights* 10 (1): 5–19.

Farmer, Paul, Jim Yong Kim, Arthur Kleinman, and Matthew Basilico, eds. 2013. *Reimagining Global Health: An Introduction*. California Series in Public Anthropology. Oakland, CA: University of California Press.

Farnsworth, Clyde H. 1988. "Micro-Loans to the World's Poorest." *New York Times*, Feb 21, 1988. www.nytimes.com/1988/02/21/business/micro-loans-to-the-world-s-poorest.html.

Forbes, Geraldine Hancock. 1996. *Women in Modern India*. New York: Cambridge University Press.

Fort, Meredith, Mary Anne Mercer, and Oscar Gish, eds. 2004. *Sickness and Wealth: The Corporate Assault on Global Health*. Cambridge, MA: South End Press.

Freedman, Lynn P., and Stephen L. Isaacs. 1993. "Human Rights and Reproductive Choice." *Studies in Family Planning* 24 (1): 18–30.

Freire, Paulo. 1970. *Pedagogy of the Oppressed*. Translated by M. B. Ramos. New York: Continuum.

_____. 1998a. "The Adult Literacy Process as Cultural Action for Freedom." *Harvard Educational Review* 68 (4): 480–98.

_____. 1998b. "Cultural Action and Conscientization." *Harvard Educational Review* 68 (4): 499–521.

Fritzen, Scott. 2007. "Strategic Management of the Health Workforce in Developing Countries: What Have We Learned?" *Human Resources for Health*. no. 5: article 4. human-resources-health.biomedcentral.com/articles/10.1186/1478-4491-5-4.

Gang, Ira N., Kunal Sen, and Myeong-Su Yun. 2011. "Was the Mandal Commission Right? Differences in Living Standards between Social Groups." *Economic and Political Weekly* 46 (39): 43–51.

Ghosh, Anindita, ed. 2007. *Behind the Veil: Resistance, and the Everyday in Colonial South Asia*. New Delhi, India: Permanent Black (Macmillan).

Gish, Oscar. 2004. "The Legacy of Colonial Medicine." In *Sickness and Wealth: The Corporate Assault on Global Health*, edited by Meredith Fort, Mary Anne Mercer, and Oscar Gish. Cambridge, MA: South End Press.

Gonzalez, Roberto M., 2015. "Infant Mortality in Cuba: Myth and Reality." *Cuban Studies* 43 (1): 19–39.

Graeber, David. 2011. *Debt: The First 5,000 Years*. Brooklyn, NY: Melville House.

Gramsci, Antonio. 1971. *Selections from the Prison Notebooks of Antonio Gramsci*. Edited by Quintin Hoare and Geoffrey Nowell-Smith. London: New Left Books.

Green, Linda Buckley. 1989. "Consensus and Coercion: Primary Health Care and the Guatemalan State." *Medical Anthropology Quarterly* 3 (3): 246–57.

Gupta, Dipankar. 2005. "Caste Politics: Identity over System." *Annual Review of Anthropology* 34 (Oct. 2005): 409–27. doi.org/10.1146/annurev.anthro.34.081804.120649.

Guru, Gopal. 1995. "Dalit Women Talk Differently." *Economic and Political Weekly* 33 (44): 2548–50.

Harvey, David. 2005. *A Brief History of Neoliberalism*. New York: Oxford University Press.

Heggenhougen, H. Kristian. 1984. "Will Primary Health Care Efforts Be Allowed to Succeed?" *Social Science and Medicine* 19 (3): 217–24.

Hodgson, Dorothy Louise. 2016. *The Gender, Culture, and Power Reader*. New York: Oxford University Press.

Hogan, Margaret C., Kyle J. Foreman, Mohsen Naghavi, Stephanie Y. Ahn, Mengru Wang, Susanna M. Makela, Alan D. Lopez, Rafael Lozano, and Christopher J. L. Murray. 2010. "Maternal Mortality for 181 Countries, 1980–2008: A Systematic Analysis of Progress towards Millennium Development Goal 5." *Lancet* 375 (9726): 1609–23.

Hong, Evelyne. 2004. "The Primary Health Care Movement Meets the Free Market." In *Sickness and Wealth: The Corporate Assault on Global Health*, edited by Meredith Fort, Mary Anne Mercer, and Oscar Gish, 27–40. Cambridge, MA: South End Press.

IIPS (International Institute for Population Sciences) and ICF. 2017. *National Family Health Survey (NFHS-4), 2015–16: India*. Mumbai: IIPS. dhsprogram.com/pubs/pdf/FR339.pdf.

IIPS and Macro International. 2007. *National Family Health Survey (NFHS-3), 2005–06: India, Vol. 1 and 2*. Mumbai: IIPS and Macro International. dhsprogram.com/pubs/pdf/FRIND3/FRIND3-Vol1AndVol2.pdf.

Ilaiah, Kancha. 2004. "Caste or Class or Caste-Class: A Study in Dalit-Bahujan Consciousness and Struggles in Andhra Pradesh in 1980s." In *Class, Caste, Gender: Readings in Indian Government and Politics*, edited by M. Mohanty, 227–54. New Delhi, India: Sage Publications.

India Census. 2014. "SRS Statistical Report 2014." Office of the Registrar General & Census Commissioner, India Ministry of Home Affairs. www.censusindia.gov.in/vital_statistics/SRS_Reports_2014.html.

Ingraham, C. 2014. "Our Infant Mortality Rate Is a National Embarrassment." *Washington Post*, Sept. 29, 2014. www.washingtonpost.com/news/wonk/wp/2014/09/29/our-infant-mortality-rate-is-a-national-embarrassment.

Iyer, A., G. Sen, and P. Östlin. 2008. "The Intersections of Gender and Class in Health Status and Health Care." *Global Public Health* 3 (sup1): 13–24.

Jain, Devaki. 2005. *Women, Development, and the UN: A Sixty-Year Quest for Equality and Justice*. Bloomington: Indiana University Press.

Janes, Craig R. 2004. "Going Global in Century XXI: Medical Anthropology and the New Primary Health Care." *Human Organization* 63 (4): 457–71.

Janes, Craig R., and Kitty K. Corbett. 2009. "Anthropology and Global Health." *Annual Review of Anthropology* 38 (Oct. 2009): 167–83. doi.org/10.1146/annurev-anthro-091908-164314.

Jayawardena, Kumari, 2016. *Feminism and Nationalism in the Third World*. New York: Verso Books.

John, Mary E. 2000. "Alternate Modernities? Reservations and Women's Movement in 20th Century India." *Economic and Political Weekly* 35 (43/44): 3822–29.

John, Mary E. 2015. "Intersectionality." *Economic and Political Weekly* 50 (33): 72–76.

Kabeer, Naila. 1999. "Resources, Agency, Achievements: Reflections on the Measurement of Women's Empowerment." *Development and Change* 30 (3): 435.

Kalokhe, Ameeta, Carlos del Rio, Kristin Dunkle, Rob Stephenson, Nicholas Metheny, Anuradha Paranjape, and Seema Sahay. 2017. "Domestic Violence against Women in India: A Systematic Review of a Decade of Quantitative Studies." *Global Public Health* 12 (4): 498–513. doi.org/10.1080/17441692.2015.1119293.

Kane, Sumit, Maryse Kok, Hermen Ormel, Lilian Otiso, Mohsin Sidat, Ireen Namakhoma, Sudirman Nasir, Daniel Gemechu, Sabina Rashid, and Miriam Taegtmeyer. 2016. "Limits and Opportunities to Community Health Worker Empowerment: A Multi-Country Comparative Study." *Social Science & Medicine* 164 (Sept. 2016): 27–34.

Kapilashrami, Anuj, Ramila Bisht, and Sundaris Ravindran. 2016. "Feminist Movements and Gender Politics: Transnational Perspectives on Intersectionality." *Delhi University Journal of Humanities and Social Science*, no. 3: 171–84. journals.du.ac.in/humsoc/archive16.html#content.

Karim, Lamia. 2011. *Microfinance and Its Discontents: Women in Debt in Bangladesh.* Minneapolis: University of Minnesota Press.

Kaysin, Alex. 2010. "'Treat Them with Love': Empowerment of Community Health Workers as Agents of Change." Master's degree submission, Johns Hopkins Bloomberg School of Public Health.

Kim, Jim Yong, Joyce V. Millen, Alec Irwin, and John Gershman, eds. 2000. *Dying for Growth: Global Inequalities and the Health of the Poor.* Boston, MA: Common Courage Press.

Klasen, Stephan. 2018. "The Impact of Gender Inequality on Economic Performance in Developing Countries." *Annual Review of Resource Economics* 10 (Oct. 2018): 279–98.

Klasen, Stephan, and Claudia Wink. 2003. "'Missing Women': Revisiting the Debate." *Feminist Economics* 9 (2–3): 263–99.

Krieger, Nancy. 2000. "Epidemiology and Social Sciences: Towards a Critical Reengagement in the 21st Century." *Epidemiologic Reviews* 22 (1): 155–63.

——. 2008. "Proximal, Distal, and the Politics of Causation: What's Level Got to Do with It?" *American Journal of Public Health* 98 (2): 221–30.

——. 2011. *Epidemiology and the People's Health Theory and Context.* New York: Oxford University Press.

——. 2020. "Measures of Racism, Sexism, Heterosexism, and Gender Binarism for Health Equity Research: From Structural Injustice to Embodied Harm—An Ecosocial Analysis." *Annual Review of Public Health* 41 (April 2020): 37–62. doi.org/10.1146/annurev-publhealth-040119-094017.

Krieger, N., S. Gruskin, N. Singh, M. V. Kiang, J. T. Chen, P. D. Waterman, J. Beckfield, and B. A. Coull. 2016. "Reproductive Justice and Preventable Deaths: State Funding, Family Planning, Abortion, and Infant Mortality, US 1980–2010." *SSM-Population Health*, no. 2: 277–93.

Labonté, Ronald, David Sanders, Corinne Packer, and Nikki Schaay. 2017. *Revitalizing Health for All: Case Studies of the Struggle for Comprehensive Primary Health Care.* Toronto: University of Toronto Press.

Leacock, Eleanor. 1983. "Interpreting the Origins of Gender Inequality: Conceptual and Historical Problems." *Dialectical Anthropology* 7 (4): 263–84.

Lehmann, Uta, and David Sanders. 2007. *Community Health Workers: What Do We Know about Them? The State of the Evidence on Programmes, Activities, Costs and Impact on Health Outcomes of Using Community Health Workers.* Geneva: World Health Organization.

Link, Bruce G., and Jo Phelan. 1995. "Social Conditions as Fundamental Causes of Disease." Extra Issue: Forty Years of Medical Sociology. *Journal of Health and Social Behavior* (1995): 80–94. doi.org/10.2307/2626958.

Litsios, Socrates. 2004. "The Christian Medical Commission and the Development of the World Health Organization's Primary Health Care Approach." *American Journal of Public Health* 94 (11): 1884.

Loomba, Ania, and Ritty A. Lukose. 2012. *South Asian Feminisms.* Durham, NC: Duke University Press.

López, Iris Ofelia. 2008. *Matters of Choice: Puerto Rican Women's Struggle for Reproductive Freedom.* New Brunswick, NJ: Rutgers University Press.

Lynch, Owen M. 1969. *The Politics of Untouchability: Social Mobility and Social Change in a City of India.* New York: Columbia University Press.

Maes, Kenneth. 2010. "Examining Health-Care Volunteerism in a Food- and Financially Insecure World." *Bulletin of the World Health Organization* 88: 867–69.

Maes, Kenneth, Svea Closser, and Ippolytos Kalofonos. 2014. "Listening to Community Health Workers: How Ethnographic Research Can Inform Positive Relationships among Community Health Workers, Health Institutions, and Communities." *American Journal of Public Health* 104 (5): e5–e9.

Maes, Kenneth, Svea Closser, Ethan Vorel, and Yihenew Tesfaye. 2015. "A Women's Development Army: Narratives of Community Health Worker Investment and Empowerment in Rural Ethiopia." *Studies in Comparative International Development* 50 (4): 455–78.

"Maharashtra Zilla Parishad | Maharashtra Local Government." 2010. SocialVillage.in, April 14, 2010 (posted). www.socialvillage.in/resources/32795-maharashtra-zilla-parishad-maharashtra-local.

Mahmood, Saba. 2001. "Feminist Theory, Embodiment, and the Docile Agent: Some Reflections on the Egyptian Islamic Revival." *Cultural Anthropology* 16 (2): 202–36.

———. 2011. *Politics of Piety: The Islamic Revival and the Feminist Subject.* Princeton, NJ: Princeton University Press.

Marcelin, J. R., D. S. Siraj, R. Victor, S. Kotadia, and Y. A. Maldonado. 2019. "The Impact of Unconscious Bias in Healthcare: How to Recognize and Mitigate It." *Journal of Infectious Diseases* 220 (Supplement_2): S62–S73.

Marmot, Michael. 2017. "The Health Gap: The Challenge of an Unequal World: The Argument." *International Journal of Epidemiology* 46 (4): 1312–18.

———. 2005. "Social Determinants of Health Inequalities." *Lancet* 365 (9464): 1099–104. doi.org/10.1016/S0140-6736(05)71146-6.

Marriott, McKim, ed. 1955. *Village India: Studies in the Little Community.* Chicago: University of Chicago Press.

Mathur, Saloni. 2000. "History and Anthropology in South Asia: Rethinking the Archive." *Annual Review of Anthropology* 29 (Oct. 2009): 89–106. doi.org/10.1146/annurev.anthro.29.1.89.

Mausner, Judith S., and Shira Kramer. 1985. *Mausner and Bahn Epidemiology: An Introductory Text.* Philadelphia, PA: W. B. Saunders.

McCord, C., R. Premkumar, S. Arole, and R. Arole. 2001. "Efficient and Effective Emergency Obstetric Care in a Rural Indian Community Where Most Deliveries Are at Home." *International Journal of Gynecology and Obstetrics* 75 (3): 297–307.

Menon, Nivedita. 2015. "A Critical View on Intersectionality from India: Is Feminism about 'Women'?" *Economic and Political Weekly* 50 (17): 37–44.

Merry, Sally Engle. 2006. *Human Rights and Gender Violence: Translating International Law into Local Justice*. Chicago Series in Law and Society. Chicago: University of Chicago Press.

Mishra, Arima. 2014. "'Trust and Teamwork Matter': Community Health Workers' Experiences in Integrated Service Delivery in India." *Global Public Health* 9 (8): 960–74.

Mohanty, Chandra Talpade. 1984. "Under Western Eyes: Feminist Scholarship and Colonial Discourses." *Boundary* 2 12 (3): 333–58. doi.org/10.2307/302821.

———. 2003. *Feminism without Borders: Decolonizing Theory, Practicing Solidarity*. Durham, NC: Duke University Press.

Mohanty, Manoranjan. 2004. *Class, Caste, Gender: Readings in Indian Government and Politics*. New Delhi, India: Sage Publications.

Moodie, Megan. 2008. "Enter Microcredit: A New Culture of Women's Empowerment in Rajasthan?" *American Ethnologist* 35 (3): 454–65.

Morgan, Lynn, 2001. "Community Participation in Health: Perpetual Allure, Persistent Challenge." *Health Policy and Planning* 16 (3): 221–30.

Mukherjee, Joia. 2004. "Diagnosing Global Injustice." In *Sickness and Wealth: The Corporate Assault on Global Health*, edited by Meredith Fort, Mary Anne Mercer, and Oscar Gish. Cambridge, MA: South End Press.

Mukherjee, Joia, Jean Claude Mugunga, Adarsh Shah, Abera Leta, Ermyas Birru, Cate Oswald, Gregory Jerome, Charles Patrick Almazor, Hind Satti, and Robert Yates. 2019. "A Practical Approach to Universal Health Coverage." *Lancet Global Health* 7 (4): e410–11. doi.org/10.1016/S2214-109X(19)30035-X.

Mull, J. Dennis, 1990 "The Primary Health Dialectic: History, Rhetoric, and Reality." In *Anthropology and Primary Health Care*, edited by Jeannine Coreil and J. Dennis Mull. Boulder, Colorado: Westview Press.

Mullings, Leith. 2005. "Resistance and Resilience: The Sojourner Syndrome and the Social Context of Reproduction in Central Harlem." *Transforming Anthropology* 13 (2): 79–91.

———. 2014. *On Our Own Terms: Race, Class, and Gender in the Lives of African-American Women*. New York: Routledge.

Mullings, Leith, and Amy J. Schulz. 2006. "Intersectionality and Health: An Introduction." In *Gender, Race, Class and Health: Intersectional Approaches*, edited by Amy J. Schulz and Leith Mullings. San Francisco: Jossey-Bass Publishers.

Mullings, Leith, and Alaka Wali. 2000. *Stress and Resilience: The Social Context of Reproduction in Central Harlem*. New York: Kluwer Academic.

Mullings, Leith, A. Wali, D. McLean, J. Mitchell, S. Prince, D. Thomas, and P. Tovar. 2001. "Qualitative Methodologies and Community Participation in Examining Reproductive Experiences: The Harlem Birth Right Project." *Maternal and Child Health Journal* 5 (2): 85–93.

NABARD. 2013. *Twenty-Five Years of SHG Movement*. National Bank for Agriculture and Rural Development: Bandra, Mumbai, India.

Narotzky, Susana, and Gavin A. Smith. 2006. *Immediate Struggles: People, Power, and Place in Rural Spain*. Berkeley: University of California Press.

Navarro, Vicente. 2004. "The Politics of Health Inequalities Research in the United States." *International Journal of Health Services* 34 (1): 87–99.

———. 2007. "Neoliberalism as a Class Ideology; Or, the Political Causes of the Growth of Inequalities." *International Journal of Health Services: Planning, Administration, Evaluation* 37 (1): 47–62.

_____. 2016. "Why We Don't Spend Enough on Public Health: An Alternative View." In *The Financial and Economic Crises and Their Impact on Health and Social Well-Being*, edited by Vicente Navarro and Carles Muntaner. New York: Routledge.

Navarro, Vicente, C. Muntaner, C. Borrell, J. Benach, A. Quiroga, M. Rodríguez-Sanz, N. Vergés, and M. I. Pasarín. 2006. "Politics and Health Outcomes." *Lancet* 368 (9540): 1033–37.

Newell, Kenneth W. 1975. *Health by the People*. Geneva: World Health Organization.

Nichter, Mark. 1980. "Community Health Worker Scheme: A Plan for Democratisation." *Economic and Political Weekly* 15 (1): 37–43.

_____. 1996. "The Primary Health Center as a Social System: Primary Health Care, Social Status, and the Issue of Team-Work." *Anthropology and International Health: Asian Case Studies*, no. 3: 367.

_____. 2008. *Global Health: Why Cultural Perceptions, Social Representations, and Biopolitics Matter*. Tucson: University of Arizona Press.

Pathak, Sushmita, and Lauren Frayer. 2019. "What Headlines and Protests Get Wrong about Rape in India." *Goats and Soda: Stories of Life in a Changing World* (blog), National Public Radio, 29 December 2019. www.npr.org/sections/goatsandsoda/2019/12/29/791734411/what-headlines-and-protests-get-wrong-about-rape-in-india.

Parpart, Jane L., Shirin M. Rai, and Kathleen A. Staudt. 2003. *Rethinking Empowerment: Gender and Development in a Global/Local World*. Abingdon, UK: Taylor and Francis.

Perry, Henry B., Emma Sacks, Meike Schleiff, Richard Kumapley, Sundeep Gupta, Bahie M. Rassekh, and Paul A. Freeman. 2017. "Comprehensive Review of the Evidence Regarding the Effectiveness of Community–Based Primary Health Care in Improving Maternal, Neonatal and Child Health: 6 Strategies Used by Effective Projects." *Journal of Global Health* 7 (1): 328–41. doi.org/10.7189/jogh.07.010906.

Pfeiffer, James. 2003. "International NGOs and Primary Health Care in Mozambique: The Need for a New Model of Collaboration." *Social Science and Medicine* 56 (4): 725–38.

Pfeiffer, James, and Rachel Chapman. 2010. "Anthropological Perspectives on Structural Adjustment and Public Health." *Annual Review of Anthropology* 39 (Oct. 2010): 149–65.

Pfeiffer, James, and Mark Nichter. 2008. "What Can Critical Medical Anthropology Contribute to Global Health? A Health Systems Perspective." *Medical Anthropology Quarterly* 22 (4): 410–15.

Purushothaman, Sangeetha. 1998. *The Empowerment of Women in India: Grassroots Women's Networks and the State*. New Delhi, India: Sage Publications.

Raj, Anita, and Lotus McDougal. 2014. "Sexual Violence and Rape in India." *Lancet* 383 (9920): 865.

Rao, Anupama. 2003. Introduction. In *Gender and Caste*, edited by Anupama Rao, 1–47. Issues in Contemporary Indian Feminism. New Delhi: Kali for Women.

Rao, Mala, and Eva Pilot. 2014. "The Missing Link–The Role of Primary Care in Global Health." *Global Health Action* 7 (1): article 23693. doi.org/10.3402/gha.v7.23693.

Rege, Sharmila, ed. 1998. "Dalit Women Talk Differently: A Critique of 'Difference' and Towards a Dalit Feminist Standpoint Position." *Economic and Political Weekly* 33 (44): WS3-WS46.

_____. 2000. "'Real Feminism' and Dalit Women: Scripts of Denial and Accusation." *Economic and Political Weekly* 35 (6): 492–95.

_____. 2003a. "Feminist Challenge to Sociology: Disenchanting Sociology or 'for Sociology.'" Introduction. In *Sociology of Gender: The Challenge of Feminist Sociological Thought*, edited by Sharmila Rege. Themes in Indian Sociology. New Delhi: Sage.

_____. 2003b. "More Than Just Tacking Women on to the 'Macropicture': Feminist Contributions to Globalisation Discourses." *Economic and Political Weekly* 38 (43): 4555–63.

_____. 2006. *Writing Caste/Writing Gender: Narrating Dalit Women's Testimonios.* New Delhi, India: Zubaan (Kali for Women).

_____. 2013. *Against the Madness of Manu: B. R. Ambedkar's Writings on Brahmanical Patriarchy.* New Delhi: Navayana Publishing.

Rosewarne, Clive, Gai Wilson, and Joun Liddle. 2017. "Ingkintja: The Congress Male Health Program." In *Revitalizing Health for All: Case Studies of the Struggle for Comprehensive Primary Health Care,* edited by Ronald Labonté, David Sanders, Corinne Packer, and Nikki Schaay. Toronto: University of Toronto Press.

Ruxin, J. N. 1994. "Magic Bullet: The History of Oral Rehydration Therapy." *Medical History* 38 (4): 363–97.

Rylko-Bauer, Barbara, and Paul Farmer. 2002. "Managed Care or Managed Inequality? A Call for Critiques of Market-Based Medicine." *Medical Anthropology Quarterly* 16 (4): 476–502.

Sankaran, Lavanya. 2013. "Opinion: Can India's New Laws Stop Rape?" *Guardian*, April 03, 2013. www.theguardian.com/commentisfree/2013/apr/03/indias-new-laws-stop-rape.

Schulz, Amy J., and Leith Mullings, eds. 2006. *Gender, Race, Class, and Health: Intersectional Approaches.* San Francisco: Jossey-Bass.

Sen, Amartya K., 1992a. *Inequality Reexamined.* London: Oxford University Press.

_____. 1992b. "Missing Women: Social Inequality Outweighs Women's Survival Advantage in Asia and North Africa." *British Medical Journal* 304 (6827): 587–88.

_____. 1999. *Development as Freedom.* New York: Anchor Books.

_____. 2002. "Why Health Equity?" *Health Economics* 11 (8): 659–66.

_____. 2003. "Missing Women—Revisited: Reduction in Female Mortality Has Been Counterbalanced by Sex Selective Abortions." *British Medical Journal* 327 (7427): 1297–98.

Sen, Gita, Asha George, and Piroska Östlin. 2002. "Engendering Health Equity: A Review of Research and Policy." In *Engendering International Health: The Challenge of Equity,* edited by Gita Sen, Asha George, and Piroska Östlin, 1–34. Basic Bioethics. Cambridge, MA: MIT Press.

Sen, Gita, and Piroska Östlin. 2008. "Gender Inequity in Health: Why It Exists and How We Can Change It." *Global Public Health* 3 (sup1): 1–12.

_____. 2009. *Gender Equity in Health: The Shifting Frontiers of Evidence and Action.* Routledge Studies in Health and Social Welfare. New York: Routledge.

Sharma, Aradhana. 2008. *Logics of Empowerment: Development, Gender, and Governance in Neoliberal India.* Minneapolis: University of Minnesota Press.

Sindhuja, Pandian, and Kurunathan Raju Murugan. 2018. "A Gender Perspective on Role Performance of Elected Panchayat Leaders in India." *Journal of International Women's Studies* 19 (3): 199–214.

Singer, Merrill, and Hans Baer. 2018. *Critical Medical Anthropology.* New York: Routledge.

Skolnik, R. L. 2016. *Global Health 101.* Boston: Jones and Bartlett Publishers.

Snell-Rood, Claire. 2015. "Marital Distress and the Failure to Eat: The Expressive Dimensions of Feeding, Eating, and Self-Care in Urban South Asia." *Medical Anthropology Quarterly* 29 (3): 316–33.

Solheim, Karen, Beverly J. McElmurry, and Mi Ja Kim. 2007. "Multidisciplinary Teamwork in US Primary Health Care." *Social Science and Medicine* 65 (3): 622–34.

Srinivas, M. N. 1966. *Social Change in Modern India.* Berkeley: University of California Press.

_____. 1997. Introduction. *Caste: Its Twentieth Century Avatar*, ix–xxxvii. New York: Penguin Books.

Susser, Ida. 2011. "Organic Intellectuals, Crossing Scales, and the Emergence of Social Movements with Respect to AIDS in South Africa AES Presidential Address for 2008." *American Ethnologist* 38 (4): 733–42.

Taylor, C. E. 1992. "Surveillance for Equity in Primary Health Care: Policy Implications from International Experience. *International Journal of Epidemiology* 21 (6): 1043–49.

Taylor, Sebastian, and Alireza Marandi. 2008. "Social Determinants of Health and the Design of Health Programmes for the Poor." *British Medical Journal* 337 (7664): 266–69.

UN. N.d. "What We Do: Economic Empowerment." United Nations Women, accessed August 2018. www.unwomen.org/en/what-we-do/economic-empowerment.

Visaria, Leela, 2008. "Violence against Women in India: Is Empowerment a Protective Factor?" *Economic and Political Weekly* 43 (48): 60–66.

Wali, Alaka. 2012. "On Happiness: A Different Measure of Well-Being." *American Anthropologist* 114 (1): 6–18.

Wallerstein, Nina. 2006. *What Is the Evidence on Effectiveness of Empowerment to Improve Health?* Copenhagen, Denmark: World Health Organization.

Walsh, Julia A., and Kenneth S. Warren. 1979. "Selective Primary Health Care: An Interim Strategy for Disease Control in Developing Countries." *New England Journal of Medicine* 301 (18): 967–74.

Werner, David, and Bill Bower. 2005. *Helping Health Workers Learn: A Book of Methods, Aids, and Ideas for Instructors at the Village Level*. Berkeley, CA: Hesperian Health Guides.

Werner, David, and C. Sathyamala. 1977. *Where There Is No Doctor: A Health Care Handbook*. Berkeley, CA: Hesperian Health Guides.

Whiteford, L. M., and L. G. Branch. 2008. *Primary Health Care in Cuba: The Other Revolution*. Lanham, MD: Rowman and Littlefield.

Whiteford, Linda M., and Cecilia Vindrola-Padros. 2016. *Community Participatory Involvement: A Sustainable Model for Global Public Health*. New York: Routledge.

Whitehead, Judith. 2015. "Au Retour a Gramsci: Reflections on Civil Society, Political Society and the State in South Asia." *Journal of Contemporary Asia* 45 (4): 660–76.

WHO (World Health Organization). 1989. *Strengthening the Performance of Community Health Workers in Primary Health Care: Report of a WHO Study Group (meeting held in Geneva from 2 to 9 December 1987)*. Geneva: World Health Organization.

_____.2002. Declaration of Alma-Ata, 1978. International Conference on Primary Health Care, Alma-Ata, USSR, 6–12 September 1978. www.who.int/publications/almaata_declaration_en.pdf.

_____. 2008a. *The World Health Report 2008: Primary Health Care Now More than Ever*. Geneva, Switzerland.

_____. 2008b. "Commission on Social Determinants of Health and World Health Organization." *Closing the Gap in a Generation: Health Equity through Action on the Social Determinants of Health: Commission on Social Determinants of Health Final Report*. Geneva: World Health Organization.

_____. 2014. *Basic Documents*, 48th ed. Geneva: World Health Organization.

_____. 2015. *Trends in Maternal Mortality: 1990 to 2015: Estimates by WHO, UNICEF, UNFPA, World Bank Group and the United Nations Population Division*. Geneva: World Health Organization.

_____. 2017 "Diarrhoeal Disease." Fact Sheets, World Health Organization, May 2, 2017. www. who.int/news-room/fact-sheets/detail/diarrhoeal-disease.

_____. 2018. *WHO Guideline on Health Policy and System Support to Optimize Community Health Worker Programmes.* Geneva: World Health Organization.

Whyte, Susan Reynolds, Michael Whyte, Lotte Meinert, and Jennipher Twebaze. 2013. "Therapeutic Clientship." In *When People Come First: Critical Studies in Global Health,* edited by João Biehl and Adriana Petryna, 140–65. Princeton, NJ: Princeton University Press.

Wolf, Eric R. 1999. *Envisioning Power: Ideologies of Dominance and Crisis.* Berkeley: University of California Press.

_____. 2001. *Pathways of Power: Building an Anthropology of the Modern World.* Berkeley: University of California Press.

World Bank. 1979. *Recognizing the "Invisible" Woman in Development: The World Bank's Experience.* Report no. 9957. Washington, DC: World Bank.

_____. 2015. "Maternal Mortality Ratio (modeled estimate, per 100,000 live births)—India." World Bank Open Data. data.worldbank.org.

_____. 2016. *India's Poverty Profile: Snapshot 2012.* Infographic. World Bank Group, May 27, 2016. www.worldbank.org/en/news/infographic/2016/05/27/india-s-poverty-profile.

_____. 2018. "The World Bank Data Mortality Rate, Infant (per 1,000 live births) Country Comparison." World Bank Open Data. data.worldbank.org.

Yunus, Muhammad. 2004. "Grameen Bank, Microcredit and Millennium Development Goals." *Economic and Political Weekly* 39 (36): 4077–80.

Zavella, Patricia. 2016. "Contesting Structural Vulnerability through Reproductive Justice Activism with Latina Immigrants in California." *North American Dialogue* 19 (1): 36–45. doi.org/10.1111/nad.12035.

Zelliot, Eleanor. 2003. "Dr. Ambedkar and the Empowerment of Women." In *Gender and Caste,* edited by Anupama Rao, 204–17. Issues in Contemporary Indian Feminism. New Delhi, India: Kali for Women/Women Unlimited.

INDEX

Page numbers in *italics* refer to figures, maps, or tables.

CPSIA information can be obtained
at www.ICGtesting.com
Printed in the USA
LVHW020400111120
671309LV00010B/983

9 780826 500236